WRUNG

THE NEW AMERICAN CANON

The Iowa Series in Contemporary Literature and Culture

Samuel Cohen, series editor

WRONG

A Critical Biography of Dennis Cooper

by Diarmuid Hester

UNIVERSITY OF IOWA PRESS | IOWA CITY

University of Iowa Press, Iowa City 52242
Copyright © 2020 by the University of Iowa Press
www.uipress.uiowa.edu
Printed in the United States of America

Design by April Leidig

Printed on acid-free paper

Library of Congress Cataloging-in-Publication Data
Names: Hester, Diarmuid, 1982– author.
Title: Wrong: a critical biography of Dennis Cooper / Diarmuid Hester.
Other titles: Critical biography of Dennis Cooper
Description: Iowa City: University of Iowa Press, [2020] | Series: The new
    American canon | Includes bibliographical references and index
Identifiers: LCCN 2019045112 (print) | LCCN 2019045113 (ebook) |
    ISBN 9781609386917 (paperback) | ISBN 9781609386924 (ebook)
Subjects: LCSH: Cooper, Dennis, 1953– | Gay authors—United States—Biography. |
    Poets, American—21st century—Biography. | Motion picture producers and
    directors—United States—Biography. | Cooper, Dennis, 1953—Criticism and
    interpretation.
Classification: LCC PS3553.O582 Z67 2020 (print) | LCC PS3553.O582 (ebook) |
    DDC 813/.54 [B]—dc23
LC record available at https://lccn.loc.gov/2019045112
LC ebook record available at https://lccn.loc.gov/2019045113

Cover photo: *Dennis Cooper* © Sheree Rose

For George Mind

Contents

Acknowledgments

THIS BOOK IS the product of more than a decade of close engagement with the work of Dennis Cooper. Incorporating extensive archival research and new interviews, it offers detailed readings of Cooper's poetry, prose, films, performances, and HTML works from the 1970s to the present. Some receive their first extended treatment here; others prompt new assessments that demonstrate their continued importance. But if this work is comprehensive, it's not exhaustive. A critical biography holds in tension two modes of writing: biography, which generally observes chronology, and critique, which pursues an argument. Negotiating between them has been an exciting challenge that, with any luck, has made for a book that will interest different kinds of readers, but the form and limitations of space have also precluded an in-depth examination of every instance of this prolific artist's work. Daniel Kane once told me that, at its best, scholarly work is a conversation; this book is thus envisaged as a contribution (a significant one, I hope) to an ongoing conversation about Dennis Cooper's work, the cultural contexts he has created, and the ones through which he has moved. It's far from the final word.

A project in gestation for this long accumulates debts to many. Thanks are owed especially to Dennis Cooper, for supporting the project at every turn with his friendship and generosity, and Daniel Kane, who supervised the doctoral research this book is based on. Thanks to my colleagues and friends who helped to shape this work: Kasia Boddy and Peter Boxall, who first suggested I write a critical biography; Thomas Houlton and

Laura Ellen Joyce for their support in the initial stages; Sarah Franklin and Heather Stallard of lgbtQ+@cam for helping me to feel at home at the University of Cambridge; and Claude Grewal-Sultze and Julie Hrischeva for tiny books and enormous kindness. I am very grateful to the following people for their support, intellectual and otherwise: Kris Beaghton, Gavin Butt, Lisa Darms, Jacob Engelberg, Laure Fernandez, Kristin Grogan, David Grundy, Helen Hester, David Hobbs, Nick Hudson, Kevin Killian, Wayne Koestenbaum, Robert Macfarlane, Geoffrey Maguire, Leo Mellor, Michael O'Rourke, Jules O'Dwyer, Mike Rowland, John David Rhodes, Jordan Savage, Sophie Seita, Natasha Tanna, Lynne Tillman, David Trotter, Bernard Welt, and David Winters. To my mother and father, Doireann, Cathal, Harry, and Róisín; to my friends Sam Nesbit, David Bramwell, Josh Schneiderman, and Jim Macairt; and to my partner George Mind: to you I owe the greatest debt of gratitude for your unfailing love and support. *Go raibh míle maith agaibh.*

For their expert assistance in archival matters, I am very grateful to Marvin Taylor, Charlotte Priddle, and the staff of the Fales Library and Special Collections, New York University. Thanks also to Sam Cohen, for his unwavering enthusiasm for the project, and the team of the University of Iowa Press, especially Ranjit Arab, who took the book on, and Meredith Stabel, who took it over, and about whom I'd like to write reams of praise, but as we both know I'm over my word limit.

Many thanks to those who gave me permission to quote from their work and correspondence: Mike Amnasan, Paul Curran, Jonathan Galassi, Amy Gerstler, Mark Gluth, Ron Koertge, Jonathan Mayhew, Eileen Myles, Thomas Moore, Sheree Rose, Marvin Taylor, Brian Tucker, Matias Viegener, Bernard Welt, and George Wines.

This book was researched and written with the financial support of an Arts and Humanities Research Council doctoral scholarship and a Leverhulme Trust Early Career Fellowship, with additional funding from the University of Cambridge Faculty of English and the Isaac Newton Trust.

Selections from "An American Poem" are used by permission from *I Must Be Living Twice: New & Selected Poems* by Eileen Myles. Copyright © 2015 by Eileen Myles. Courtesy of HarperCollins Publishers.

Chapter 3 was originally published as "A Poetics of Dissociability: Poetry and Punk in Los Angeles, 1976–83," *American Literature* 91, no. 1

(March 2019): 183–207. Part of chapter 11 was published as "The Anarcho-Queer Commons of Dennis Cooper's Blog, *The Weakings*: A Brief History," *GLQ: A Journal of Lesbian and Gay Studies*, 24, no. 4 (October 2018): 522–27. Part of chapter 12 was published as "Queer Cryptograms, Anarchist Cyphers: Decoding Dennis Cooper's *The Marbled Swarm: A Novel*," *Studies in the Literary Imagination* 45, no. 2 (Fall 2012): 95–112.

WRONG

Wrong | The Adolescence of an Iconoclast

1 IN THE MIDDLE of the photograph, a man stands with his hands in his pockets on the pavement in front of a suburban bungalow. He wears a pale, short-sleeved shirt and dark trousers. Judging by the style of the house behind him and the identical one behind it, it looks like somewhere in California—there's also a palm tree growing out of the guy's head. The tree is actually behind him, but the way the photographer's caught it, it looks like it's sprouted from his head. His face is mostly in shade and he's pretty far away and out of focus, so it's difficult to make out his expression, but from his demeanor, it looks like he might be in on the joke. Or perhaps the way he's holding himself indicates something else. A kind of pride, maybe? In which case it could be *his* house he's standing in front of; maybe he's just bought it and stashed the "For Sale" sign behind the station wagon parked in the driveway. Some of its tailgate reverses into the frame from the right, as part of a succulent bush encroaches on the scene from the left. That would mean that whoever took this amateurishly composed photo, standing too far back and divided from their subject by a vast swathe of road in the foreground, could be married to the man who's standing in front of their new family home. The caption underneath the photo, one word in large black capital letters, reads, "WRONG."

Dennis Cooper first saw John Baldessari's 1968 artwork *Wrong* on a high school field trip to the Los Angeles County Museum of Art (LACMA) when he was around sixteen years old. He doesn't seem to have cared about visual art before then, or taken much notice of it, but he remembers that

1

WRONG

John Baldessari, *Wrong*, 1966–68. Photoemulsion with acrylic on canvas, 59 × 45 in.
Courtesy of the estate of John Baldessari.

the trip to LACMA was incredibly important: "I was really struck by this John Baldessari piece called *Wrong*. I don't know why, but for some reason I was startled by that, and I thought 'Wow.' There was something about the fact that it's art. I was completely fascinated by it, and I thought it was hilarious and strange" (2015).[1] Conceived as a response to an instruction booklet for amateur photographers that illustrated the "right" and "wrong" way to take a photo, Baldessari created the piece, he said, because "I loved the idea that somebody would just say that this is right and this is wrong. So I decided I would have . . . a work of art that was wrong—which seemed right to me."[2]

From the weird framing that fills the foreground with a band of unremarkable tarmac, to the subject's blurry features and the tree that emerges as if from his head, there's a lot that's formally "wrong" with this picture, as the caption laconically states. It's witty too: in the same way a joke works by setting up expectations and undermining them, *Wrong* declares itself an artwork (with all the attendant expectations of beauty and skilled composition) while simultaneously subverting the criteria of good photography—and good art. But as Abigail Solomon-Godeau points out, *Wrong* "obviously surpasses the realm of the one-liner," and Baldessari's joke also addresses larger aesthetic issues.[3] Pushing its artistic standpoint to the extreme, it suggests that in order to be art, a piece *must* be "wrong"—conventions must be shattered, the aberrant must be included; the amateur is also an artist. Baldessari's insistence that what people think is "wrong" is, in fact, *art* has something of a proto-punk defiance about it. As we'll see, it's the kind of attitude that Cooper would later embrace under the influence of New York punk rock. Cooper would title his first collection of experimental short stories *Wrong*.

Apart from its formal elements—how it attacks and sends up artistic convention—*Wrong* also imparts a social critique that would have been evident to a gay teen like Cooper, who grew up in the 1950s and 1960s and was, even during this early period of his life, politically progressive. Baldessari's photo looks like so many other amateur photos of family life in the suburbs of midcentury America. It's the kind one might find stuffed into an old cardboard box in a junk shop or an attic: an out-of-focus, badly framed snap of Mom and Dad all smiles on their wedding day, or standing awkwardly outside their new home, or on the porch the day the baby came home from the hospital. These photos document the heterosexual family and plot its linear progression through the usual life events that American society in the postwar era deemed worthy of note: birth, marriage, entry into the workforce, acquisition of property, and so on. They guaranteed the family and its history a continuity with America's vision of the nuclear family and its unimpeded passage through (state-sanctioned) time—a time that, as queer theorists like Lee Edelman have noted, was underpinned by a "reproductive futurism," or the heteronormative injunction to reproduce, and was therefore unavailable in this period to queer people like Cooper.[4] As so many other Americans in the 1960s had done, Baldessari looked at this image of the family and suburban bliss championed by the previous generation and pronounced it wrong: wrongheaded, exclusive, and sympathetic with the logic of consumer capitalism and the military-industrial complex that would lead most disastrously to the United States' war in Vietnam.

Solomon-Godeau writes that Baldessari's *Wrong* reflected the "antiauthoritarian, democratic, and ludic impulses" of countercultural California in the 1960s, but Cooper also connected with the piece emotionally—unconsciously ("I don't know why").[5] A darker interpretation of the artwork that Cooper would have been drawn to sees it hint at a wrongness or corruption underneath suburban America's pleasant, conservative veneer. Calling the image "wrong," Baldessari imbues it with an unsettling menace (what Cooper remembers as a "strangeness") by implying that there may be something amiss here, which contrasts with the innocent, domestic, even humorous scene it depicts. Viewed in this way, *Wrong* anticipates the work of later artists such as David Lynch, who most famously exposed the nightmarish underbelly of the suburban American dream in films like *Blue Velvet* (1986). Baldessari's piece thus overturned the conventions of traditional photography while satirizing postwar America, but when the young Cooper saw it first at LACMA, he may have been most startled by the artwork's uncanny familiarity—how it seemed to echo his experience growing up and his sense that, regardless of appearances, life in the California suburbs could indeed be very wrong.

CLIFFORD DENNIS COOPER was born on January 10, 1953, to a wealthy family from West Covina in Southern California. Known simply as Dennis from an early age, dropping his first name helped to distinguish him from his father, also named Clifford, who had come West from Oklahoma twenty years earlier with dreams of making it as a writer. When that didn't work out, he embarked on a successful career as an agricultural policy consultant before setting up the Cooper Development Corporation, an aerospace manufacturer that made parts for America's first space satellite, the Explorer 1. Cooper's mother, Ann, had similarly thwarted artistic aspirations. Trained as a concert pianist, she gave up her musical ambitions to marry Cooper's father—a decision that seems to have troubled her for the rest of her life. With a failed-writer-turned-entrepreneur for a father and a frustrated-musician-cum-housewife for a mother, Cooper recalls that when he was growing up, his family home wasn't especially hospitable to his early artistic attempts: "It was not an artistic household, that's for sure. The book shelves were full of *Reader's Digest* condensed books that would just fill out the shelves and make them look like they had books in them" (2012).[6]

The kind of creative stimulation he yearned for came instead from his mother's side of the family and his maternal grandmother, K. D. Thompson, in particular. According to her obituary in the *Courier-Gazette* of McKinney, Texas, Thompson had a locally celebrated talent for drawing and painting. After receiving an art education, she worked as an art instructor at the Jones Academy in McKinney, where she taught painting for a number of years before she was married; her obituary states that "throughout her life, Mrs. Thompson continued painting and because of the excellence of her work, her paintings have been much in demand."[7] Cooper fondly recalls visiting his grandmother in Texas as a child, where he was exposed to her art and her efforts at amateur taxidermy: "She was kind of amazing," he says, "she was very creative. She would always tell these really crazy stories to us as kids, and I remember being very taken with those" (2015).[8] His mother's brother, Jon King, seems to have inherited Thompson's artistic talent, becoming a painter and moving West from the family home in Texas to the suburbs of Los Angeles. King had bipolar disorder and was an alcoholic, however, and, unlike Cooper's grandmother, he wasn't very encouraging of the young author's creativity. Cooper remembers that when he was eight, King "blew his brains out with a shotgun."[9]

His uncle's suicide is one of a number of traumatic events from his childhood that Cooper remembers vividly and to which he sometimes credits the arousal of his longstanding interest in exploring violence in his writing. Another example comes from the time he was eleven, when, in the middle of building a fort together, his best friend split Cooper's head open with an ax.

> There was no shovel so I found an ax and my friend was digging a hole with the ax. I crawled out the wrong way and the ax went right into the top of my head. I was knocked unconscious for I don't know how long and my friends freaked out and took off. I woke up and blood was just spurting, volcanoing, all over the joint. I reached up and felt my brain. [Laughs.] It was horrifying, I almost died. (2001)[10]

During Cooper's convalescence, the friend who bludgeoned him wouldn't talk to him or even look at him. He did send Cooper long letters, however, announcing that he wanted to kill himself as a kind of punishment for what he'd done. He also wanted Cooper to beat him and torture him as revenge; "I didn't, but I found these letters very erotic. It was the first time I had seen such things in written form, and I used to fantasize about hurting and torturing him, using the letters as pornography and justifying my fantasies to myself because he had issued the invitation."[11]

Shortly after he recovered from the ax incident, Cooper read a newspaper article about three adolescent boys his age who had been found raped and murdered in the hills behind his house. It was a discovery that held a curious interest for him. He was, he recalls, "simultaneously terrified and titillated and very confused" by his fascination with the murders, a fascination that wasn't shared by the friends he tried to confide in, who all thought "it was awful and gross and they had no interest in talking about it."[12] He managed nonetheless to convince one of them to hike to the place where the boys had been found. "We eventually did locate what I believed was the spot where the murders had taken place—I think there was still some pieces of police tape around the location. We camped there for two days. Being there was incredibly powerful, erotic, kind of religious, and frightening to me," says Cooper.[13]

Around this time, his parents also divorced—a distressing event for any child, but it seems to have been especially difficult in Cooper's case, given its impact on his mother's mental health. She had always been a drinker, and this was only exacerbated by her brother's suicide and increased tensions in her marriage; by the time she filed for divorce, Cooper claims that her alcoholism had taken a turn for the worse. With his father barred from the family home, he says "she became very erratic and bizarre," subjecting her children to a campaign of physical and emotional abuse that lasted for years.[14] She regularly threatened to kill herself in front of them by taking sleeping pills that Cooper and his siblings would have to desperately wrest from her grasp. Standing at the top of the stairs of their two-story home, she would declare that she was going to jump to her death. She would flirt with their friends, shut off the power in the house for days at a time, and smash up the children's toys. Cooper remembers that one time she gathered them all together in her car, set off down the street, and suddenly drove full speed at a wall, "saying she was going to kill us all."[15] "Every night she would drink until she was a kind of monster," he says, but "during the days she was totally normal and would deny that any of the nighttime stuff happened, claiming I was a liar" (2006).[16]

Under these circumstances, it's little wonder that Cooper saw much to identify with in John Baldessari's *Wrong*. When he saw it at LACMA as a sixteen-year-old, he already had firsthand experience of just how "wrong"—how terrible, traumatic, violent, and unjust—life in the picture-postcard suburbs of the United States could be. But by this time, he had also started to write about these experiences, which in some ways legitimized them for him and, he says, "helped me start to get away from a life that had been very confusing and unstable" (2006).[17] Like Baldessari, Cooper had started to think about art's connection to what was "wrong" and the role art could play in exploring, elucidating, or even distancing oneself from the disturbing, perverse, or occluded—those things conservative American society considered "wrong." Also pivotal in this regard, as we'll see in the next chapter, was Cooper's discovery of the Marquis de Sade's *120 Days of Sodom* and the poetry of Arthur Rimbaud around the same time.

"FIFTEEN WAS a really important age for me," Cooper says. "I decided to become a writer" (2006).[18] He was attending Flintridge Preparatory School in La Cañada near Pasadena at the time, after he was taken out of public school in the eighth grade because he was bullied. At Flintridge he'd finally found his feet, becoming friends with a group of like-minded, arty

George Miles, yearbook photo, 1968.
Courtesy of Dennis Cooper.

young people who were also into rock music and drugs, who respected him, and who thought he was cool. While he was there, he also met a fellow student named George Miles, a twelve-year-old boy who would become the single most important figure in his life. He remembers:

> George Miles was a kid I met when I was in ninth grade. He was the younger brother of a friend of mine. He was twelve when we became friends, and I was fifteen. The school we both attended went from fourth grade to twelfth, so we were fellow students. One night, I was at a school dance when my friend, his brother Jay, came to me and said "My little brother took acid and he's freaking out, and he's twelve years old." I had taken a lot of acid and everybody knew it. He said, "Maybe you can help him. Maybe you can talk him down." Jay led me to George and, yeah, he was tripping pretty heavily. I took him out to the football field and just sat with him for about four hours and tried to talk him through it. We really bonded that night, from then on, we were really close. (2011)[19]

After they met at the school dance, Cooper and Miles became in-separable, spending evenings and weekends together, riding their bikes around the neighborhood and listening to records at Cooper's house. Miles was welcomed into Cooper's gang of older friends, who all liked him and thought he was a warm, funny kid. His parents weren't happy that he was spending so much time with these new, older friends, how-ever, and began to suspect Cooper of ulterior motives—that he might have been infatuated with his young schoolmate. In fact, according to Cooper they totally misread the situation: two weeks after they'd first met, Miles had declared his love for *him*. "He said, 'I've gotta talk to you. I'm in love with you.' I said, 'I really don't think you are. . . . You're the most amazing person in the world and I love you. You're great but I can't feel that way about you. You're really young.'"[20] Miles didn't take the rejection well and in frustration threw a rock through a nearby window. To calm him down, Cooper proposed a deal:

> He got really upset that I didn't feel the way he did. So we talked about it. I said, "Look, if you were older I'd probably be able to fall in love with you. Let's make a deal to be best friends and if you still feel this way in a couple of years, tell me. I think in a couple of years it's possible that I might feel differently. But right now I just can't." (2018)[21]

Whenever they met from that point on, Miles would remind Cooper of their deal and gently inquire if his feelings had changed. They hadn't, and they wouldn't—at least for a while.

Convinced that Cooper was somehow taking advantage of their son, Miles's parents finally banned him from seeing Cooper. The two friends had to resort to hanging out in secret, getting together at a friend's house or setting up clandestine meetings after school. "That went on for a while but it was fucked up and just made things more intense between us," Cooper recalls.[22] The ban remained in place for a while until, at the age of fourteen, Miles suddenly became very depressed and was diagnosed with manic depression (bipolar disorder). Things would get so bad that he would spend days in bed in an almost catatonic state; his mother, desper-ate to help him in any way she could, asked Cooper to come over. "He was literally lying in his bed staring at the ceiling," says Cooper. "He tried to engage but he was having a really hard time. I sat there for a really long time. He got a little better and I left" (2018).[23] Although she didn't like him, Miles's mother was struck by the positive effect Cooper's presence had on her son and asked him to visit more often. Eventually she relied on Cooper to come over and try to raise Miles's spirits whenever he was depressed, which happened quite a lot.

For the next few years Miles would continue to experience many more severe depressive episodes; doctors tried various combinations of drugs to help alleviate his symptoms, but they had no lasting effect. Cooper stuck by him through it all—even when his group of friends, in the callous way of some teenagers, asked Miles to stop hanging out with them because he'd become such a drag. In time, Cooper's feelings for Miles changed. He recalls that when he was nineteen (Miles was fifteen), "I started to realize I had more than friendship feelings for him. It was very complicated because he was such a mess but I did have them."[24] Miles was in love with him too, but once they'd talked it out, it became clear that nothing could happen between them: they knew Miles's mental health issues would ruin any chance they had of making it work. So he and Cooper decided to wait until he got better—or at least until his medication evened him out. As Cooper tells it, "Basically we decided 'OK we're in love, but we're not going to do anything about it right now'" (2018).[25]

Miles didn't get better. Shortly afterward, he attempted suicide and was committed to a psychiatric hospital. When he was released, he became a fundamentalist Christian and left high school for a time to live in a Christian commune. Having a girlfriend was a recurring fixation for him that exacerbated his confusion and depression. Heterosexual relationships promised his compliance with social norms and a psychological stability that he yearned for; when he was unable to give himself physically and emotionally to relationships with women, this promise was swiftly withdrawn and exposed for the fraud it was. According to Cooper, "George had this idea that if he had a girlfriend he would be normal. Not just that he would *seem* normal (although that was important too), but that it would *cure* him. It didn't make any sense, but he had it for his whole life" (2018).[26] Cooper ventures that Miles was probably bisexual and that he struggled with his sexuality throughout his life.

The pattern that marked the early years of their friendship—the intimacy between them stalled and derailed by Miles's psychological problems and the interference of his parents—would recur in subsequent years. They finally had sex in Cooper's dorm room at Pitzer College in 1975 (Cooper remembers that "it was kind of amazing: I was like 'Wow, why didn't we do this years ago?!'"), but their plan for Miles to join Cooper there and for them to live together was ruined by Miles's parents, who refused to pay his college tuition.[27] A few years later they got together again while Miles was at college in northern California, this time for an extended period, but it was clear to Cooper that his friend had changed in the intervening years. Mental health–wise, he'd gotten much worse.

> It was amazing but it was different. He was different. I don't know what happened to him, but he wasn't the same anymore. He just didn't have hope anymore; he was very cynical. He said to me, "I'm never going to get better." He always used to believe he would but it'd been four years and I think it was really hard for him up there [in northern California]. I think he tried to kill himself. . . . But we would be together and he would become himself again. He would become, at times, completely like the George I remembered: he'd be really happy and funny and great for a lot of the time. Then he would just . . . Tilt. (2018)[28]

The tilts and mood swings ultimately became too much, and Cooper and Miles agreed to cool things off; although they talked on the phone all the time (even when Cooper moved to New York in 1983), they were ostensibly on a break.

In the early 1980s, Cooper told Miles that he wanted to create an artistic tribute or memorial to him that would honor him and their long, profound, extremely complicated relationship. From the time Cooper started writing as a teenager, he'd wanted to write a large, elaborate, literary work that would stand the test of time, and meeting Miles turned out to be the key to the whole endeavor.

> I realized that George was very important to me and that if I put George in it, if I made the project a tribute to him, it would have its heart. I wanted to do something for him, because even at that point it was very clear that although he was on medication and fairly okay, his emotions and psychology and energies were engaged in such a battle within him. . . . I felt that he would get lost in life, and I wanted his name to mean something.[29]

When Cooper talked to Miles about his idea and told him his plans for what would become the George Miles Cycle, Miles approved: "He said, 'Sure, you can do that. That's nice'" (2011).[30]

Work on the Cycle began in 1985, when Cooper moved to Amsterdam; unfortunately, during that time he also lost touch with Miles, who was thousands of miles away and eight hours behind. "I wrote George a bunch of letters and he never wrote back, but people do that," says Cooper.[31] His repeated attempts to contact Miles when he returned to the States a couple of years later were fruitless, and only when he'd published the fourth of the five novels in the George Miles Cycle did he finally find out that Miles had killed himself in 1987. *Closer*, the first novel in the Cycle, was published in 1989: Miles had never seen a single page of the celebrated work that was inspired by him and written as a monument to him. In the aftermath of his discovery, Cooper was overcome with grief: "I spent about eight months trying to find out what had happened, checking microfilm of newspapers from that time, searching cemeteries for his grave, trying to locate mutual friends, anything I could think of," he says. "I eventually found his mother, and she told me he had killed himself, blown his head off with a shotgun in his childhood bedroom on his thirtieth birthday" (2011).[32]

It's impossible to accurately assess the impact of George Miles on Cooper's work: Cooper himself admits that Miles was "the most important person I've ever known. I always write about him. In some ways, he's in all of my characters" (2011).[33] A whole book could be dedicated to their friendship—how Miles affected Cooper's writing, his psychological makeup, his physical type—but any such work, as Cooper found out in 2012 when he tried in vain to write a memoir focused on Miles, would inevitably fail to capture the subtleties of their relationship and their complicated emotional dynamic. And yet Cooper's feelings for Miles are palpable in the novels. The George Miles Cycle might have been called "blank" by hasty readers dazzled by the sheen of Cooper's prose, but to more careful readers it's obvious that the writing overflows with emotion—profound affection; frustrated, unfulfilled longing; and a desperate desire to care for a loved one and be cared for in return.

Miles is a flickering presence in the Cycle: he's the inscrutable George of *Closer*, whom everyone fucks but nobody knows; in *Frisk* he's Kevin, spliced with a young Keanu Reeves; in *Try* his bipolar disorder animates

George Miles (left), 1970. Courtesy of Dennis Cooper.

the disturbed, adorable Ziggy; in *Guide* he's refracted through the narrator's memory and locked up in a psychiatric hospital. All of *Period*'s troubled teens are haunted by him. In these novels, Miles is apprehended only in fragments, and perhaps this is the reason why Cooper's feelings for him are so readily apparent. He appears in the Cycle as he appeared to Cooper: in fragments. The Cycle offers elusive glimpses of a beloved, goofy kid Cooper first met outside a school dance at Flintridge Prep, distorted through the prism of psychosis and separation.

OF HIS SCHOOL DAYS at Flintridge, Cooper says "that was where I kind of blossomed" (2012).[34] His friendship group at the school and his attachment to Miles offered him some relief from the ongoing drama at home. In particular, he says, "I could focus my thwarted wish to cure my mom or protect my siblings on George, who was deeply troubled, but, at the same time, someone not unlike myself, and who seemed to really flourish within my love and support for a long time" (2006).[35] He also started to write in earnest. Having previously spent much of his time alone in his bedroom, "obsessing over rock music and television shows, drawing pictures and writing naïve poems and stories" (2006), as one of the school's most artistic students, at Flintridge Cooper found a small but appreciative audience that was eager to hear what he'd written. "I was the school's writer and artist," he remembers (2012).[36]

His writing from this time bears the obvious hallmarks of a youngster growing up in 1960s California, surrounded by a burgeoning counterculture that expressed its dissatisfaction with the politics of the day and the warmongering of American politicians with a growing voice. It wasn't a view shared by Cooper's conservative parents: the family had profited enormously from his father's political connections. Cliff had worked with people like Herbert Hoover and Harry S. Truman on agricultural policy, and he was happy to cozy up to political figures to advance his fortune, later becoming close friends with Richard Nixon. He even named their second son, Richard, after him. As Cooper's early poems and stories show, Cliff's eldest son was far more hostile to the political establishment.

Sweetly sincere and alternately utopian and liberal, Cooper's teenage writings have titles like "Reform," "The Life and Stupidity of L. B. J.," and "Ballad of a Segregated Relationship." Some were collected in a binder with the enigmatic title *I'm Sorry I Bent Your Feathers So Long* doodled on the cover in bubble letters. His poems and stories are divided into sections labeled things like "Life and Death in the Present Mediocre Society," "Protesting Time," and "War." A poem called "Death of a Common Man" approaches the style of a folk protest song in its arresting account of a political demonstration, scattered before the billy clubs of the police (Cooper was a fan of Bob Dylan at the time).

What's that sound
Liberty bells
Motorcycles
Thousands in terror
Running for their lives
Trampling buffaloes
Ho Chi Min [*sic*]
Jackie Kennedy
Fear Fear Fear

A surreal dialogue called "A KITV Talk Show" pits the host against a rambling, anti-Semitic bigot who is quickly hustled off the set before he's revealed to be the rambling, anti-Semitic (and homophobic) pastor, Billy Graham. Meanwhile, "The Life and Stupidity of L. B. J.," written in 1968 as Lyndon B. Johnson's controversial presidency was drawing to a close, rages: "He led our country for five years. He killed our boys in Vietnam for five years. He mangled this country for five years and now he retires after he has almost completely ruined our land. . . ."[37]

Consistent with the ideals of the hippie movement (one page carries an illustration of a flower accompanied by the phrase "flower power"), Cooper's juvenilia are a little naïve, and he has dismissed all of his writing from this period, but they nonetheless evoke the fertile ground out of which the author's political radicalism would later grow. These pieces are of course much more explicit in their engagement with politics than his later work—none of his published poetry or prose advances the same kind of impassioned criticism of the political establishment that these early poems do, calling out politicians by name. But we will see that even as Cooper's engagement with extant politics becomes less explicit, his actual political stance shifts from the kind of hippie liberalism evoked by these early writings to a more recognizably anarchist position following his encounter with punk rock.

Unfortunately, Cooper's time at Flintridge was relatively short. Taken to be the leader of a small group of clever, arty teenagers who were taking drugs and listening to rock music (Cooper also became a vegetarian—and has remained one throughout his life), Cooper was identified by the school as a subversive element. "We were just bad kids in a private boy's school and we were considered bad influences," he remembers. "And because of George, the younger kids became friends with us too. The school authorities were panicked because of the weird hippy degenerates having all these twelve-year boys hanging out with them" (2001).[38] All of Cooper's friends were kicked out when drugs were found on them; when they couldn't get him for drug use, Cooper was finally expelled on a trumped-up charge in the eleventh grade, and he returned to public school education in Los Angeles in 1969.

After Cooper graduated from high school in 1970, he headed to Pasadena City College to study poetry. His two years there seem to have been uneventful, although classes with poets like Jerene Hewitt and Ron

Koertge introduced him to a wider LA poetry scene, which he and his friends would set out to revolutionize a few years later. Koertge, a poet and novelist who still teaches at Pasadena City College, remembers Cooper as "an extraordinary student": "He was sophisticated and well-read, and even in those days . . . someone who wrote and was interested in publishing on his own terms. In short, he struck me as a real writer."[39]

While at college, Cooper also first encountered the New York School of poets, who would become a major influence on his poetry and writing life. After he found Sade and Rimbaud as a teenager, he sought out other French writers, including Baudelaire, Lautréamont, Apollinaire, and Reverdy. Although he admits to being interested in experimental American fiction in high school and reading people like Richard Brautigan, Thomas Pynchon, and Ishmael Reed, who were "very cool and fashionable" at the time, it didn't excite him in the same way, and when he started college, he was reading only French writers (2011).[40] Once he discovered New York School poetry, however, he was hooked. He recalls that its impact was "huge":

> I'd been pretty much exclusively interested in French poets up until then, but discovering the second generation of the New York School poets was a huge revelation. Their work was so fresh and exciting and just so relevant, and it had an interest in style and form that created a kind of bridge from the French poets I loved, who were all dead, and the world I occupied, which revolved around rock music and drugs and rebellion and poetry. (2006)[41]

The influence of the New York School is tangible in Cooper's first collection of poetry, a self-published chapbook called *The Terror of Earrings*, which he put out in 1973. A mishmash of styles, in these poems Cooper has yet to develop the remarkably flat tone of his later poetry, and he's obviously still experimenting with different styles and approaches. The subjects of these poems are themselves a rather varied bunch and range from the crystalline glimpses of domestic strife of "Save This Marriage (A Plea)" to the epidemiological "History of Disease." Rock-and-roll musicians like David Bowie and Jim Morrison are recurring presences, however, as are Hollywood stars, drugs, and death. "The Plague and Boredom Are Getting Married" describes a hallucinatory travelogue that finds the poem's speaker driving through California with Pinocchio, Neil Young, and a "mescaline baby."

> The Mazda climbs the hill into Altadena.
> Pinocchio and Neil Young swap life stories in the back seat.
> The silence is swallowing me in the front seat so I shove
> my hand into the tape player
> and scream.
> Neil pretends to barf, tells me
> "You watch too much T.V."[42]

Transferring Disney's Pinocchio into its drugged-up demotic, Cooper's poem echoes the New York School poets' characteristic improvisations on cartoons and comic strips, such as those found in John Ashbery's "Farm Implements and Rutabagas in a Landscape" (1963), which features the cast of Popeye—or even Joe Brainard's adult reimaginings of Nancy and Sluggo where the two iconic characters smoke cigarettes and have sex. But in this poem, as elsewhere in the collection, Cooper brings a certain morbidity to bear on a New York School theme as his Pinocchio finally dies on a two-bit doctor's operating table, attended by the speaker and Neil Young: "Moments later . . . gasp . . . school's out. / He's gone dead."[43]

This kind of sinister deflation of New York School whimsy is evident in another poem, called "#19," which seems to respond to Frank O'Hara's wry remark in "Personism: A Manifesto" (1959) that while he was writing a poem at work, "I was realizing that if I wanted I could use the telephone instead of writing the poem."[44] Stephanie Burt's gloss on this finds that, for O'Hara, poems "are only one kind of intimate communication, and ought to be at least as impressive, at least as personal perhaps, as the others (even if their forms differ). Every poem is or could be a 'Personal Poem' . . . with an 'I' and a 'you,' and a hope, not that Heaven will favor the poet, but that 'one person out of the 8,000,000 is / thinking of me.'"[45] In "#19," Cooper seems to take these ideas and bury them in the ground.

> the effect of these poems is to dial
> then (dead things)
> the mouths are all dead

> the telephone box looks dead thru
> the trees
> the sun is amazing   to be dead[46]

In the opening line, the speaker indicates his familiarity with O'Hara's statement and evokes the latter's comparison between poetry and telephony. After that, the line between O'Hara and Cooper goes dead. In contrast to the kind of "Personal Poem" Burt takes as exemplary of O'Hara, there's no "I" or "You" here, and no communication is established between the poet and the reader; variations on "dead things" ("all dead," "dead thru the trees," "to be dead"), stacked on the right-hand side, obstruct the poem's rhythm and impede any attempt to understand it or get a read on what the poet means. O'Hara's typical exuberance is evoked in "the sun is amazing," which sounds like something he might write (punctuated with an exclamation mark, perhaps), but it appears to have been grafted onto the poem, away to the left and separated from the sense of the line. It's almost as if in this poem Cooper is trying to connect with O'Hara—as the image of the telephone box evokes—but his interest in death and the macabre shorts that connection.

In effect, "#19" foregrounds the fact that a New York School aesthetic may be ill-suited to a treatment of darker subjects such as those addressed by Baudelaire and Lautréamont. In place of a hybrid form, Cooper is left with a cluster of weird contradictions. This was far from Cooper's final word on O'Hara, however, and it might be better to consider this poem as the beginning of what would become a long negotiation with New York School aesthetics in his poetry. Daniel Kane points out that "as much as Cooper was indebted to the New York scene, he was also clearly determined not to ape his heroes," and, as in the case of "#19," Cooper's subsequent poetry would continue to adopt, critique, and often torture the style of his beloved forebears.[47]

IN 1975, COOPER LEFT Pasadena City College and started at Pitzer College in Claremont, California, where he continued studying poetry and took classes with the likes of LA poet Bert Meyers. Although he was only there for a year, his time at Pitzer was significant in large part because it was where he met his lifelong friend and fellow poet, Amy Gerstler. In her, Cooper found a kindred spirit who was similarly passionate about the New York School and who would later partner with him in putting together an exciting young punk poetry scene in Los Angeles. She remembers that they met early in their first year at college through his roommate Brian Tucker, with whom she'd been taking acting classes. "One day Brian said, 'You're interested in poetry—you should meet this guy Dennis, he's a total poetry nut.' I was already curious about this 'Dennis Cooper' because he had taken to lightly plastering our tiny campus with Xeroxes of what he called 'THE WEEKLY POEM,' or something like that, where he wrote out a poem he loved, with a little contextual info, and Cooper commentary appended. I first encountered the work of poet Russell Edson, for example, through Dennis's weekly poem postings."[48]

Gerstler, a 2018 Guggenheim Fellow who won the National Book Critics Circle Award in 1991 for her collection *Bitter Angel* (1990), regards Cooper as a literary mentor and recalls that when she first met him, he struck her as an "incredibly powerful presence" who "took himself absolutely seriously as an artist."

> His intelligence, his mind-energy, the force of his personality, his magnetism were staggering for me to encounter at 17, as was his voraciousness about every kind of art. He was (and is) incredibly articulate, focused, charismatic. He was a guy who made things happen around him, interesting, important, affecting things. He curated his life and the lives of those who fell under his sway (and that was definitely me) with an almost single-minded passion for cultivating generative artistic and cultural immersion.[49]

For his part, Cooper says quite simply, "Amy's the best" (2018).[50] A confidante and trusted peer with whom he has always shared his writing and from whom he always received thoughtful critiques, Gerstler's important influence on his life and work is repeatedly recognized in many of his books, and her name is a fixture of Cooper's list of acknowledgments.

Cooper settled in quickly at Pitzer, hanging out with Gerstler and his roommate Tucker, with whom he had also become close. Tucker, who would continue to be Cooper's roommate for the best part of a decade, later remembered going to countless performances, readings, films, and gigs together. When Cooper got a spot on the college radio station, 88.7 FM, hosting a music show that went out on Monday and Friday mornings,

Tucker did the artwork for the promo posters Cooper stuck up around campus. Nevertheless, after just a year Cooper left college and never returned. Devastated that George Miles wouldn't be able to join him at Pitzer after they had finally consummated their relationship and made plans to live together as boyfriends, he cared less and less about his college education. His departure was hastened by an encounter in the hallway with his teacher Meyers. Cooper explains:

> I was always rattling on to [Meyers] about poetry as a visionary practice and carrying a Rimbaud book everywhere I went. One day I was walking down the hall pontificating to him and he grabbed me, threw me against a wall, and told me that if I really believed what I was saying, I should quit school and live my life and see the world at large and be a writer and not just some student speculating wildly about the practice. And I did—I quit school at the end of the semester, and I owe him, because he was absolutely right. (2011)[51]

That summer he set out to explore the world at large with Tucker in tow, and the two young friends toured Europe in June and July of 1976. At Cooper's behest they made a trip to Charleville-Mézières, the birthplace of Arthur Rimbaud in northern France, where, Tucker remembers, Cooper made a solemn journey alone to Rimbaud's tomb: "The trip to his grave was almost a sacred pilgrimage to Dennis, so I remained in town while he went out to the gravesite. He came back with two or three pill bottles filled with dirt from the site. I recall that he intended to give one of them to Patti Smith."[52] Cooper and Tucker also went to England and caught a fateful gig at London's Roundhouse on July 4, featuring the Ramones and the Flamin' Groovies, which arguably kick-started the UK punk scene in earnest (more on this later).

Once they returned to the States, as per Meyers's suggestion, Cooper also got serious about being a writer and published a second book of poetry, *Tiger Beat*, in 1978 with his newly created Little Caesar Press. Like his earlier efforts, these poems attested to his abiding interest in California youth culture, pornography, and the numbing glamour of American TV shows. The iconography of rock music was also a recurring concern, and stars of pop and rock continued to make cameos: "Boy Talk" takes place in the aftermath of a Blondie gig, where singer Debbie Harry has left the poem's speaker with "chills on [his] skin,"[53] while "David Cassidy" is an extended homoerotic fantasy staring the teen idol of *The Partridge Family*.

> David Cassidy picks me on the Dating Game.
> I walk around the partition
> and there he is. A quick kiss,
> then Jim Lange gives us the good news.
>
> "David, we'll be flying you and your date
> to . . . . . . Rio de Janeiro! You'll be
> staying at the luxurious Rio Hilton
> and attend a party in your honor!"
>
> At the Hilton we knock the chaperone
> out with a lamp, then we jive around,
> smoke a little Colombian.
> David says something to let me
> know he's willing, and I get
> to chew his clothes off.[54]

Even though the previous collection's darker elements surfaced once again here (one piece, "Dean Corll, American Mass Murderer," hints at a subject that Cooper would return to many times), the influence of New York School poetry was still readily apparent in the collection. People like Allen Ginsberg picked up on it immediately, exclaiming that "*Tiger Beat* is imaginative, sexy, funny, TV pop high school masculine muscles and hair plus some high irony cadenzas out of the extravagances of 'N.Y. School' mind." Joe Brainard also offered his praise, stating rather more laconically, "I like it a lot."[55]

Sturm und Drang | Rimbaud and Sade

2 COOPER'S FIRST widely distributed poetry collection, *Idols*, was published in 1979 by Felice Picano's progressive gay SeaHorse Press. A selection of Cooper's poetry written between the ages of sixteen and twenty-five, it includes almost a decade's worth of work, but unlike his previous, more erratic collections, there is a remarkable consistency to Cooper's choice of subjects. The reader is struck from the outset by the continual circulation in the space of the collection of numerous sexually adventurous teenage boys masturbating in high school locker rooms, lounging on street corners turning tricks, or caressing each other's pale bodies in hotel rooms in Amsterdam. Yet Cooper's preoccupation with teenagers doesn't stand apart from the way he tells their stories—it often determines how the poems are written. More than a mere subject to be disinterestedly described or applied to a poetic form, in a number of these poems adolescence bears upon their style. "High School Basketball," for instance, sketches fast-paced flashes of scenes from an afternoon of pickup basketball games at the high school gym.

> When boys wanted to toss the ball around they'd use ninth period
> when nothing was going on. I'd see a herd of them heading down the
> gym stairs. I'd join them if no one had brought any Hendrix records
> or dope. I'd be in the middle of that crowd, trampling the steps like
> water in front of a busted dam. We'd hit the cool of the locker rooms.
> We couldn't stop moving around, too ready. Jockstrap never washed.
> Short blue trunks. Blue tee-shirt or not. Dirty white socks to our
> knees. Tennis shoes (white or black) with our names.[1]

Cooper's rush of short, punchy sentences spill out like water from "a busted dam." Quickly swamping the speaker's rather removed "I" and carrying him away in a plural "we," the poem simulates the energy and excitement of its youthful subjects as they sprint up and down the court, watched by "a few girls in the bleachers talking boys with their faces close together."[2] Shifting and erratic, flitting from one image to the next, the poem is "too ready" to "stop moving around" and seems to derive this incessant motility from its "herd" of aroused teens.

The poems in *Idols* are also preoccupied with how adolescence affects one's perception of time. Written during and just after Cooper's teenage years, in these poems adolescence is either something being lived through or something that has been left behind, whose loss is felt acutely. Many of the poems take the latter approach; the opening series of eight poems called "Boys I've Wanted" insists on a temporal dislocation between the speaker and the teenage figures who drift into his retrospective mirror. In the poem "Greg Tomeoni," the speaker remembers a scene of fumbling adolescent sex from a removed present: "I was in eighth grade / when he was in seventh," he remembers, noting that "we didn't cum (too young I think)."[3] Throughout the series, a pervasive past tense distances the poetic voice from the events and individuals described such that they occasionally assume the character of objects separate from the speaker, now much older. The subject of "Bill McCall" is offered to the reader like an old photograph, yellowing at the edges.

Friends, see how pale
his skin was. It
glowed. And his lips
with a trace of teeth, and
ears like boats for tongues.[4]

In these poems and others like them from the collection, the poet tries to encapsulate the events and beloveds of his youth from the position of the present. But detachment dogs his representations such that their artificiality, their constructedness, their rerouting through the screen of an older poet's mind constantly comes to the fore. Cooper here seems to insist that the lived experience of an adolescent—even the poet's own adolescence—can't be translated into the experience and language of a mature adult without doing a certain violence to it. This may account for the flat, descriptive tone of the series and its subdued affect: Cooper is perhaps reticent to speak for the adolescent other or speculate about their emotional states in words that are not their own. In short, in the "Boys I've Wanted" series, adolescence takes place *in another time*: not just an earlier time but a lived temporality that is qualitatively different from the poet's own and exists beyond his attempts to represent it.

This conjunction of poetics and adolescence appeared a little unusual to Robert Peters, one of *Idols'* first reviewers, who wrote, "Until recently, I knew of no poets who capture the rich fantasy life of the adolescent in poetry worthy of the name. Leonard Cohen's self-pitying, beaver-shot, teenybopper poems don't quite make it. But Dennis Cooper's new poems, *Idols*, do."[5] Peters shouldn't have been that surprised, however—the concept of adolescence as described and popularized by G. Stanley Hall's two-volume study *Adolescence* (1904) in fact marked poetic production since the early decades of the twentieth century.

Hall famously defined adolescence as a time of rapidly accelerated growth and development when the individual is forced to give up the protected seclusion of childhood and assume his or her place in the social collective. Adolescence, he famously argued, is

> suggestive of some ancient period of storm and stress [Sturm und Drang] when old moorings were broken and a higher level attained. There is much passivity, often active resistance and evasion, and perhaps spasms of obstinacy, to it all. But the senses are keen and alert, reactions immediate and vigorous, and the memory is quick, sure, and lasting, and ideas of space, time, and physical causation, and of many a moral and social licit and non-licit, are rapidly unfolding.[6]

Hall's study identified a constellation of ideas that would come to define the way people thought and talked about teenage life in the years that followed. Delinquency, the adolescent's pursuit of excitement, susceptibility to the media's influence, and propensity for "relational aggression" like rumor and gossip: these kinds of ideas and their widespread circulation not only changed what people thought were appropriate topics for poetic treatment, they also changed how poems were written.

Poets such as William Carlos Williams tried to bear witness to the experience of adolescence through a modulation of poetic form and diction. Williams's work is one of the earliest examples of a modern adolescent poetics, incorporating contemporary youth culture into his writing with the hope of catalyzing a rejuvenation of art and poetry. Adolescence is not just a recurring subject for works like *Spring and All* (1923) and *The Descent of Winter* (1928); their composition also appears to emerge out of an adolescent's pursuit of new sensations—charging ahead, lines left half-written, orthodoxy dismissed with the impertinence of youth. Williams's critics were not initially convinced by his irreverent, unpredictable poetics, however, and Marion Strobel in particular took issue with the timorous, juvenile machismo of his poems, writing that "[Williams] is like an adolescent boy who, while loving something of soft-petalled beauty, scoffs at it, so that he will be considered a He-Man."[7] Cooper nonetheless seems to gesture toward Williams's importance to the development of a poetics of adolescence by giving him a cameo in the high school homework assignment of John F. Kennedy Jr., featured in the series of poems in *Idols* titled "Some Adventures of John F. Kennedy Jr."

> . . . he slogs through poets,
> hates them all until William Carlos Williams.
> "You mean this is poetry?" He leaps
> on his notebook. "I can write this stuff
> by the ton." And so he does, a twenty pager.[8]

Long before he heard about Williams, however, Cooper had already encountered Arthur Rimbaud's *Illuminations* (1886). Remarking on his earliest influences, Cooper says, "When I was fifteen, I read an interview with Bob Dylan and he mentioned Rimbaud. So I bought one of Rimbaud's books and I was staggered. Everything changed. His poetry, his biography, the fact that he wrote such incredible things and was so ambitious when he was my age were hugely inspiring" (2011).[9] While still a teenager, therefore, Cooper had found in Rimbaud a paradigmatic combination of youth and poetic form. In her survey of the intersections of youth and poetry, Stephanie Burt affirms this combination when she states that Rimbaud is "the closest nineteenth-century predecessor for the modern English-language poetry of adolescence. . . . Composed in the 1870s, Rimbaud's poetry seemed to him and to its later readers rebellious, uncontrollable, immature, unstable, hostile to received authority, radiant with sexual energy, sensitive to urban social change (i.e., the Paris

Commune), and in search of an extraordinary new language. Not coincidentally, Rimbaud was himself in his teens."[10]

The most pertinent aspect of Rimbaud's work is its pervasive energy and an affirmation of incompletion, which repeatedly curbs development. In Burt's estimation it demonstrates an "absolute resistance to *Bildung*, to any and all attempts to mold, from a youthful life, an adult life course or a career."[11] Works collected in the *Illuminations* especially display Rimbaud's resistance to normative notions of maturity and psychological development. Leo Bersani argues that these poems repudiate conventional models of the mature individual, and "the poetic imagination tends to become a slide projector that ejects each slide almost at the very instant it is lighted up."[12] The poem "Childhood," for instance, is made up of numerous stubborn impediments to progress or narrative continuity and comprises successive "slides" of half-beheld consciousness tethered to a precarious, positional "there is":

> In the woods there is a bird; his song stops you and makes you blush.
> There is a clock that never strikes.
> There is a hollow with a nest of white beasts.
> There is a cathedral that goes down and a lake that goes up.
> There is a little carriage abandoned in the copse or that goes running
> down the road beribboned.[13]

For Cooper, adolescence evokes Rimbaud, and Rimbaud's poetics is defined in large part by his adolescence. We can see this at work in a number of pieces from *Idols*, where he combines an emphatically adolescent milieu with a form reminiscent of a Rimbaldian poetics. In these poems, temporality is once again brought into play.

> Jim, my best friend,
> gives me five dollars
> when I am sixteen
> to lie face down on his bed
> while he feels my ass,
> long hair passing for a girl's.
>
> Jim, caught by his mom
> on the night I sleep over

with my used underwear
pressed up to his nose
while I perch nearby
pretending to sleep.

I, pulling up his
wet swimmer's silks
over my white ass
in front of the mirror
and Jim, from behind,
slips his palms inside.

Jim, my oldest friend,
watching me dress out
in gym class, grabbing me,
snapping my butt with
wet towel, leaves marks
on me, red as his mouth.[14]

"Early Riser" shows that on those occasions when Cooper tries to describe adolescent experience, time is an essential vantage from which to explore and represent it from the inside. The poem conveys a sense of logical continuity (e.g., when the speaker refers to "his wet swimmer's silks," the reader can infer correctly that these are Jim's), but it unfolds as a series of vignettes, illuminated momentarily and arranged without transition from one scene to the next. Its form recalls Bersani's description of a Rimbaldian "slide projector," and, as in the French poet's work, only the incident that is underway right now is significant: Jim *"gives* me five dollars / when I *am* sixteen." If the poem is logically continuous, therefore, it is certainly not temporally so—each end-stopped line does not so much interrupt the action as strictly define its limits within the space of each isolated stanza.

Unlike other poems from the collection that go to great lengths to remove their teen subjects to a distant, unassailable past, "Early Riser" is marked by the insistence of the present. We watch as Jim hands over the money, gets caught sniffing the speaker's underwear, gropes the speaker in front of a mirror. The language illustrates a sequence of moments placed in a continuous present, and Cooper's employment of present participles

in the final stanza in particular ("watching," "grabbing," "snapping") locates the events he recounts in an elongated instant: the intimate lives of
these two adolescents appear before the reader in a continual *now*. This
effect resonates intimately with one found in Rimbaud's *Illuminations*
(we recall the insistent "There is" of "Childhood"), as Cooper's delicate
warping of the poem's temporality around the sex lives of his teenage
protagonists refuses narrative progress. Concentrating sexually charged
activity in an enduring instant, "Early Riser" is emblematic of Cooper's
ongoing explorations of the time of adolescence—an exploration that is
only made possible by his initial encounter with Rimbaud.

FOR COOPER, the most exciting and enduring features associated with
the young French poet—Rimbaud's iconoclastic energy, his radical resistance to authority, his aesthetic innovation—indicate the possibilities
of adolescence in general. Cooper's work affirms a potential he perceives
in adolescence, against a society that on the one hand adores childhood
and on the other lionizes maturity, that effectively normalizes social ac-
culturation and dismisses adolescence as a temporary aberration or an
unfortunate excrescence that must be overcome. As he passionately states
in an interview with Ira Silverberg, "The fact that teenagers were routinely
disrespected, objectified, exploited, and disempowered was a huge issue
to me [at fifteen] and one that has remained very important to me as I've
become an adult." He continues:

> Now I can inhabit the thoughts and emotions and motivations of
> adults who see teenagers as problems, as reminders of their own
> youth, as sex-objects or triggers of sentimentality, as a dismissible,
> transitional, short-lived species that occupies some sort of dark age
> between childhood and adulthood, both of which are seen as more
> legitimate stages of life. But my concentration is on resisting that
> supposed wisdom. (2011)[15]

Implicit in this analysis is a radical attitude toward time, which emerges
in tandem with the idea of adolescence and with Rimbaud by proxy: instead of a stage in a normative process of psychological and social development, adolescence is rather a *state* that Cooper's work investigates and
enshrines.

A similar idea runs through Kristen Ross's *The Emergence of Social Space* (1988), which reads Rimbaud together with the Paris Commune, a "semianarchistic" uprising that began on March 18, 1871, and ended seventy-two days later in a bloody massacre of twenty-five thousand Parisians by the federal army.[16] Inaugurating a "horizontal" system of government via a network of self-governing *arrondissements*, the Commune was endorsed at the time by the anarchist Mikhail Bakunin, who acclaimed its "spontaneous and continued action" that brought about "a bold, clearly formulated negation of the State."[17] Bakunin was nonetheless wary of heaping too much praise on such a short-lived uprising, and modern historians have followed suit, giving it relatively short shrift. But according to Ross, the Commune represents an important insurrectionary moment, and its dismissal on the basis of its ephemerality is symptomatic of a normative view of time that privileges longevity—a notion that is challenged by the Commune itself. Temporality in the Commune, Ross argues, was untimely or "saturated."

> The publicity of political life, the immediate publication of all the Commune's decisions, and proclamations, largely in the form of *affiches*, resulted in a "spontaneous" temporality whereby citizens were no longer informed of their history after the fact but were actually occupying the moment of its realization . . . we can describe the sensation as being a simultaneous perception of events passing by quickly, too quickly, and of each hour and minute being entirely lived or made use of: saturated time.[18]

The Commune is therefore a rupture with the idea of historical progress, imbued with a latent potentiality that turns the concept of time on its head. Reminiscent of theories of the event found in the continental tradition of European philosophy (espoused by such thinkers as Maurice Blanchot, Jacques Derrida, and Gilles Deleuze), Ross's refiguring of the Commune in fact most closely resembles the anarchist writer Hakim Bey's notion of a Temporary Autonomous Zone, or TAZ. Bey's influential take on poststructuralist thought affirms the capacity of small-scale uprisings to create "a bit of land ruled only by freedom," beyond State control. "A certain kind of 'free enclave'" comes into being, he declares, not via a much-awaited revolution and its attendant annihilation of all inequalities but rather through localized insurrections like the Commune, which frequently go unrecognized by the status quo. Necessarily spatial, he argues that such enclaves also have an inherent relationship to time, often existing only as temporal scramblings of the hegemonic code, but also constituting epiphanic discontinuities within the normative notion of time and historical progress: "The uprising is a moment that springs up and out of Time, violates the 'law' of History. If the State IS History, as it claims to be, then the insurrection is the forbidden moment, an unforgivable denial of the dialectic."[19] While Bey is evasive and lyrical when it comes to defining the TAZ, the impression he conveys parallels Ross's rather more deliberate examination of the Commune, adolescence, and Rimbaud. "The Communards are 'out of sync' with the timetable of the inexorable march of history," she states. "Like adolescents they are moving at once too fast in their unplanned seizure of power and too slowly."[20]

As the poet of the Commune and the poet of adolescence, Rimbaud's work also bears witness to an "evental" time: his *A Season in Hell* is a *récit*, or the account of an "exceptional event," which inhabits a temporality wholly different from the "everyday, mundane time" of the bourgeois novel.[21] While the nineteenth-century realist novel imposes a linear development on its narrative and the motivations of its characters, Rimbaud's *récit* is an anti-genre that dispenses with development and resists the formula of the bildungsroman. Poet laureate of the TAZ, according to Ross, Rimbaud "proposes the impossible: a narrative that consists of pure transformational energy, pure transition or *suradolescence.*"[22] This is Cooper's Rimbaud: iconoclastic *suradolescent* idol whose life and work allow one to view askew the social adherence to "mundane" time. This idiosyncratic take on temporality, so reminiscent of Bey's anarchist ideas, is therefore an indispensable element of Cooper's take on adolescence and Arthur Rimbaud.

The adolescent effect in *Idols* is not limited to time, however. Adolescence also lends the work its solitary, egocentric air. The way Cooper thinks about adolescence seems to tally with developmental psychologist Jean Piaget's influential model of intellectual development, which finds the teenager enclosed within a self-contained psychological loop. According to Piaget, as individuals grow through childhood into adolescence, they begin to recognize others' capacity for thought, yet they cannot see that the objects preoccupying others differ from those that they themselves are preoccupied with. Consequently, they think the thoughts of others are the same as the thoughts they have. Having filled everyone else's heads with their own thoughts, in public adolescents believe they stand before people who assess them as harshly or as approvingly as they assess themselves. In their mind, therefore, they construct an insular, solipsistic—and profoundly lonely—vision of the world composed solely of solitary impressions: "The young adolescent, because of the physiological metamorphosis he is undergoing, is primarily concerned with himself. Accordingly, since he fails to differentiate between what others are thinking about and his own mental preoccupations, he assumes that other people are as obsessed with his behavior and appearance as he is himself. It is this belief that others are preoccupied with his appearance and behavior that constitutes the egocentrism of the adolescent."[23]

Yet where Piaget argues that such egocentrism is overcome with age, Cooper's work seems to suggest that growing up doesn't solve the problem. In *Idols* the teenager's experience is taken as a particularly potent example of conditions that persist into adulthood: for Cooper, solitude, non-relationality, and egocentrism are fundamental features of subjective experience. As we shall see, Cooper draws a radical conclusion from the rather banal idea that personal impressions color the way we see the world. If subjectivity always inflects one's experience of reality such that one interacts not with the world per se but with a subjectively mediated *impression* of the world, no human being can ever experience a truly intersubjective encounter with another. Human individuals are thus ever alone with their representations. An early encounter with the Marquis de Sade curses Cooper with this egocentric worldview, which he is destined to continually confront and contest with little hope of success.

IF *THE TERROR OF EARRINGS* was the first book Cooper published, it wasn't the first book he made: in a number of interviews he has referred to an epic but now lost prose work completed in his teens and modeled on the Marquis de Sade's *120 Days of Sodom*. Describing its fate to Slava Mogutin of *Honcho Magazine*, he says:

> DC: I tried to imitate *120 Days of Sodom*, and wrote this 800-pages-long extreme novel. It was about this party in the high school where my friends and I got all these different cute guys to come

to the party, and then we kept them there and tortured and killed them. It was a really long thing, totally horrible and ridiculous.

SM: Basically you tried to be as kinky as possible.

DC: Yeah, evil and cool. Then one day I realized that my mom was going through my stuff and reading my diary. It was a long story. She made me go to a psychiatrist. I was really afraid that she was going to find it. It was hidden in my bedroom. So I burned it. And years and years later I was putting my book together and I found one page that got somehow out of that.[24]

Although only a solitary page remains of his teenage tribute to *120 Days of Sodom*—included in *Idols* as the prose poem "Mike Robarts (page from a porno novel I wrote at sixteen)"—the effect of Sade's book persists in Cooper's writing, and he frequently claims that Sade is one of a handful of writers who had the greatest impact on his development. Considering the sadistic scenes for which Sade is known and the exaggerated fantasies of murder and rape that made Cooper's novels somewhat infamous in the 1990s, it may be tempting to conclude that Sade's influence on Cooper extends only as far as offering him a model for the depiction of sexualized violence. Matias Viegener goes a little further by suggesting that, as a philosopher and pornographer of power, Sade's presence haunts Cooper's novel *Frisk*. "As in de Sade," Viegener writes, "Dennis Cooper's work is a series of speculations on what are essentially philosophical issues, but they are recast in contemporary terms in and on the body."[25]

Yet the impact of Sade's thought on Cooper's work is simultaneously more profound and more diffuse than Viegener's otherwise excellent analysis allows, and Sade's influence is not limited to *Frisk*'s imagined scenes of murder and mutilation or Cooper's recurring interest in the body. Rather, the effect of his early exposure to Sade and his reception of Sade's work through the interpretive lens of Simone de Beauvoir and Maurice Blanchot reverberate throughout his writing. Speaking with the *Paris Review*, Cooper talks about reading Sade as a teenager and, significantly, notes that "the Grove Press editions of Sade's books that I read had super-heady essays on and in defense of Sade's work by Beauvoir and Blanchot, so I knew what he was doing was serious literature" (2011).[26] The essays he refers to here, Blanchot's "Sade" (1949) and Beauvoir's "Must We Burn Sade?" (1952), offer two of the earliest and most enduring examinations of Sade's philosophy of egoism. Turning to Beauvoir's and Blanchot's texts, we can see that this egoism represents a fundamental problematic for the entirety of Cooper's work—one that initially appears to lapse into anguished solipsism only to later form the basis of his interest in anarchist ideas.

In the introduction to *120 Days of Sodom*, Sade has his libertine hero the Duc de Blangis voice one of the more succinct appraisals of his egoist worldview. The Duc asserts that conventional morality and ethics, which dictate that one should strive to be virtuous and just, are without an impartial or universal foundation. Notions of the just and unjust "have never been anything if not relative. . . . The stronger has always considered exceedingly just what the weaker regarded as flagrantly unjust, and that it takes no more than the mere reversal of their positions for each to be able to change his way of thinking too."[27] Getting rid of this kind of vacuous and illegitimate ideology, he states that the only recourse is to behave just as he likes: "I do my choosing without hesitation, and as I am always sure to find pleasure in the choice I make, never does regret arise to dull its charm. Firm in my principles because those I formed are sound and were formed very early, I always act in accordance with them; they have made me understand the emptiness and nullity of virtue; I hate virtue, and never will I be seen resorting to it."[28] Beholden to neither gods nor masters, the Duc does what he wants, and, "as he was a man of the greatest possible wit," Sade's narrator exclaims, "his arguments had a decisive ring."[29]

Passages like this are the foundation of Blanchot's essay, included, as Cooper points out, in Grove Press's 1965 edition of *Justine, Philosophy in the Bedroom, and Other Writings*. Here Blanchot constructs a clear picture of Sade's philosophy as one based on systematic negation, which sets the sovereign individual at its head. According to Blanchot, Sadean thought advances one principle above all others:

This philosophy is one of self-interest, of absolute egoism: each of us must do exactly as he pleases, each of us is bound by one law alone, that of his own pleasure. This morality is based upon the primary fact of absolute solitude. Sade has stated it, and repeated it, in every conceivable form: Nature wills that we are born alone, there is no real contact or relationship possible between one person and another. . . . These principles are clear.[30]

This is Blanchot's strong claim: that Sade's egoism proceeds via an axiomatic belief in the solitude of the subject. Other individuals, if they appear at all in the world of the Sadean man, exist for him only as shapes of his consciousness, always already negated in the abstract. Thus the Duc reminds participants in his forthcoming orgies that "it is not at all as human beings we behold you, but exclusively as animals one feeds in return for their services, and which one withers with blows when they refuse to be put to use"; undifferentiated and dehumanized, he indifferently tells them that they are "already dead."[31] Sovereign, supreme, untouched, and unmoved by other individuals, "what is especially striking," Blanchot says, "is the fact that the world in which the Unique One lives and moves and has his being is a desert; the creatures he encounters there are less than things, less than shades. And when he torments and destroys them he is not wresting away their lives but verifying their nothingness."[32]

Although her essay is more obviously marked by existentialism, Beauvoir's analysis proceeds in much the same way as Blanchot's earlier work; like him, she aims to demonstrate the fundamental egoism of Sade's writing. Sade, in her account, repudiates the notion of a universally applicable system of morality or ethics on the basis of "a heterogeneity of values, not only from class to class, but from individual to individual."[33] His system finds its clearest expression in the Duc de Blangis, and thus, according to Sade and the Duc, "there is no reality other than that of the self-enclosed subject hostile to any other subject which disputes its sovereignty."[34] For Beauvoir as for Blanchot, Sade's egoism arises out of a self-imposed solitude that refuses to imagine a relationship with another individual.

> [For Sade] nothing has truth for me other than what my experience envelops, and the intimate presence of the other radically escapes this experience; therefore it does not concern me and cannot dictate any duty to me. "We mock the torment of others: and what would this torment have in common with us?" And again, "There is no comparison between what others experience and what we feel; the strongest pain for others must surely be nothing to us, and the least tremor of pleasure we experience touches us."[35]

Each of these pivotal essays triangulates Sade's system via intersecting concepts of non-relationality, solitude, and egoism. No two subjective worldviews are compatible; therefore, in Sade's reckoning, the individual is sundered from the world and from others, condemned to live in an emotional and spiritual solitude that echoes Sade's own isolation in French prisons and asylums for over thirty years. It is this aspect of Sade's work that has the most profound effect on Cooper's writing. If later works like *The Tenderness of the Wolves* and *Frisk*, known for their transgressive combinations of scatology, sex, and death, display a more legibly Sadean style, *Idols* explores the ideas that lie beneath, in particular the concept of subjective isolation and the human condition of non-relation.

In the "Boys I've Wanted" series, non-relation defines the association between the figures that appear in the poems as much as it marks the temporal relationship between the speaker and his past. In pieces like "Scott Van Der Karr," the speaker's desire for communion with another is continually negated by the physical boundary of bodies and the unfathomable otherness of his beloved. Opening with an acknowledgment of the separation between them, the poem quickly shifts to a linguistic suturing together of the writing "I" and the desired "you" in a shared, communal "we":

> It was the Christmas dance
> wasn't it? My rock band
> played. You joined the dance floor.
> We had knocked over the big tree.
> We had opened the mock packages.[36]

Here, first- and second-person pronouns meet and join momentarily before almost immediately defying poetic contrivance and withdrawing to their previous positions: "My band was the Stones. I, Jagger. / Your eyes were closed. You knew your way."[37] Cooper's choreography of pronouns is accentuated when the speaker joins Scott on the dance floor and initiates some passing corporeal intimacy between them.

> Later I danced beside you, drunken,
> stumbled into you again and again.
> And I could smell your sweat and your breath.
> Everyone could. Did you notice?[38]

Although the speaker may repeatedly stumble into Scott, they are both bounded by individual bodies that seem, for Cooper, to emphasize the separation of each and circumscribe their interaction. The bathetic and ever-unanswerable question that concludes this poem—"Did you notice?"—also insists on the psychological separation between the self and the other. The other's mind will forever escape the understanding of the speaker, and this, the reader is led to infer, will forever obstruct their combination in a wished-for, intersubjective "we."

The sense of ubiquitous separation in the "Boys I've Wanted" series appears in other poems in the collection where Cooper continues to locate his characters at a distance from one another. "First Sex" emphasizes the dissociation between the speaker of the poem and a desired other and details the disappointing divergence between his imagined lover and the one he finds before him. "This isn't it," he thinks, comparing his dreams of erotic union with the stark, unpleasant reality he's confronted with:

> I try to get his shoulder blade between my teeth.
> He complains, pillow in his mouth.
> Doesn't mean it.
> Means it.
>
> He rolls onto his back,
> face raw and wet as fat,
> like it has been shaken from nightmares.
> I don't know how to please this face.[39]

The question that concludes "Scott Van Der Karr" is echoed in this last line, in the evident illegibility of the lover's desire and the speaker's acknowledgment of an empathetic wall between them. But "First Sex" also confronts an important corollary of *Idols'* recurring interest in the non-relational: with the obstruction of understanding between the self and the other and in the absence of a coveted intersubjective experience, the speaker is isolated and alone with his fantasies.

> Tomorrow when he has made breakfast
> and gone, I will sweep
> the mound of porno from my closet,
> put a match to its lies.[40]

Imagined erotic scenarios generated with the aid of "a mound of porno" are here contrasted with real referents, and the latter are found wanting: "This isn't it."[41] Hanging on the ambivalent "match"—a pun that suggests both a search for equivalence and a means to incinerate that search—the poem's conclusion suggests that the speaker considers forsaking the immediate, actual encounter with his lover for the solace of his fantasies.

This reading finds support in the masturbatory scenes that appear in a number of poems from the collection. "If I Were Peter Frampton" sees the speaker projected into the body of the English rock star and, once inside, desperately wishing to "finger fuck [himself] / in front of a one way mirror." Although he would take pleasure in trying to have sex with Mick Jagger and hiring punk bands to open for his shows, the speaker tells us that "the best / part is the masturbation, looking / down at my own famous body."[42] This onanistic fantasy is directed by a kind of radical self-containment, in which the speaker dreams about being Frampton only to lock this fantasy up in an erotically self-referential loop. Like "First Sex," what turns the speaker on is not the other but fucking his own *fantasy* of the other.

Poems like this epitomize the broader argument *Idols* attempts to make regarding the relationship between the individual and the world. In this collection the non-relational looms large and appears, for the poet, to constitute a fundamental feature of his interactions with others: as the thoughts and feelings of another remain largely indecipherable, no intermingling of discrete selves may occur. Concomitant with this attempt to plot the distance between individuals is Cooper's focus on intellectual and emotional isolation—without the capacity for an intersubjective encounter, the individual is forever alone, hemmed in by a solitary subjectivity. Non-relationality and solitude: these two aspects make up the recto and verso of Cooper's conceptual framework and highlight his indebtedness to the Marquis de Sade.

Cooper suggests throughout this work that, subjectivity being inescapable, one does not communicate with the world directly but rather through a subjective membrane. Experience is forever mediated through subjective representation, and therefore others can be considered mere images of consciousness; "less than things"; "shades" of the mind. The unhappy upshot of this for Cooper is that relationships consist not of an immediate contact between the self and the other but rather of a frottage between the self and the self's perception of the other. The masturbatory scenes depicted in the poems of *Idols* seem to insist that every form of encounter, even one comprising sexual intimacy, is ultimately an onanistic procedure. If the self only interacts with its representation of others, it seems to follow for Cooper that making love to another is just like jerking off. Yet this existential situation seems to sadden and infuriate Cooper ("I've held love" he writes, but alas it's been "at arm's length"), and although he can see no alternative, his work refuses to affirm and acclaim it.[43] Thus while Cooper's thought seems contiguous with Sade in their comparable belief in subjective solitude, his response to this condition is very different.

Sade's affirmation of subjective solitude in *120 Days of Sodom* is implicit in the libertines' refusal to relate to their victims or even countenance the notion that their victims might possess interiority; as Beauvoir points out, "Remorse and disgust are unknown to them; at most they have occasional feelings of satiety. They kill with indifference."[44] The only system of morality and ethics appropriate to such an unsympathetic view of human relations is one of supreme egoism. The only way to live is as an egoist. Cooper struggles with the repercussions of this egocentric worldview. The solitude of the individual and the lack of communion with others are inescapable ideas in *Idols*, yet such conditions aren't celebrated as they are by Sade's Duc de Blangis. Instead, these poems attest to a profound anguish at individual isolation, and the pieces assembled in this collection encompass repeated, fruitless struggles to overcome this dismal state. *Idols* is not just another of Cooper's adolescent imitations of Sade: poems in this work limn a desperate life of quiet isolation as their speakers valiantly attempt to form connections with other individuals but find these attempts repeatedly frustrated. Although they acknowledge that subjectivity is inescapable and that representation is an insurmountable barrier to intersubjective contact, from first to last these poems are tortured by this state and constantly rage against it. The opening poem of *Idols*, "Craig Tedesco," for instance, carefully depicts the object of the speaker's unrequited affection by patiently conducting the beloved's features through the text.

This smile knew
girls, kissed
mother and burgers.
This smile was
turned against me;

"Hey asshole,"
it grinned. This hair
was red, and face
tanned by freckles.
No beard dimmed this chin.[45]

The repeated "this" that prefaces each description announces the speaker's intention to overcome the distance that stands between him and the perceived other and declares his attempt to induce an intimate encounter in language: possessing and proffering, "this" tries to draw the beloved near. The concluding section of the poem reveals this closeness to be impossible, however: the oneiric setting manifestly empties "this" and "these" of content and reveals them as poetic conceits. Like the "mock packages" featured in a later poem, they possess nothing except a poet's dreams of intimacy.[46]

In my dreams
these eyes clenched
beneath me.
This smile was bound,
or not a smile,
or it was softened
and smeared by mine.[47]

"Jeff, After a Long Time," the final poem of *Idols*, also voices the speaker's desire to gather a loved one close in language. Oscillating between motifs of distance and proximity, in this piece the speaker sees an old lover from across a crowded bar and remarks, "our eyes . . . still touch across the distance, didn't forget."[48] He yearns to unify their respective minds and bodies and join the present with the past, but he finds there are "Just our feelings / to hold us together / now when our minds / are off in directions / our bodies tag behind." In writing, however, the speaker finds a brief, if provisional connection, allowing him to reconstruct this scene and imagine an emotional closeness between them. "And just a poem," he writes,

to show when I grow
tender, you remain

that friend that
I am reaching for.[49]

Forever incomplete and unfulfilled, this unrelenting "reaching for" (a friend, a once-cherished lover, the poet himself in his adolescence) characterizes the dominant trajectory of these poems. As Cooper says in an interview with Steve Lafreniere before the republication of *Idols* in 1989, "My things are about this kind of weird detachment and longing for attachment and all that stuff," and these poems are tortured by the fundamental solitude of the subject but continually strive to surmount this condition.[50] Raging against isolation, they *reach for* an embrace of the other.

A Poetics of Dissociability |
The Punk Poets of Los Angeles

3 IN THE SUMMER OF 1976, Cooper traveled to England, where he would experience the emergent British punk scene firsthand. In London on July 4, he and Brian Tucker caught the Ramones supporting the Flamin' Groovies at London's Roundhouse, a gig that is widely recognized as an important moment in the development of UK punk. In attendance that night were the Stranglers (who were the opening act), Marco Pirroni of Siouxsie and the Banshees, the Damned's Captain Sensible, and, if they are to be believed, almost every other young punk in the British Isles. Documentary evidence of Cooper and Tucker's presence at the gig is provided by Danny Fields, the manager of the Ramones, who photographed the surging throng of British fans cheering for the New York punks with two young Californians in their midst.

During the trip Cooper also found himself knee-deep in a rising tide of UK punk zines, including Mark Perry's influential *Sniffin' Glue*, which, like John Holmstrom's New York–based *Punk*, transposed the look of Richard Hell's safety-pinned shirts into a print collage of scrawled reviews, interviews, and concert photos. This combination of an electric, emergent punk community and an offbeat, improvised aesthetic had a huge impact on Cooper. He remembers: "When I got back to LA it seemed like the right time to give it a shot myself—have a small group of friends and people that I liked do a magazine without a center. Also try to pull some of the New York stuff in, the music and all" (2007).[1] The result of

The Ramones, at London's Roundhouse, July 4, 1976, attended by Dennis Cooper (bottom right, in front of the stage) and Brian Tucker (on Cooper's right, with glasses). Courtesy of Danny Fields from his book *My Ramones* (London: Reel Art Press, 2018).

this was *Little Caesar* magazine, which Cooper set up with his friend Jim Glaeser in 1976. (The editors amicably parted ways after the first issue, leaving Cooper with sole responsibility for editing, collating, typesetting, and distributing the following ten issues until 1982.)

Little Caesar aimed to introduce the iconoclasm of a punk attitude into the usually staid confines of a poetry journal. The editors were convinced that punk could fundamentally alter the form and status of literature in the 1970s, and as a punk poetry zine, *Little Caesar* tried to make such a change manifest. In his introduction to the first issue, Cooper writes:

> I have this dream where writers are mobbed everywhere they go, like rock stars and actors. A predilection? You never know. People like Patti Smith are subtly forcing their audiences to become literate, introducing them to Rimbaud, Breton, Burroughs, and others. Poetry sales are higher than they've been in fifteen years. In Paris ten year old boys clutching well worn copies of Apollonaire's [*sic*] ALCOOLS

put their hands over their mouths in amazement before paintings by Renoir and Monet. Bruce Lee movies close in three days. This could happen here.[2]

Casually situating the outlook of the editors and their contributors within a cluster of major themes and influences (e.g., rock and roll, film, youth culture, surrealism, Rimbaud), Cooper's mission statement draws these together under a standard borne by Smith, the doyenne of Downtown New York punk rock with whom Cooper had corresponded since 1974. In this manifesto, Smith's punk is celebrated for staging a paradigmatic union of high and low art. As I demonstrate in this chapter, Smith would later prove exemplary for antithetical reasons—her *separation* from the New York poetry scene foreshadowed Cooper's and his friends' efforts to dissociate themselves from an older generation of LA poets.

While Cooper's dream that writers might one day enjoy moments of Beatlesque mania is to date largely unrealized, *Little Caesar* would bear out his aspiration to combine high and low art with a punk ethos and aesthetic to great effect. Interest in the magazine was such that two years after its inception Cooper launched Little Caesar Press, which would go on to publish twenty-four books by established and up-and-coming poets, all of whom had at some point contributed to the magazine. In his history of postwar LA poetry, Bill Mohr maintains, "[*Little Caesar*] quickly gained a vociferous readership because of [Cooper's] eclectic editorial blend of articles on punk and popular music, film criticism, and a huge swath of casually deft poetry. He also caught the attention of older poets because of his unabashed but thoughtful enthusiasm for how lively the scene was in the late 1970s and for his willingness to be specific about his favorite local poets."[3]

Such distinguished locals included the likes of Ed Smith, Ron Koertge, Jim Krusoe, Jack Skelley, David Trinidad, Bob Flanagan, Benjamin Weissman, and Amy Gerstler. He'd set out to explore the literary scene in LA with Gerstler; unimpressed by what they found, Cooper attempted to set up one more suited to them in the pages of his magazine, in the catalog of Little Caesar Press, and later in his poetry reading series at LA's Beyond Baroque Literary Arts Center. In addition to pieces by these LA poets, Cooper published work by New York artists and writers, particularly those associated with the second-generation New York School and Andy

Warhol's Factory scene. In its dozen issues, *Little Caesar* included writing by Ted Berrigan, Ron Padgett, Tom Clark, Lewis MacAdams, and Joe Brainard, as well as Lou Reed, Nico, Gerard Malanga, and Rene Ricard.

Of course *Little Caesar* aimed at being more than just a poetry periodical. What made its volumes stand out was the sheer variety of material Cooper chose to include. A special Rimbaud-themed issue from 1978, for instance, featured new translations of Rimbaud's work alongside Rimbaud-inspired pieces by people like Tim Dlugos, Ricard, and Malanga, as well as photographs of modern Rimbaud "live-a-likes," including James Dean and Johnny Rotten. Cooper's friend and later spearhead of San Francisco's New Narrative movement, Steve Abbott, contributed a comic strip that reimagined scenes from Rimbaud's life. In one panel a yawning Rimbaud exclaims, "Paul, you reek of Absinthe and nasty bourgeois values," to which Verlaine replies, "Bitch!" Although they arrived too late for inclusion in this issue, a later *Little Caesar* would also feature sixteen photographs from David Wojnarowicz's now-famous "Rimbaud in New York" series. Wojnarowicz's photos depict his friend and lover Brian Butterick idling in various locations in Downtown Manhattan wearing a Rimbaud mask photostatted from the cover of *Illuminations*. In each shot, Rimbaud's starkly pale features and bored, arrogant gaze simultaneously negate and endorse the situations into which his image is dragged: Rimbaud/Butterick is pictured riding a subway car plastered with illegible graffiti, shooting heroin, cruising the abandoned piers in the Hudson River, masturbating naked and recumbent.

In its promotion of an alternative tradition of poetry and attempt to gather a community of contributors around a shared artistic vision, *Little Caesar* is part of a tradition of little magazines associated with the literary avant-garde in the twentieth century. Littles such as Robert McAlmon and William Carlos Williams's *Contact* (1920–32), John Ashbery, Kenneth Koch, and Harry Mathews's *Locus Solus* (1961–62), and LeRoi Jones (Amiri Baraka) and Diane Di Prima's the *Floating Bear* (1961–69) all anticipate to varying degrees *Little Caesar*'s use of the small-circulation poetry periodical to forge a group identity in opposition to conservative poetic trends. *Locus Solus*, for instance, gave a group of little-known poets somewhere to publish their work, which to that point had been largely ignored by more mainstream outlets like *Poetry* and the *Partisan Review*. Ashbery states, "[Harry Mathews and I] probably talked about how nice it would be to have a magazine that would publish our work, and also the work of people we liked but who could never get published."[4] This, according to David Herd, led the magazine to carry the New York School poets' "collective imprimatur. Part of its purpose, accordingly, and within the bounds of an aesthetic that aimed to resist all conventions of style, was to identify and distinguish the New York School."[5] The magazine's curation by and circulation among friends charted the outlines of a collective group identity by offering a manifesto of sorts: certain styles of innovative midcentury poetry were endorsed through their inclusion, and the names that fill its pages constitute a who's who of New York School poets. Along with work by the editors and Frank O'Hara, *Locus Solus* included contributions from Jones, Malanga, Bill Berkson, Jane Freilicher, Barbara Guest, Fairfield Porter, and others.

Magazines edited by Cooper's beloved second generation of New York School poets took a comparable approach. Berrigan's mimeographed *C: A Journal of Poetry* (1963–66) and Lewis Warsh and Anne Waldman's letterpress-printed *Angel Hair* (1966–78) similarly sought to evoke a shared aesthetic sensibility and situate a poetic community. *C*, for instance, produced a sense of second-generation community through the appearance of the same poets and poetic styles throughout its run, and poems by Padgett, Berrigan, and Dick Gallup appeared in most of its thirteen issues. For its part, *Angel Hair* also featured a rotating roster of New York School poets of the first and second generations, including editors Warsh and Waldman, Berrigan, Gallup, Padgett, Kenward Elmslie, Koch, Ashbery, and others.

Expanding the remit of their predecessors, the pages of *C* and *Angel Hair* advance a radically inclusive vision of poetic community, permeable and open to all kinds of influences and styles. Berrigan's editorial stance at *C* offered a particularly salient example of this in his apparent attempt to dismantle divisions between poetic cliques and stage a rapprochement between estranged avant-gardes. "*C* will print anything the editor likes," Berrigan writes in his editorial statement, and a glance at the names of poets featured in its issues attests to a broad and varied aesthetic taste.[6] Ranging beyond Ashbery, O'Hara, and the usual suspects (although these are represented), *C* also featured contributors far from the peripheries of a quintessentially New York School aesthetic. Such a varied roster of writers leads Harry Thorne to remark that in his work at *C*, Berrigan "eschewed the codification of a poetics in favor of contrast and idiosyncrasy."

He writes, "Berrigan did not present any kind of theoretical framework or manifesto in his magazine that would separate New York School poets (who were themselves hardly a homogenous group) from non–New York School poets. The resulting mix of poets and poetic styles and approaches in *C* means that it is almost impossible to discuss the magazine in terms of a unified poetic grouping."[7]

Thorne also notes Berrigan's attempt as editor of *C* to bridge a long-standing dissociation between the New York School and the Factory scene through the inclusion of cover art by Warhol. In Thorne's account, such a move circumvents O'Hara's antipathy for Warhol's art by including the work of both within the magazine. Commissioning work by Warhol demonstrated a desire "to question group allegiances and open the magazine to wider avant-garde influences. While Berrigan would certainly not have wanted to alienate O'Hara . . . it does show that despite his fervent admiration of O'Hara's work, Berrigan did not want his magazine to reproduce the artistic tastes of his literary hero."[8]

With *C*, Berrigan sought to forge an inclusive and especially diverse community made up of different—and not always sympathetic—poetic and artistic traditions. Daniel Kane suggests that this may be read as Berrigan's "microcommunity building that both echoed and complicated the utopian aspects of 1960s counterculture."[9] Similarly utopian aspects had prevailed in Los Angeles's little-known countercultural poetry scene in the 1950s, which grew up around Venice West and determined the trajectory of poetry in LA for the following two decades. Cooper found such a situation intolerable, however, and worked to radically transform the LA scene and how poetry was seen there: not only did his efforts *not* echo 1960s counterculture, but they were directed against it and the idea of community it fostered. Although Cooper's skeptical regard for collective endeavor distinguished him both from earlier LA poets and the poets of the second-generation New York School, this nonetheless dovetailed in certain respects with the attitude of his correspondent and occasional idol Patti Smith.

DURING THE LATE 1950S, Los Angeles's Venice West became known as a Beat hangout, serving as the setting for Lawrence Lipton's classic, *The Holy Barbarians* (1959), which celebrated a sun-drenched, drug-infused,

Southern California society at the margins of America. This countercultural community was briefly home to a small group of poets, including Stuart Perkoff and Bruce Boyd, who were both featured in Donald M. Allen's groundbreaking anthology *The New American Poetry* in 1960. Exemplars of a Beat ethos and aesthetic, such poets advocated the use of illegal drugs like pot and peyote as part of their creative process, and their poems echo the work of Allen Ginsberg and Gregory Corso in an apparent pursuit of authenticity and transcendence. "Venice Recalled," one of Boyd's poems included in Allen's collection, regards the community from the vantage point of one who had departed for San Francisco and wistfully recalls the Venice West poets' shared commitment to the notion of poetry as a collective quest for spiritual communion, summed up by the poet's vow "always to prefer the common."

> there, with us
> a new poem always was something
> the making, something
> that asked to be shared at once: seldom a "result"
> to praise or blame, & never this only, we mostly looked
> behind it for the ways that came together,[10]

Lipton's bestselling book features transcribed conversations between prominent Beats like Ginsberg and members of the Venice West scene. Boyd's insistence here on the oral tradition of poetry ("that asked to be shared at once"), the process of poetic composition as a channeling of creative energies that seemed to exist "behind it," and the appreciation of process or "the making" at the expense of the finished product or "result" epitomizes certain qualities of a Beat poetics. Boyd's peers also identified his work with the pursuit of authenticity: according to an audience member who saw him read in San Francisco, "Everybody present recognized that [he] had struck it rich and had written an absolutely authentic poem."[11] Due to its inhabitants' increased dependence on hard drugs and the incarceration of Perkoff—arguably the lynchpin of the scene, who was responsible for founding the Venice West Cafe and its weekly poetry reading series—Venice West quickly disintegrated in the 1960s, leaving Los Angeles once again without a notable literary hub.

In 1968 the reading series and writing workshops at Venice's Beyond Baroque helped to resuscitate LA's moribund scene. Poets in the city flocked to George Drury Smith's storefront property on West Washington Boulevard to read and discuss their work, in the hope of finding a community of like-minded literati. According to Mohr, a cluster of LA poets yearning for mutual support and encouragement quickly formed around the Beyond Baroque building and its NewComp Graphics Center, which allowed neighborhood poets to typeset and paste up their work cheaply on the premises.

> Beyond Baroque provided the poets in the region with the opportunity to have a poem critiqued on Wednesday night, test the revision out loud at an open reading before the featured poet on Friday, type and paste it up for publication during the following week, and subsequently bring it back from the printer to be shelved at the library and sold at the bookstore. . . . Beyond Baroque presented very little in the way of impediments to an artist's decision about how mature she or he was as an artist, and its institutional projection into the development of the community continually favored potential rather than enactment.[12]

Such a description evokes the sense of a poetic community at Beyond Baroque. Like the one at St. Mark's Church-in-the-Bowery on Manhattan's Lower East Side (the site of the famous Poetry Project) and in *C* and *Angel Hair*, the Beyond Baroque community was inclusive and supportive of its members, if perhaps not terribly critical of the poetry presented at its workshops. Mohr's description also connects Beyond Baroque to the Beat ideology of Venice West as articulated by Boyd's poem, in particular the latter's insistence that a poem is symptomatic of a creative process, not an object in itself to be "praise[d] or blame[d]" by other poets. Indeed, poets from Venice West like John Thomas, who were not yet strung out on drugs or locked up for criminal activity, often turned up at Beyond Baroque readings and were welcomed into the fold. The early groupings that gathered at West Washington Boulevard, like the Venice Beats, thus seemed simply "to prefer the common"—sharing space and poetry with one another in a city that was dominated by the film industry and had no time for this least lucrative of arts.

Following the acquisition of a new lease, Beyond Baroque moved into the disused Venice City Hall in 1979, and Cooper shortly took over as director of the reading series. He and Gerstler had come to Beyond Baroque in the mid-1970s, looking for poetry they connected with and a group of peers that would support and challenge them. Initially, they didn't find what they wanted there: in Cooper's estimation, the community that orbited the reading series before he inherited it was too minor and "provincial."[13] However, having made connections with poets across the continent through *Little Caesar* and finding himself in charge of the reading series at the new location, Cooper was in a strong position to revolutionize the poetry scene at Beyond Baroque. He set out to establish an alternative community of poets whose influences and ambitions matched his own. "Basically Amy and I tried to assemble a kind of group; we wanted to have a group of writers," he recalls. "We were very interested in the New York School poets and how the scene around St. Marks was, and we were interested in trying to have a group of writers that we were peers with" (2012).[14] Cooper's work with Gerstler culminated in the development of a distinct grouping of LA poets that Brian Kim Stefans in his anthology of overlooked LA poetry calls "the poets of the punk era."[15]

Channeling the *Geist* of a highly literate, individualistic, and even elitist Downtown punk rock headed up by Smith, which was different in character from the more brazenly philistine and communal ethos of British punk and hardcore, one of Cooper's first acts as reading-series organizer was to put an end to open readings. Cooper remembers, "I wanted there to be a lot of energy and I wanted people to be really serious about their writing. So I was picky. . . . And to all the people who had always automatically gotten readings there I said no, you're not good enough, you can't read here."[16] With Jack Skelley, director of the music and performance series, Cooper also sought to shake up the usual format of poetry programming by booking punk bands like X and organizing themed events like a birthday party for Rimbaud, where a Rimbaud impersonator was hired to "piss on people and spit on them" (2007).[17] These kinds of events also helped to solidify associations between Beyond Baroque and the burgeoning LA art and performance scene based around Los Angeles Contemporary Exhibitions (LACE) and the Los Angeles Institute of Contemporary Art (LAICA), which included young artists like Mike Kelley, Jim Isermann, and Bruce and Norman Yonemoto. Kelley recalls: "Through Benjamin Weissman and Tim Martin, who went to CalArts with me, I got to know writers associated with Beyond Baroque like [Dennis Cooper] and Bob Flanagan and Jack Skelley and Amy Gerstler. . . . A lot of writers associated with Beyond Baroque were exploring mass culture in a manner I found new and inspiring. I think the intermixture of writers, musicians, and artists and video makers in LA then was remarkable."[18]

Cooper abolished the policy of free admission to Beyond Baroque readings, enabling the center to apply for grant funding by offering evidence of income from its events; admission fees and the connections Cooper formed through *Little Caesar* allowed him to invite a much wider range of poets to the reading series than ever before. Journalist Craig Lee contemporaneously notes that before Cooper's appointment as reading-series organizer, "the series mostly featured local Venice poets [while] Cooper immediately pressed for national recognition, often inviting poets from outside Southern California."[19] Guests included Steve Benson, Elaine Equi, Ted Greenwald, Ginsberg, Carla Harryman, Christopher Isherwood, LeRoi Jones, Jerome Sala, Ron Silliman, and many others from across the United States.

Cooper also cultivated a community at Beyond Baroque that would be receptive to the readings he organized. Mohr cites an anecdote by a previous director of programming, Jim Krusoe, in which a reading by Kenward Elmslie under Krusoe's tenure was attended by only six people: "Three of them left after intermission."[20] Given that Cooper and Gerstler were both enamored of the New York School, under Cooper's tenure as reading-series organizer such an affront to a second-generation New York School poet would have been unthinkable. As Stefans points out, the so-called punk poets of Los Angeles all shared an affection for writers like O'Hara and Brainard and "self-consciously tried to adapt modes of New York school writing to Los Angeles."[21] This interest in the New York School not only characterized Cooper's and Gerstler's work and friendship, it also formed the basis of their association with other young poets, including Trinidad, Equi, Flanagan, and Weissman, whose ideas and influences were different from their predecessors. Each of these poets vehemently attests to the vibrancy of Beyond Baroque at the time and to Cooper's impact in particular. In an interview with D. A. Powell, for instance, Trinidad remembers his first meeting with Cooper, and his account offers a vivid impression of the scene.

That November [1979], at a memorial reading for Rachel [Sherwood], Dennis Cooper sought me out. He'd seen some of my poems in

Beyond Baroque magazine and wanted to include me in an anthology of poets in their twenties, *Coming Attractions*, that he was editing. I think Amy Gerstler and Jack Skelley were with him that night. Later we all became friends. Their work had a big impact on me. Dennis created a lively scene at Beyond Baroque, which lasted until he moved to New York, in '83 or '84. He brought a lot of interesting poets from around the country to read at Beyond Baroque. I met Tim Dlugos that way, and Elaine Equi and Jerome Sala. Those were very exciting days. Everyone had their own magazine and/or press, or ran a workshop or reading series. We'd all show each other our new poems. There was a real sense of camaraderie, of mutual support. Dennis introduced me to the work of the New York School poets.[22]

Although she rarely spent extended periods of time in Los Angeles, as Trinidad mentions, the Chicago-based poet Equi also became an intimate of the Beyond Baroque group: Cooper regularly showcased her work in *Little Caesar*, and her second collection of poems, *Shrewcrazy*, was published by Little Caesar Press in 1980. Her recollections of Beyond Baroque, like Trinidad's comments, attest to Cooper's influence and the LA punk poets' improvisation on a New York School aesthetic.

Eventually in the early '80s [Jerome Sala and I] got invited to read at Beyond Baroque when Dennis Cooper ran the series. It was one of my all time favorite readings. We felt so at home there and met a lot of cool poets who are still among my best friends—people like David Trinidad, Amy Gerstler, Jack Skelley. . . . I loved the sensibility of most of those writers. Their work was so witty and edgy. What fascinated me most was how pop it sounded. If it had been a big deal for Frank O'Hara to write about James Dean, these L.A. poets seemed to have grown up, like myself, watching hours and hours of TV.[23]

Flanagan, the performance poet, member of the LA punk-rock trio Planet of Toys, and soon-to-be "supermasochist," also fondly recalled the Beyond Baroque scene Cooper had brought into being, claiming that it "turned my life around. I came from knowing nothing about poetry at all—from writing awful rhyming stuff—to poetry as a life style. It was an incredible learning experience."[24] Benjamin Weissman, meanwhile, remembers that when he stumbled upon the reading series in the early 1980s, "[Dennis] was very cool and supportive. I also fell in love with my wife at Beyond Baroque—Amy Gerstler, the foxy librarian. Beyond Baroque rocks."[25] Cooper, Gerstler, Trinidad, Flanagan, and Weissman, along with Jack Skelley and Ed Smith— this group of friends made up the core of a new generation of LA poets—"punk poet mutants"—that observers like Laurel Delp of the *Los Angeles Herald Examiner* found were "breathing life into the local poetry scene."[26]

COOPER COLLECTED THE WORK of a number of these poets in *Coming Attractions: An Anthology of American Poets in Their Twenties*, edited with the assistance of Dlugos and published by Little Caesar Press in 1980. The collection includes LA poets like Flanagan, Skelley, Trinidad, and others associated with Beyond Baroque and *Little Caesar*, including Equi, Sala, and Eileen Myles, as well as poets from the Mass Transit scene in Washington, DC, like Bernard Welt and Donald Britton. In his introduction, Cooper reveals that his decision to group these poets together arose out of a desire to highlight those who "are doing writing which is both promising in relation to their future as artists and indicative of new feelings among younger writers toward poetry and the world."[27] Later, when Cooper revealingly admits, "Being in one's twenties sets up certain limits and forms certain bonds," he hints at what he thinks this "new feeling" might be. The poets Cooper included in the anthology effectively address the problems of their age. Not coincidentally, these were the same problems faced by Cooper and his friends at Beyond Baroque: how to locate the boundaries of the self and how one might connect with others in ways that are consistent with those limits. Setting themselves apart from the previous generation of poets, whose ethos of radical inclusivity they plainly disagreed with, and influenced by their contemporaries in punk rock, the outlook of members of this younger generation was rather more individualistic in character and more protective of their individuality than their immediate predecessors.

The poems assembled in *Coming Attractions* bear this out. From Trinidad's triumphal celebration of his inebriated "outcast tongue" to the discontinuous logic of Skelley's splatter-horror poems that fail to dislodge the lyric subject loitering "in the hills, on the beach, other lonely places," these poets insist upon the distinction of the self and the separation

Beyond Baroque poets outside the Ear Inn, New York, 1981 by Sheree Rose. Left to right: Bob Flanagan, Dennis Cooper, Amy Gerstler, Michael Silverblatt. Used by permission of Sheree Rose. Source: Dennis Cooper papers, box 8, folder 444, Fales Library and Special Collections, New York University Libraries.

between the self and others.[28] Yet they also consider the conditions under which connections might be possible; Flanagan's contributions exemplify these ideas. "Houses" in particular focuses on the dissociation that exemplifies the poet's perception of the world and locates his speaker, still and unchanging, at the center of a maelstrom of flux and mutability.

> As each unit is a constant, so is Bob,
> his flashlight here, now there;
> spider, mouse, pipe, table, cup,
> An arc of white light sweeps across the sky.
> The crocuses work their way toward the surface
> until the pale tip of a finger
> points to some star,
> not a star, but a planet,

then, finally, a space,
the space between two fence posts.
The neighbors are busy moving.
Who moves at this time of night?
Not even a street light of a moon,
just a bulb
shining through a window.[29]

Here everything the speaker's eye alights upon appears as a distinct entity or "unit"—even the speaker himself as "Bob"—and the flashlight that picks out these things and distinguishes one object from another stresses a dissociative perspective. These units are the theme of the poem but so too is the space between them, and this stanza imitates its "pale tip of a finger," which at first points to "a planet" and then to the vacuum that gives the planet its definition. This space is not some abstract mass overhead that fails to penetrate the speaker's life—he sees it all around him, even in "the space between two fence posts." Elsewhere in the poem Flanagan says that "there are long gaps between what we see and what we hear," and this distance between things—especially the distance that marks the speaker's relationship to the world—is a recurring idea.[30]

However, if objects are isolated from each other, and the speaker's relationship to the world is one of distance and dissociation, "Houses" hardly laments this fact; the solitary, domestic "bulb / shining through a window" lights a lonely scene, but it is also starkly beautiful in its integrity. "As each unit is a constant, so is Bob," the opening line runs, and the poem repeatedly endorses the isolation and unitary wholeness of the self in particular.

There are long gaps between what we see and what we hear.
We hear the glass breaking but the windows are still intact.
No one is getting married. Everything back the way it was.
The ground lies flat again, undisturbed.
The world goes in and out, building and dismantling.
Some days a certain lamp seems much brighter than usual
and other days much dimmer.
There's an urge to change,
to knock out a wall or plant a flower bed.

As if we've come to the end of everything we know
and somehow these new things will attach themselves to us,
changing the way we look or how we talk.[31]

The nucleus of this stanza is the constant self that stands adjacent to an unstable world. Whether on a grand scale ("the world goes in and out, building and dismantling") or more trivially in his garden, the poet observes that change is always underway. Later in the poem he writes of the change that has overtaken the places from his past: "yes, the very ground where his house was, / where he can now drive that freeway past his old school / and watch his market, and his drug store, and his trees / blur past him in a muddy wash."[32] He even admits that the ongoing flux of the world may "[change] the way we look or how we talk." Yet these changes are cast as merely cosmetic: they fail to fundamentally alter the subject to which they "attach themselves." Change happens, it seems, but does not trouble a constant, distant self who regards it all with disinterest.

Can bonds with others be formed in such an atomized universe? Well, as Flanagan's poem continues, "no one is getting married"; nonetheless, connections do occur:

George and Mary throw rocks at the windows of an abandoned house. He says, "Let's make a wish." He wants to go someplace exotic like Africa or Tahiti. She has a different wish, and hers comes true.[33]

The relationship between George and Mary is sympathetic but somewhat antagonistic: although they join in a shared and quintessentially delinquent endeavor, they are nonetheless different entities with distinct aspirations. To put this into context, if George and Mary are lovers, their relationship with each other is the antithesis of the version John Donne famously presents in "The Good-Morrow," where he champions the idea that love should dissolve the distinctions between individuals. He writes, "If our two loves be one, or, thou and I / Love so alike, that none do slacken, none can die."[34] In Flanagan's poem, conversely, lovers' freedom from each other and the separation between them is paramount. Provisional alliances are therefore possible in Flanagan's world, but only between subjects that retain their independence. This stanza may be read as emblematic of the punk poetry scene at Beyond Baroque, where Flanagan joined with other delinquent poets at a rundown literary arts center just off Venice Beach to lob poems like rocks at the previous generation's decrepit forms.

The changes Cooper and his friends made were not always appreciated by the crowd that had previously frequented Beyond Baroque, and his tenure aroused no small amount of animosity. A reflective Mohr contends, "Other poets in Los Angeles who were not part of what appeared to be a new inner circle at Beyond Baroque began to grumble at their reduced stature at Beyond Baroque. After years of building a scene into prominence, they felt that they were being relegated to supporting roles and walk-on parts."[35] Regarding the fallout from his abolition of the open readings policy, Cooper maintains, "Everyone was furious at me, literally punching me and throwing things in my face. Because that's all they had. They would go there every week and read their poems at the open reading and that was their thing" (2007).[36] Elsewhere he comments on the pervasive hostility directed toward himself, Skelley, and their friend Jocelyn Fisher, then president of Beyond Baroque: "We were seen as pretty elitist by the local scene" (2012).[37] Craig Lee, who wrote a profile of Cooper for *L.A. Weekly* under the headline, "The Little Caesar of L.A.'s Poetry Scene," reports, "The fraternity of younger poets, whom Cooper describes as 'his group' are often denigrated by other poets ([Venice Beach poet] Lynne Bronstein calls them a 'poetry mafia')."[38]

IN THE EARLY 1980S, Beyond Baroque was effectively the setting for an ideological struggle that was underway throughout the United States at the time, as the flower power of the 1960s helter-skeltered into a far less idealistic 1970s. LA's earlier poetry scene, inclusive and radically porous, preferring what Bruce Boyd calls "the common" and communion with others, was in constant conflict with Cooper's young, somewhat exclusive set. This incessant antagonism between the old crowd and the new even contributed to a split in the Wednesday-night workshop and led to the establishment of a splinter group that moved out of Beyond Baroque and into the nearby Social and Public Art Resources Center. It also resulted in Cooper's resignation as the reading-series coordinator in 1983, after more than three years in charge. The shift away from a community that valued collective endeavor over the individual efforts of any one poet provides a useful vantage from which to differentiate between the social formations of the second-generation New York School and those endorsed by Cooper and his friends, which might be thought of as the post–New York School generation.

Kane contends that the second-generation poets "resuscitate" the practices of appropriation and collaboration used by previous avant-garde movements like surrealism, such that in certain works the voices of individual contributors become so braided together that the reader cannot be sure who has written any single line or word.[39] From Berrigan and Waldman's landmark collaboration "Memorial Day" (1971) and Berrigan and Robert Creeley's "Think of Anything" (1971–72) to book-length collaborations such as Berrigan, Padgett, and Brainard's *Bean Spasms* (1967), these kinds of collaborative experiments participate in what Kane elsewhere calls the second generation's "poetics of sociability," which acts as the glue for the community even as it critiques the culturally enshrined notion of a lone poetic voice by transcribing the clamor of a poetic community. Kane writes, "Second-generation work manifested more clearly than previous groupings had done before that the place of the solitary and muse-inspired author could productively give way to a poetics of sociability that, at least temporarily and by virtue of the collective, could help create a truly alternative site of resistance against the literary and political establishment of the era."[40]

By contrast, although they hung out together all the time, the circle of younger poets at Beyond Baroque had little interest in developing a *poetics* of sociability. They accepted the isolation and solitude that defined the world around them, and their work looks favorably on independence and individuality. Consequently, they seem to have been much more wary of sacrificing their individual voices to the flux and anonymity of collaboration, and collaborations between Cooper, Gerstler, and the other poets of the LA set are quite rare. Indeed, Trinidad appears to be the only member of the group with any real interest in the practice, collaborating with Flanagan on their book-length *A Taste of Honey* (1990), with Dlugos on "Columbus Day" (1982), and with Cooper on the unpublished poem "S.O.S.," written in January 1985.

It would seem that even though poets such as Berrigan and Waldman expanded the range of material available to subsequent generations of poets inspired by New York School poetry, offering models of poetic engagement with subjects like sex, drugs, and rock and roll, Cooper and his friends didn't enthusiastically embrace the older poets' model of a poetic community. There is a clear generational difference here: the LA punk poets' reluctance to collaborate (which is significant given their intimacy with Berrigan, Brainard, and others) and their antipathy for Beyond Baroque's older poetry scene is symptomatic of a disagreement between succeeding generations about the place of the individual within social formations.

This disagreement has a precedent and in fact characterized Patti Smith's relationship with New York's Poetry Project in earlier years. Arriving in the East Village in the late 1960s and eager to make a name for herself as a poet, from the outset Smith sought to establish her independence from the poetry community that had taken up residence at St. Mark's Church, which included Berrigan, Waldman, and other members of the second-generation New York School set. Kane's study of Smith's association with the Downtown poetry scene finds her identifying not with the progressive forms of community fostered at the Poetry Project but with poets like Rimbaud in an attempt to "aggressively . . . reinstate uniqueness to the figure of the poet."[41] "Read consistently as agitating if not outright repudiating affiliation with a collective," Rimbaud was Smith's example of antagonistic individualism, Kane argues, and buying into his "outlaw aura" helped her dissociation from the community and poetics of the Poetry Project: "Rimbaud and related figures are practically epic demigods for Smith, whose heroic individualism she contrasts, in an implicitly disparaging way, with the cheerful flocks assembled at St Mark's."[42] Kane takes a rather dim view of Smith distinguishing herself from the group at St. Mark's Church, and he sees her actions as those of a twenty-four-year-old's "youthful arrogance."[43]

Kane's association of Smith's individualism with youth and Rimbaud is instructive: as we saw in the previous chapter, Rimbaud, whom Carrie Noland names "a model of antisocial innocence," necessarily signifies the state of adolescence and its attendant egoism for those who were influenced by him.[44] Yet where Kane perceives only a "reactionary" bent to Smith's shunning of the practices of a "neo-Dada collaborative scene," one might also see a quasi-anarchistic attempt by her to reclaim a piece of individual autonomy in the face of a social grouping for which the idea of

Flyer for reading and performance at Beyond Baroque, January 6, 1985. Source: Dennis Cooper papers, box 10, folder 800, Fales Library and Special Collections, New York University Libraries.

individual uniqueness was not only anathema but positively regressive.[45] Kane's second-generation New York School poets produced a poetics of sociability that Smith resisted; Los Angeles in the late 1970s saw the rise of a poetics of *dissociability* that reinstated the idea of individuality and allowed for a separation of the individual poet from the efforts of the collective. As a punk-rock attitude was transposed to the West Coast through Cooper, it facilitated a necessary separation from the (older) collective at Beyond Baroque and the generation of an alternative punk poetry scene that regarded the singular more sympathetically.

A poetry community that cleaves to a quasi-anarchist principle of individual freedom, whose punk attitude insists on the right of individual independence from the collective, and that is erected on a poetics of dissociability is not built to last. In 1983, seven years after the punk excursion that started it all, Cooper stepped down from his position at Beyond Baroque. Speaking with Kate Wolf, he describes the night he decided to quit: "I quit because of this really bad night. I got attacked on stage by the writer Kate Braverman who felt I had never given her due. I gave her a reading, and she just really attacked me the whole night. I was just sitting there and I was like, fuck this, I'm done. I got so upset that I was being attacked in my own space that I quit" (2012).[46]

In spite of having supported his fellow punk poets for years through his magazine, press, and reading series, at this crucial moment when he most needed their support, none of them were willing to defend him and the work he'd done. With a heavy heart Cooper closed Little Caesar Press, packed his bags, and headed for New York—a move he'd thought about making for years. Without his charismatic influence and with the center's dwindling funds, the poetry community he helped to establish at Beyond Baroque collapsed and was finally scattered to the California winds. Turning his back on Los Angeles, Cooper also turned his back on poetry, and by the time he returned to live in the city five years later, having spent the intervening years in New York and Amsterdam, he'd given up poetry entirely to focus solely on prose. This transition was heralded by "A Herd," an extended prose poem from Cooper's second major collection of poetry, *The Tenderness of the Wolves* (1982).

"I'm Yours" | Frank O'Hara, Paul Goodman, and *The Tenderness of the Wolves*

4 IN HIS LIFE AND WORK, Cooper continually negotiates between a desire for togetherness and an endorsement of individuality. While he was at Beyond Baroque, he and his friends repudiated a model of poetry and community that prioritized "the common" and communion with others, yet the poems of *Idols* are always "reaching for" another, regardless of the fundamental solitude of the human subject. The way Cooper embraces independence and commits himself to community building at the same time seems somewhat paradoxical—at the very least there's a tension between these contrary tendencies. It's worth stepping back for a moment to spend a little time with this apparent paradox and to think through some of the political and literary factors that might have contributed to its appearance.

Cooper has often said that he is an anarchist, and indeed the tension that characterizes his work can be detected in the writings of other anarchist thinkers. Emma Goldman, for instance, wrestles with it in her essay "The Tragedy of Woman's Emancipation" (1906) when she writes, "The problem that confronts us today, and which the nearest future is to solve, is how to be one's self and yet in oneness with others; to feel deeply with all human beings and still retain one's own characteristic qualities."[1] It is a problem for Pierre-Joseph Proudhon too, who argues that an individualistic orientation and a wish for community are "the two faces of our nature, ever adverse, ever in course of reconciliation, but never entirely reconciled." Proudhon's anarchism is thus marked by the oscillation between dissidence and harmony: "In a word, as individualism is the primordial fact of humanity, so association is its complementary term; but both are in incessant manifestation."[2]

Cooper's difficulty is therefore hardly new or exclusive to this writer at this particular time, but a productive comparison might be drawn between his ongoing mediation between individual and communal concerns and a similar dialectic that emerges in the work of Frank O'Hara. Cooper was of course a great admirer of O'Hara, who was arguably as important a figure to him and his friends as Rimbaud was. While he was still head of the Beyond Baroque reading series, Cooper followed up his Rimbaud birthday party in 1980 with a Frank O'Hara birthday party in June 1982. The event included readings of O'Hara's poetry by Trinidad, Gerstler, and others; a screening of a film featuring O'Hara reading his work in his New York apartment; and a wine reception at which O'Hara's favorite music was played (Debussy and Erik Satie). At the intermission, O'Hara's favorite meal was served: breakfast, with cornflakes, orange juice, and donuts.

The first-generation New York School poets are widely considered to be totally apolitical: David Lehman writes that unlike the Beats, "the poets of the New York School pursued an aesthetic agenda that was deliberately apolitical, even antipolitical."[3] But a patient analysis of O'Hara's work and the intellectual culture in which he moved reveals that the provenance of what has come to be called his "coterie poetics" is much more radical than some have previously held. In this chapter, I make a rather unusual claim—possibly a surprising one, given that Cooper's work is hardly known for mimicking O'Hara's characteristic enthusiasm. Nonetheless, in what follows I show that O'Hara's influence on Cooper goes deeper than "kangaroos, sequins, chocolate sodas!" (or indeed, cornflakes or donuts): O'Hara's critique of the common, I argue, resurfaces in Cooper's poetry and community building with a punk rock hue.[4] Tracking the percolation of this critique through the New York School poet's work, I argue that Cooper's work may be viewed as an engagement by proxy with the ideas of the anarchist intellectual Paul Goodman.

THE SENSE OF COMMUNITY that the New York School poets' little magazine *Locus Solus* produced within its few issues in the early 1960s reflected in its contents the kind of community that Frank O'Hara had attempted to cultivate in his poetry for more than a decade. Now commonly called his "coterie poetics," critics have recently focused on O'Hara's commitment to relationality in poetry and the ways his work attempts to transcribe the intimate bonds between members of his group of friends. In *Frank O'Hara: The Poetics of Coterie* (2006), for instance, Lytle Shaw finds that O'Hara's poetry and art criticism express a desire to replicate and interrogate in writing the social fabric of the New York School, their friends, and associates: "The idea of O'Hara as a coterie poet emerges both from his intimate links to a circle of famous artists and writers and from the intimate referential practices of his work, in particular his conspicuous use of proper names, especially those of his friends."[5]

Dropping the names of his friends, like John (Ashbery), Jimmy (Schuyler), Kenneth (Koch), and LeRoi (Jones, aka Amiri Baraka), O'Hara's texts gather a small community of people brought together in friendship and poetry. Critics including Shaw have attributed the emergence of this coterie poetics to the influence of Paul Goodman's "Advance-Guard Writing in America: 1900–1950," published in the *Kenyon Review* in 1951. An influential text for a number of emergent poetry communities in the United States at the time, O'Hara read Goodman's essay as a master's student at the University of Michigan in the summer of 1951 and wrote excitedly to Jane Freilicher: "I read Paul Goodman's current manifesto in *Kenyon Review* and if you haven't devoured its delicious message, rush to your nearest newsstand! It is really lucid about what's bothering us both besides sex, and it is so heartening to know that someone understands these things."[6]

Goodman's article is at once a rather bewildering history of the European avant-garde in the first half of the twentieth century and a lucid exploration of the role of the "advance-guard" of American letters as the twenty-first century approaches. For Goodman, the United States was still in a state of shell shock following World War II.[7] As a result of increased technologization and the resurgence of consumer culture in the postwar years, American society was also defined by conformity and abstraction, where the individual was separated from the power to act and Americans were alienated from one another. However, a radical revision of these social formations was possible. The avant-garde artist in particular could help to break down the anonymity and emptiness of modern society by establishing "intimate communities" through art. In a lengthy passage often quoted by O'Hara scholars, Goodman writes:

> The essential aim of our advance-guard must be the physical re-establishment of community. This is to solve the crisis of alienation in the simple way. If the persons are estranged from one another, from themselves, and from their artist, he takes the initiative precisely by putting his arms around them and drawing them together. In literary terms this means: to write for them about them personally, and so break the roles and format they are huddled in. It makes no difference what the genre is, whether praise or satire or description, or whether the style is subtle or obscure, for anyone will pay concentrated attention to a work in which he in his own name is a character. Yet such personal writing can occur only in a small community of acquaintances, where everybody knows everybody and understands what is at stake; in our estranged society it is just this intimate community that is lacking. Of course it is lacking! Then give up the ambitious notion of a public artist.[8]

O'Hara effectively took up Goodman's challenge, writing for and about a small community of friends, using their proper names, having his work embrace them as a group, and courting the danger of its circulation among the members of a small coterie rather than the public at large. As Andrew Epstein observes, "O'Hara's enthusiastic response to Goodman's essay offers a tantalizing clue about the origins of O'Hara's distinctive poetic stance: in particular, his penchant for writing poems to and about his friends, his preference for occasional poetry, and his notorious, controversial practice of nonchalantly citing his friends' proper names in his poems, leaving some to wonder how the reader is supposed to have any idea who 'Jane' or 'John' are."[9]

But what of the origins of Goodman's idea of an "intimate community," which O'Hara so enthusiastically endorsed? A poet and literary critic, Goodman was also the most outspoken and controversial anarchist intellectual in the United States during the 1950s and 1960s, notorious for his virulent criticisms of American society and for his openly bisexual lifestyle. In a culture of widespread conformity, Goodman's work took aim at the status quo and what he called Americans' "powerful psychological resistance" to thinking the contemporary situation otherwise; such resistance cast alternatives to the absurdity and alienation of modern life as impractical and "utopian."[10] He writes, "There is no doubt that the term 'utopian thinking' is importantly used to conceal the statement: *The structure and folkways of our society are absurd, but they can no longer be changed. Any hint of changing them disturbs our resignation and rouses anxiety. Cruelly, for things are well enough as they are.*"[11] Goodman warned that "mankind seems to be galloping toward the condition of a social beehive or termitary in which individual uniqueness, creaturely contact, neighborly charity, the satisfactions of local community, and the high culture of real cities, are all increasingly irrelevant."[12]

His proposed alternatives to the absurd structures and folkways of society—including his idea of an avant-garde "intimate community"—thus sought to accommodate and attend to these virtues. According to Goodman, the education system spent too much funding on the infrastructure of teaching and not enough on teachers: "Why not try, as a pilot project, doing without the school building altogether for a few hundred kids for most of the day . . . using the city itself as the material for the curriculum and the background for the teaching."[13] In urban areas like New York, he declared elsewhere, city planners bowed to the cult of the automobile by bulldozing enormous highways through old neighborhoods, obliterating communities, and accentuating the alienation of modern life with a road to the suburbs. His proposition? Ban the private automobile from metropolitan areas: "By banning private cars and reducing traffic, we can, in most areas, close off nearly nine out of ten cross-town streets and every second north-south avenue. These closed roads plus the space now used for off-street parking would give us a handsome fund of land for neighborhood relocation."[14]

In these kinds of "utopian" proposals, Goodman consistently fought against the contemporary attitude "that things are well enough, there is nothing to be grievous or angry about, and anyway our situation is inevitable," offering suggestions that stemmed from an anarchistic belief in the inviolability of individual uniqueness and the practicality of small-scale community building.[15] In "Poem Read at Joan Mitchell's," written by Frank O'Hara the day before Jane Freilicher's marriage to Joe Hazan in February 1957, we can read echoes of Goodman's ideas in O'Hara's negotiation between a desire for individuality and a dedication to togetherness.

The poem spins a complicated web of friendships from references to New York School intimates like Ashbery, Koch, Freilicher, and LeSueur. The epithalamion opens by addressing to the bride to be: "At last you are tired of being single / the effort to be new does not upset you nor the effort to be other / you are not tired of life altogether." It later continues:

> This poem goes on too long because our friendship has been long,
>   long for this life and these times, long as art is long and
>   uninterruptable,
> and I would make it as long as I hope our friendship lasts if I could
>   make poems that long[16]

From the outset O'Hara's poem makes good on his commitment to Goodman's idea of an intimate "advance-guard" community, referencing in its title a named friend (the painter Joan Mitchell) and intimating the presence of a group of avant-garde friends at the poem's initial reading. Yet this communal intimacy is quickly abraded by the opening lines, where the speaker offers an equivocal statement on Freilicher's impending union and sees in it the demise of her uniqueness and individuality: "At last you are tired of being single / the effort to be new does not upset you nor the effort to be other / you are not tired of life together." The state of "being single" (i.e., unattached or independent; one instead of two) is here equated with newness and otherness or variety, two cardinal virtues in O'Hara's poetry. The speaker also attributes a kind of heroism to the maintenance of one's independence by recognizing the "effort" it takes—an effort that the bride-to-be has "tired" of, capitulating instead to a life of ease and togetherness. The first stanza, therefore, seems to undercut the title's apparent encouragement of friendly attachment by championing the individual who separates herself from the drift toward unity with another.

In the following stanza, however, the speaker seems to revise his earlier dismissal of the "life together."

city noises are louder because you are together
being together you are louder than calling separately across a
    telephone one to the other
and there is no noise like the rare silence when you both sleep[17]

The speaker now appears to recognize his error: previously portrayed as the result of a failure of fortitude or of giving in to exhaustion, the state of "being together" is here affirmed as vigorous and necessary. It is also treated more tenderly, and these lines are replete with the speaker's own yearning for such a connection, which might undo the lonely separation of "being single" epitomized by "telephone" calls that never seem to connect "one to the other." Andrew Epstein writes that "[O'Hara's] poems are filled with a strange, agitated mixture of optimism and sadness, a thirst for togetherness and a yearning for solitude," and these first ten lines establish a motif that will recur throughout the rest of the poem, where we find the poet balancing the individual and the communal, oscillating between fervent support of togetherness and wariness about the loss of self it might bring about.[18]

Of the commentaries that address the connection between O'Hara's writing and Goodman's thought, most attend almost exclusively to the significance of the *Kenyon Review* piece and usually dismiss the fact that Goodman and O'Hara moved within intersecting social circles in New York throughout the 1950s and 1960s. Such a constricted focus might lead us to assume that O'Hara's familiarity with Goodman and his work extends only as far as this essay, when O'Hara actually owned at least three of Goodman's books and was reasonably well acquainted with him personally. Joe LeSueur, O'Hara's friend and roommate for more than a decade, to whom he dedicated his *Lunch Poems*, was even introduced to O'Hara by Goodman in 1951 at a New Year's Eve party thrown by John Ashbery. LeSueur had met Goodman in Los Angeles in 1949, and they were occasionally lovers for some years afterward. In his memoir, *Digressions on Some Poems by Frank O'Hara*, LeSueur writes:

> I met Frank on New Year's Eve 1951, at a party given by John Ashbery. Paul Goodman said, "There's a poet named Frank O'Hara I think you'll like," and led me across the room to him. And that, of course, was my real introduction to Frank, the one that took. It led

somewhere and for that reason became etched in my memory. At the time, Paul—the first intellectual, the first poet, and the first bohemian or non-conformist I ever got to know—was still in my life, still of some importance to me, and the hold he had over me, sporadic in the three years we'd known each other, came to an end once and for all when, by introducing me to Frank, he unwittingly turned me over to him.[19]

More curiously, Shaw, Epstein, Brad Gooch, and Terence Diggory also fail to recognize Goodman's status as a prominent anarchist intellectual and that his work as a whole is anarchistic in origin, consistently drawing on anarchist sources and aligning itself with a tradition of anarchist thought. Carissa Honeywell for one finds that "Goodman utilized the anarchist tradition to formulate his distinctive critique of contemporary America according to the principles of decentralization, participatory democracy, autonomy, and community."[20] Only Lehman's *The Last Avant-Garde* names Goodman as an anarchist—but it doesn't make the connection between his advance-guard essay and O'Hara's poetics.[21]

It seems, therefore, that there exists in the critical commentary on Frank O'Hara's coterie poetics a desire to separate O'Hara from Goodman and muffle the anarchistic tones of Goodman's ideas and consequently O'Hara's poetics. Granted this may be the result of mere oversight or of modern critics' underestimating the extent of Goodman's influence—an influence that, as Susan Sontag pointed out, was grossly underestimated even at the time of his death. Despite "the extent to which Paul Goodman's ideas were repeated," she wrote, "as the assessments come in now that he is dead, he is treated as a marginal figure."[22] In any case, given O'Hara's avowed admiration for Goodman, their long—and sometimes fraught—acquaintance, and their circulation within the same milieu, it seems reasonable to conclude that when he adopted Goodman's model of an intimate avant-garde community, O'Hara (if not, perhaps, his later critics) was well aware of the radical underpinnings of Goodman's thought.

It is not my intention here to portray O'Hara as an anarchist poet like Goodman or suggest they were close friends. LeSueur, for instance, points out that in spite of O'Hara's admiration for Goodman's work, "at best theirs was a tenuous friendship, one that never got off the ground."[23]

I simply wish to suggest that, due to the influence of Goodman's thought, O'Hara's coterie poetics resonates more closely with anarchist ideas than previous criticism will allow and that these ideas are more overtly actualized when Cooper comes on the scene. Enthused by Goodman's work, O'Hara's poetry orients itself toward microcommunity building while retaining traces of an anarchist's belief in individual autonomy; given that a struggle between individual isolation and intersubjective communion already marks the poems in *Idols*, Cooper's writing and his efforts at Beyond Baroque are receptive to O'Hara's (and thus Goodman's) ideas.

Cooper's introduction to Goodman through O'Hara's poetry and indeed Cooper's acquaintance with punk rock introduces a modulation into his thought. With his exposure to anarchism at one remove comes a renewed appreciation for individuality and a wariness about certain aspects of the common and of communal endeavor. *The Tenderness of the Wolves* begins to reflect this newly attenuated position, and the title itself indicates that the work may be viewed as a meditation on the qualities of communal life; that the wolf's tenderness is offered only to its own suggests a judgment about the conformity often demanded of the collective. Without doubt more sensational than O'Hara's "Poem Read at Joan Mitchell's" and utterly distinct from the earlier work in tone and technique, "A Herd," Cooper's long poem from this collection, nonetheless presents a critique of communion and the common that is comparable with O'Hara's and evokes the devastating—even murderous—erasure of individuality that a pursuit of intersubjectivity may engender.

COMPOSED IN 1980 while Cooper was working at Beyond Baroque, poems in *The Tenderness of the Wolves* explore similar themes to the ones in *Idols*, and notions of solitude and isolation are ubiquitous within the collection's teenage milieu. However, such ideas are expressed in much wilder, more sexually explicit, and more violent ways than the previous collection, which appears relatively tame by comparison. In *The Tenderness of the Wolves*, the Sadean individualism that marked Cooper's earlier work meets identifiably Sadean practices for the first time, and these poems deal with extreme, mostly anally-fixated sexual encounters, along with rape and murder. The poem "Dinner" circles back to the distance that defines relationships between the protagonists of *Idols*' poems but does so via an explicit treatment of the practice of anal fisting (introducing one's hand into a sexual partner's anus and rectum). Here a nameless mustachioed older man leads teenage Tom from a gay bar to the parking lot outside; they strip and fuck in the back of a car and the man begins to finger Tom's ass, noting that "the handsome young face was far away. . . . The boy was as distant from these moves as God from his priests down on earth."[24] This sense of separation endures throughout; even as the tempo of their fucking quickens toward a climax, "both the men's breaths blew in ever altering rhythms, manned by the shapes of words which, because of the distance between them, neither could quite comprehend."[25] Despite this chasm of distance and incomprehension, the man persists, and in a pornographic parallel of *Idols'* rather chaste last lines, the poem draws to a conclusion with his reaching for (or rather, *into*) another.

> Now the man churned three fingers deeper into the well-stretched-out hole, withdrew them a little and pushed four back in. He squeezed the thumb up. Then he dialled and dialled until his hand was enclosed. The anus handcuffed the wrist. The boy was breathing so deeply the man thought that he might be dangerous or in danger.

> Suddenly, Tom shot off on his fingers. His body shuddered. His head clunked forward on the glass.[26]

From "Dinner" onward, the collection builds in intensity, arriving at a tipping point with the eponymous "The Tenderness of the Wolves" series, where the influence of Cooper's contemporaneous scrapbooks on sex and serial killing is evident. Collected in *Gone: Scrapbook 1980–1982* (published in 2014), the content of these scrapbooks is torn from the pages of magazines and newspapers like *Inside Detective*, the *National Enquirer*, and the *Los Angeles Times*, which recount in detail the rape and murder of boys and young men by male serial killers around Los Angeles in the 1970s and 1980s. "I made it to try to understand my relationship to the material I was interesting [*sic*] in writing about at that time, which was largely the sex/violence/emotion axis that I had been preoccupied secretly and imaginatively with since I was a kid," says Cooper. "At the time I was making the scrapbook, that particular axis was being acted out and illustrated all around me via the concurrent spate of serial killers who were committing their acts and coming to light in that period" (2014).[27]

These poems explore the same axis. "Grip," for instance, begins, "While raping a boy / slide your hands / around his neck / closing your grip / until he is dead."[28] The following poem, "Darkens," is more legibly indebted to the scrapbook's contents, written from the perspective of an unnamed murderer who drugs, rapes, and kills his young male victim: "First he's impeccable, tense, too ideal. Then he is / weeping, annoys me. Then limp, cool, unprevailable, / dull. Then sprawled saint-like on the floor; gazing / upward. I dump that in the river and he is gone."[29] The final poem in the series is even clearer about where its subject matter comes from—"Late Friends" is dedicated to Robert Piest (the final victim of serial murderer John Wayne Gacy) and references the Des Plaines River where Piest's body was found: "you are raped, strangled, and dropped / in the Des Plaines river. The man who does it feels / spiritual and light."[30]

The subjects of these poems are more transgressive than the ones that precede them, but their themes are contiguous. *The Tenderness of the Wolves* shows that Cooper is still thinking about subjective isolation and the possibility of communion with another. Like all of his characters, the figures who surface in this collection suffer from a "weird detachment" or are victims of another's "longing for attachment" (1988).[31] These poems nonetheless appear to test the limits of Cooper's previous conclusions. If you pursue an impossible intersubjective encounter because you cannot countenance the alternative embrace of egoism, where does this pursuit end? If intersubjectivity equals a disintegration of discrete subjects and an obliteration of difference between the self and the other, is the sum of such ideas death? Can reaching for another turn into a murderous stranglehold? The poem that closes the collection dramatizes such ideas and seems to criticize *Idols*' quest for togetherness, casting it in a new, negative light.

"A Herd" is a twelve-page, twenty-four-part prose poem that depicts the lives of some loser high school kids and their grisly deaths at the hands of a gay serial killer named Ray Sexton. The poem drifts with apparent aimlessness between sections—floating through scenes set in the locker rooms and bleachers of a California high school, the lamp-lit bedrooms of laconic teenagers, and the dark basement of the murderer's home where adolescent boys meet their doom. Its narrative repeatedly returns to Sexton, however, who is described without much psychological depth and seems bored and tired. He seizes, sedates, restrains, and tortures his victims with a kind of indifference before wearily doing them in. As for his motivations, the poem does not reveal a lot, but we are told that Sexton's actions alleviate his feeling of being "cold and empty": killing is a compulsion, and "in every cool body something could warm without reason. His hands would veer from his work and anchor him at the flesh."[32] This warmth and connection are only momentary, and once rigor mortis set in, we are told "he felt nothing."[33]

Sexton's cold and empty loneliness is thus dissipated by occasional intense contact with another, a murderous intersubjective encounter in which he convinces himself he has wholly incorporated his victim's self, and all of what his victim is (or was) is his in ecstasy; in Sexton's day-dreams, one of his victims signs an autograph, "I'm yours."[34] Yet when his boys necessarily expire as a result of their ordeal, his encounter with them dwindles into insignificance. Emptiness and his attendant desire for plenitude set in once again: "The ideal had grown sour and he was left holding the bag and looking around for something to fill it. There had been nothing. Then, gradually, the longing came back."[35] Sexton is essentially representative of the point at which the search for intersubjectivity turns pathological, and his killing spree is underwritten by a compulsive desire for communion with others, specifically teenage boys. For Sexton, being single is not just tiring, as it is for O'Hara's Freilicher, it is *unbearable* and repeatedly sends him out on the hunt for a boy with whom he can experience the state of "being together."

One upshot of this psychotic pursuit of intersubjectivity is that it erases the specificity of the other in the abstract. Apart from the imperative that they conform to his type, the particularities of each individual victim matter little to Sexton, and this fact is repeatedly emphasized in the text by the equivalence the poem draws between his adolescent victims and "a herd" of hapless animals. We are told that Ray tears his victims' photographs out of the morning newspaper and pins them in a row on a bulletin board: "Five heads hung high by a hunter." We also read that he "put bodies down in the crawl space, like beasts into a cage."[36] A more sustained comparison likens his most recent casualty to a pet dog.

> He thought about the backs of boy's necks where the haircut stopped and a soft trace of it trailed just a bit down the skin. He'd place his hand there with fingers resting behind the ears, caressing there as a

man does his dog, to relax it. A dog's mouth would drop open and tongue plop over its edge. A boy's lips would moisten, swing around as though guided by radar, leak their tongue and its peace.[37]

As this last sentence indicates in its swift transition from the singular, if indefinite, article of "a boy" to the plural possessive pronoun in "their tongue," the correlation between victims and animals has its roots in a negation of individuality and a drift toward the generic and undifferentiated that persists throughout the poem. The murderer's prey is repeatedly drawn under the sign of the common: describing the high school's denizens and its "shadowy herd of victims," the speaker insists on collective terms like "rabble," "slew," and "load."[38] Teenagers are also "crowded" into locker rooms, and Ray chooses from "ranks" of boys.[39]

This repeated emphasis on the common is joined by the lack of detail given to this rather anonymous crowd of vulnerable young beasts. In the locker rooms (whose "four parallel rows of green lockers" are as uniform as the adolescents using them), boys pull on "grey teeshirts emblazoned with crude block letters: Smith, Wojnarowicz, Peters, etc."—the use of "etc." quickly effacing any nominal specificity that preceded it.[40] Even when the poem closes in on Jay Levin, Sexton's latest victim, his face is described as "nondescript, pimply white, ruled by blue, bloodshot eyes."[41] We also read that a need for resemblance among his teenage boys and vagueness of their features are characteristics of Sexton's murderous desire: "The magazine's stars were Ray's angels, freed from the limits of IQs and coordination, whose distant looks had a cloudy, quaalude effect. Teen stars' perfection haunted him and a vague resemblance to one or another could more often than not, be gleaned from the face of a boy he had killed."[42]

Employing these techniques simultaneously throughout the poem, Cooper suggests that Sexton's suspension of any ethical or moral code arises out of the intersection of the animal and the common. Sexton may torture, rape, and murder his victims with indifference because they are denied uniqueness; their "being single," in O'Hara's words, is negated and they find themselves drawn together as a *genus*, quickly dispatched without conscience. A similar idea is implied in the Duc de Blangis's speech in Sade's *120 Days of Sodom*, cited in an earlier chapter, when he warns his victims that "it is not at all as human beings we behold you, but exclusively as animals one feeds in return for their services, and which one withers with blows when they refuse to be put to use."[43] Cooper seems to be responding to these kinds of ideas in "A Herd," aiming them at the idea of the collective. The common and the realm of animality into which Sexton's victims drift, in a way, condemns them to death: individuality and difference negated in advance, his ax hacks them up into an anonymous mass of flesh "until no owner could claim it."[44]

Spurred on by his ongoing arguments with the older Beyond Baroque crowd at the time of the poem's composition, in "A Herd" Cooper radicalizes O'Hara's interrogation of togetherness. Cooper's poem offers a gruesome, bilateral critique of the ruination of individuality and difference that the common and an attendant pursuit of intersubjectivity can threaten. The poem stakes out a more nuanced position than the one found in *Idols*, where communion with others was desperately sought even if subjectivity was acknowledged to be proscribed and insurmountable. Here subjectivity is less a state from which the poet wishes to escape and more the ground from which individuality grows—a source of uniqueness that should be prized and protected from the predations of the common.

Safe and the Aesthetics of Distance

5 IN 1983 *ROLLING STOCK*, a cultural newspaper published in Boulder, Colorado, by Black Mountain poet Ed Dorn and his wife, Jennifer, announced in their fifth issue the winners of the 1983 AIDS Awards for Poetry. In recognition of what the editors and their collaborator Tom Clark called "AN EPIDEMIC OF IDIOCY on the poetry scene," awardees were offered a prize, large and luridly depicted on the page: a beaker of blood, presumably contaminated with the AIDS virus, its infected contents overflowing. "To date 1300 cases of AIDS POETRY have been reported in the U.S.," read the caption.

This rare and rather dubious honor was bestowed on five writers. Clayton Eshleman was condemned for his *L.A. Times* review "attacking a dead—and thus harmless—Elizabeth Bishop," Allen Ginsberg received an AIDS Award for the apparently incorrect claim that he wrote lyrics for the Clash, Robert Creeley wrote book blurbs that *Rolling Stock* deemed worthy of infection with an incurable disease, and Steve Abbott went around "accusing everybody who doesn't like him or his poetry of 'rabid homophobia'" (one presumes the AIDS Award did little to assuage this supposed paranoia). Dennis Cooper, meanwhile, received his award for writing the most "AIDS-like line" of the year in his chapbook *My Mark*. The line ran: "Mark's ass is wrinkled, pink, and simplistically rendered, but cute." Assuming their readers were similarly disgusted by this plague of AIDS poetry (and not the homophobic awards themselves), the editors held open a sixth spot for the readers' "WRITE-IN CANDIDATE" of their choice: "Fill in the name of your favorite POETRY IDIOT here," it jovially declared.[1] (Jennifer Dunbar Dorn declined to give me permission to reproduce the image.)

Composed two years into an AIDS crisis that had no end in sight, which fueled the fire of state-sponsored bigotry, and which, before it was eventually brought under control through the efforts of AIDS activists, would result in the deaths of hundreds of thousands of Americans and millions of people worldwide, *Rolling Stock*'s 1983 AIDS Awards for Poetry was in sickeningly bad taste. "It's not at all funny," Eliot Weinberger wrote in *Sulfur* magazine at the time. "It has only one reading: if AIDS is 'idiocy,' then clearly the 'idiots' are AIDS-victims—that is, gay men. For Cooper, Ginsberg, and Abbott, who are publicly known as homosexual, it means: Those faggots should drop dead. For Creeley and Eshleman, publicly known as heterosexual, it means: They're idiots, therefore faggots, therefore they should drop dead from faggot disease."[2] Abbott, who died of AIDS-related complications in 1994, responded to the AIDS Awards in his *View Askew: Postmodern Investigation* (1989), writing in the epilogue that "they mock us as we die, knowing full well anti-gay humor leads to anti-gay violence. Language and ideas can kill just as surely as viruses, clubs, and guns."[3] Writer Kevin Killian, a friend of both Abbott and Cooper, was apoplectic and confessed to being "hysterical" about *Rolling Stock*'s stunt: "As far as I'm concerned, Edward Dorn is nothing less than a war criminal in the war against AIDS. . . . I ask you, what kind of person devises an 'AIDS Award for Poetic Idiocy'?"[4]

Who, indeed. "I once would have thought Dorn and Clark to be unlikely mouthpieces for Reagan America," a shocked Weinberger wrote, but in retrospect the AIDS Awards are of a piece with the antigay prejudice of Dorn in particular, which became more pronounced in his later years. The homophobic rhetoric of his *Abhorrences: A Chronicle of the Eighties* (1990), for instance, is reminiscent of the Christian Right's loud denunciation of homosexuality as synonymous with promiscuity and antisocial behavior. "Aid(e) Memoire," a poem composed a year after the publication of the AIDS Awards, supposed that if you're constantly "screwing" and being "screwed" by "everyone you meet," all day, every day, then you should expect to "get a disease," "So why not forego / the gamble and drink directly from the sewer."[5] In poet CAConrad's succinct reading, "Dorn actually blames the victim here in this poem, saying, HERE, it's YOUR FAULT because you fuck all day long you dirty fucking pig, you should just drink from the sewer!"[6] Elsewhere in the same collection, a poem called "Condom mania: the ins and outs" held that condoms had holes punched into them by bored factory employees; such vindictive persons have the same motivations as some with the HIV virus, the speaker says, "whose / industrial revenge is not saying no / but passing it on—."[7] Not only were those with HIV-positive blood promiscuous, therefore, they were malicious too and possibly even homicidal. According to CAConrad these sentiments have damaged Dorn's reputation irreparably and made him a *persona non grata* in certain circles: "The things Dorn said has put him in the category of Pound's open support of fascism for some people."[8]

As for Clark, his contribution to the AIDS Awards—or at least the nomination of Cooper for writing the most "AIDS-like line"—from one perspective was more personal than it was ideological. Cooper and Clark were once friends. A second-generation New York School poet and sometime poetry editor of the *Paris Review* who was friendly with the likes of Ron Padgett, Alice Notley, and Ted Berrigan (and published a biography of the latter, *Late Returns*, in 1985), Clark wrote the kind of pop-inflected poetry Cooper, Amy Gerstler, and the other young poets at Beyond Baroque loved and sought to import into the staid LA scene. Cooper read Clark's work and knew about its connections to the New York School as early as 1972. By 1979, as the editor of a leading underground literary magazine, he was in a position to approach Clark and ask him to contribute some poems to *Little Caesar*. As reading-series organizer at Beyond Baroque, he also asked Clark to come out to Los Angeles to read. The two quickly established a rapport, and in 1980 Little Caesar Press published Clark's poetry collection, *The End of the Line*.

After Clark, Cooper went on to publish other New York School poets in *Little Caesar* magazine and Little Caesar Press, including books by Joe Brainard (*Nothing to Write Home About* in 1981) and Eileen Myles (*Sappho's Boat* in 1982). According to Cooper, he and Clark "became pretty friendly, by mail, phone, and I went up to visit him where he was living in Santa Barbara a couple times, and I read there with him and Ed Dorn once" (2018).[9] Clark published Cooper's 1981 chapbook, *The Missing Men*, as part of the Immediate Editions series he edited for Am Here Books. He even made cover art for Cooper's book, a simple line drawing of Cooper in profile, his eyes searching the horizon, his ear unusually prominent, centered in the middle of the page, listening out perhaps for the return of those eponymous missing men.

Things started to go south in late 1982 when Cooper ran out of money. His mother, who had bankrolled Little Caesar Press and the magazine from the start, finally told him she could no longer foot the bill for his increasingly ambitious endeavors. Speaking years later, he admitted that "I basically coerced my mother into paying for [*Little Caesar*]. I guilt-tripped her. But my whole thing with *Little Caesar* was to sell it for incredibly cheap, so it never ever earned back what it cost. And of course the stores never paid me for selling it, so I lost tons of money.... There got to be a point where my mother said, 'I cannot do this anymore!'" (2007).[10] Cooper had no option but to put everything on hold, with most of *Little Caesar* magazine's thirteenth issue typeset and four new books earmarked to be published by the press in 1983, including a novel by Tom Clark. Explaining the situation to his authors while also telling them he was on the lookout for other sources of funding to publish their books, Cooper gave them an out: they could publish elsewhere if they wished. Everyone said they were happy to wait and see. "Shortly thereafter," Cooper remembers, "Tom just kind of flipped out on me" (2018).[11]

Convinced that Cooper had not been honest with him, in the winter of 1982–83 Clark sent him a barrage of postcards and letters demanding more information about the matter of "the books" (when typesetting would be done, what the publication date might be, if Cooper was going to use the cover art he selected, etc.). He followed up his voluminous correspondence with calls to Cooper's answering machine on which he left, according to Cooper, "weird, accusatory messages multiple times a day and even late at night" (2018).[12]

Something of Clark's state of mind at the time is conveyed by the postcards themselves, each cut from the same large patterned white card but differing wildly in sentiment one week to the next. In densely packed handwriting he is alternately threatening and solicitous, conciliatory and cajoling; now demanding the return of his manuscript, now urging Cooper to "forget the past and start over."[13] One of his postcards from November is written as Cooper himself and requests that the recipient pick from multiple options the one that best describes how he feels. Cooper could tick the box next to "I don't want to have to return the mss to you so you can submit it elsewhere" or "the typesetting is being done now and I will soon bring it out to show you" or, most disconcertingly, "you're just an aging white cripple whom [*sic*] nobody likes in New York, so why don't you just get off my cloud & blow away."[14] Reading through Clark's intensely erratic correspondence recalls Wayne Koestenbaum's evocation of John Ashbery's "Lazy Susan"—the way the "gesture of incorporation" in his poems "breaks down, wanders backward, loses count, decides to nap or listen to a different song, makes fun of our process of trying to understand, has a shyness spasm, grows sexually aroused, hides the 'boner,' turns erudite, throws a pie in the elucidator's face, wants Mother, gets big for its britches, calms down, plays cards, bemoans the weather, ends the poem, publishes it."[15]

But in spite of Clark's pedigree as a poet in the New York School tradition, his correspondence is not a long poem uncoiling across stacks of smudged postcards. Rather, it's the unhappy story of how a once-productive friendship—a creative partnership, really—can, with distance and paranoia, implode, ending in bitterness and acrimony. "You are congenitally irresponsible," Clark's final postcard to Cooper runs. "You were brought up rich, taught to regard the world as your entertainment, and have no idea that other people exist."[16] For his part, Cooper ended their correspondence with a long letter formally addressed to "Tom Clark" where he wrote, "I never used to understand how people could have once been your friends and then have become so angry at or far away from you, but I certainly do now. I may have fucked up or made mistakes along the line but your mistrust, incredible selfishness, viciousness and more are unprecedented in my experience with human beings."[17] Defending his work with Little Caesar Press, he continued:

> I publish books so great work or work I think is great will get into print and out there. I spend much of my time on it, doing 98% of the work myself, and spending money I could be living on to do it. It's more work than I can logically do but I've been trying to do it, and I don't need harassment and bullshit from people like you when I'm in a particularly strapped position. You may be a great writer but you're a fucking ingrate. . . .

Despite the palpable anger, a modicum of sympathy toward Clark remained as Cooper concluded his letter with some friendly counsel: "If you'll take my advice, whatever it's worth, you'll take your family and move somewhere less isolated where you'll be less isolated and your paranoia will not be allowed to fuck you and a lot of other people over by growing far out of bounds."[18] Cooper never spoke to Clark again.

AS FAR AS CLARK'S involvement was concerned, Cooper's nomination for an AIDS Award in *Rolling Stock* thus appears to have been the public face of a private grudge, which accounts for the disparity between the innocuousness of the awardees' "idiocies" and the monstrousness of the award itself. Weinberger observed that "as 'idiocy' goes—even poetry idiocy—these strike me as rather obscure misdemeanors."[19] The line taken to be most "AIDS-like" (whatever that might mean), "Mark's ass is wrinkled, pink, and simplistically rendered, but cute," isn't even drawn from a work in which AIDS is a principal or a prominent focus. *My Mark* and *Safe* (the novella it was ultimately part of) contain no references to AIDS. In truth, such large, immediate problems for the gay community and society as a whole are held somewhat at a distance in the text. Relationality in a more abstract sense is instead the recurring theme of *Safe*: how one relates to others; how one relates to one's body and one's feelings; writing's relation to intimacy and reality in general.

Cooper's first full-length prose work, *Safe*, was published in 1984 by Felice Picano's SeaHorse Press, which had previously published *Idols*. Offering Cooper his book contract, Picano wrote, "I hope *Safe* is scandalous, and I trust it will be."[20] A short narrative in three parts, the novella follows a twenty-something gay Los Angelino named Mark Lewis as he moves in and out of the lives of the men who love him. Its opening section, "Missing Men," juxtaposes various incidents from Mark's doomed relationship with his writer boyfriend Rob and itemizes Rob's repeated attempts to write a novel where feeling is "blanketed" by "stylization."[21] The following section, "My Mark," depicts Mark's sexual encounters with older men and includes a number of fragmentary, introspective passages written by an unnamed author that reflect on his relationship with Mark and his efforts to capture him in prose, "safe, in a sense, from the blatant front lighting of my true emotion, though it creeps in."[22] Finally, "Bad Thoughts," set in the aftermath of Mark's death from undisclosed causes, follows his quietly grieving ex-boyfriend Doug as he superimposes Mark's face onto a succession of new lovers. At Mark's funeral, we are told, Doug "couldn't conjure up anything close to tears."[23]

Drawing explicitly on aspects of the author's life—Cooper was once obsessed with a guy named Mark Lewis, who came to a poetry reading he did with Tim Dlugos in Washington, DC—and tracing the movement of characters around an elusive object of their desire, the book is something of a model for many works that Cooper would later write. Recalling his doomed relationship with Lewis, Cooper says, "When he never called me, I was incredibly disappointed. In my mind, he had become a kind of one boy consensus of so many themes in my life and in my work. So I sat down and wrote *My Mark* about him, making him the ultimate object of my fantasies and emotional needs, similarly to what I would later do with George Miles in my novel cycle."[24]

It also draws on the work that came before it, and the alienated world-view put forward by Cooper's poems is here in abundance. *Safe*, like the earlier poetry, goes to great lengths to demonstrate that solitude is an intrinsic part of human experience, and distance between ourselves and others, even those we love—*especially* those we love—is unavoidable. As the character Doug and his young lover Skip know, subjective isolation is a condition that can be alleviated in sex, if only occasionally and all too briefly:

> [Skip's] ass and Doug's balls meet up with a light slapping sound. Their breathing only embellishes it. They're in different worlds, but with each slap realize they're not alone . . .[25]

Moments like this draw attention to what Dodie Bellamy in her review of the book calls Cooper's "aesthetics of distance"—how he emphasizes his characters' existential solitude, their loneliness, their removal from one another: "For [Cooper's characters] all sex is essentially masturbatory. It takes the slapping sound of fucking to remind them they're not alone."[26] Bellamy finds that "*Safe* is a sex novel bent on distancing the corporeal," and Cooper's aesthetics of distance, in her perceptive reading, is not only visible in the way he presents relationships between the characters in his work, we can also see it in his characters' relationships to their own bodies and emotions.[27] This marking out of distance and a ubiquitous sense of alienation from other people and oneself pervade the work. They even determine the relationship of the reader to the text and, as Bellamy points out, "we [the readers] are distanced from the narrative by humor, over-inflated language, convoluted syntax, and intrusions of an author discussing his feelings and technique."[28]

This aesthetics of distance is created in *Safe* largely through its channeling of Robert Bresson. The influence of the French filmmaker is everywhere in the novella, and if Cooper's earlier poetry bore the mark of his encounters with Rimbaud and Sade, *Safe* demonstrates the impact of Bresson as the last in a trio of major influences he has repeatedly acknowledged and celebrated. Speaking with Robert Glück, for instance, he enthused, "[Bresson's] work is so powerful and meaningful to me that I find it almost impossible to talk about" (2006).[29] Elsewhere he claimed that films like *Quatre nuits d'un rêveur* (*Four Nights of a Dreamer*, 1971), *Lancelot du Lac* (1974) and *Le diable probablement* (*The Devil, Probably*, 1977), "really changed my world and thoroughly influenced my writing. . . . When I discovered them in the late-seventies, I felt I had found the final ingredient I needed to write the fiction I wanted to write" (2011).[30]

Cooper seems to have approached Bresson in the same way as he approached Sade when he was a teenager, by trying to imitate his style and translate it into his own vernacular. The chapbook *Antoine Monnier*, published by Anon Press in 1978, was named after the principal actor of Bresson's *Le diable probablement* and, like Cooper's adolescent reimagining of Sade's *120 Days of Sodom*, drew characters and scenarios from the source text and relocated them into a quasi-pornographic story. In this short eight-page piece, an unnamed American narrator wanders through Paris, stumbling into what appears to be a scene from Bresson's film where, he observes, "at the end of a darkened alley a door stood open with French voices inside, in anger—a leader proclaiming anarchy and a group answering affirmatively. Then one wandered out bored, chased by the jeers of the others. He walked past me as quietly as though floating." The narrator persuades this beautiful yet bored and emotionally unavailable youth to have sex with him in his hotel room: "'I love you,' I repeated constantly and he said nothing though vague words rose, lost in a rush of breath or moaning."[31] Following sections depict Antoine in various other situations (fucking someone, hanging out with pretentious friends, being murdered), all inspired by scenes from Bresson's film. Although Cooper would come to view it as "a god-awful, incompetent attempt to rewrite

Charles (Antoine Monnier) in *Le diable probablement* (1977), directed by Robert Bresson.

Bresson's film *Le diable probablement* as a pornographic novella" (2011), Rudy Kikel, who reviewed it at the time, didn't think the story was that bad, saying he thought it was "a core contribution to the growing Cooper canon."[32] As the first piece of prose writing by Cooper under the influence of Bresson, it also helps us to see which Bressonian features he draws out and brings forward into his later work.

Le diable probablement follows the character of Charles (Antoine Monnier), a skinny, impossibly beautiful twenty-something Parisian who is profoundly out of step with the world around him. "I'm not depressed," he tells his psychoanalyst. "I only want to have the right to be who I am." Attempting to find some significance in modern life, he tries out various pursuits (e.g., politics, religion, sex, psychoanalysis) and finally despairs of them all, finding them worthy only of his disdain. "I hate life. I also hate death," he declares. His friends' attempts to dislodge his profound nihilism, to connect with him and "save" him from himself, all fail, and finally he pays an acquaintance to shoot him dead in Père Lachaise Cemetery.

Monnier's beautiful, tragic youth resembles certain characters that appeared in Cooper's previous work (there is something of a John F. Kennedy Jr. in his affluence and imperiousness), and in this regard at least the film must have appealed to Cooper when he first saw it. But it's the way the film treats emotion more than anything else that seems to carry over into the text of *Antoine Monnier*. Like all of Bresson's films, the actors (or "models," to use Bresson's preferred term) in *Le diable probablement* were nonprofessionals encouraged by the director not to identify with or attempt to embody their characters' sentiments, which gives their delivery of profound emotional dilemmas a curious and uniquely Bressonian woodenness and impassivity. Gestures and reactions are heavily stylized, often appearing disconnected from the feelings they would ordinarily communicate. Cooper interprets this in his story as a blankness: gazing at his quarry, the narrator finds, for instance, that "his eyes told me nothing but were beautiful." To the narrator who attempts to take the measure of his young idol, Antoine's apparent nonchalance is impenetrable, his facial expressions inscrutable—a smile conveys, what? "Sympathy? Contempt? Amusement?" Even sex can't bring about an imagined emotional intimacy, and after their night together, Antoine is still distant and unassailable; the narrator recalls that on leaving, "he smiled from the doorway and walked into the day, his current phone number in my hand tempered with the warning, 'You'll never get further than this.'"[33]

Apart from the supercharged nonchalance evoked by his models, what was it about Bresson's worldview that could have so profoundly affected Cooper and made him want to translate the filmmaker's vision into prose? Cooper's correspondence with Kathy Acker from the early 1980s offers some insights into his motivations. In the fall of 1981, Acker wrote to Cooper after finishing *The Missing Men*, his short, Tom Clark–edited collection of poetry that came out just before *My Mark* and would share its title with a section of *Safe*. With a bluntness characteristic of her correspondence with her peers, in her letter Acker admits that "although your poetry is clear and beautiful, the sameness of themes and the theme itself puts me off."[34] She was nevertheless sufficiently intrigued to offer some astute observations about Cooper's work and what she called the "pervasive anonymity" of his writing: "The reader is introduced to a number of characters who lack faces, innocence, depth of feeling—the only thing definite about most of them is their thirst for physicality. Whether they're all seeking an intimacy that is beyond them, or even trying to regain something through all the sex (innocence?), it's difficult for me to sympathize or identify with them because there's so little insight into what motivates them."[35]

Cooper immediately composed a long and appreciative reply in response to Acker's challenging critique (which also demanded to know if Cooper foresaw a time "when you will feel that sex in your writing will have outrun its usefulness or relevance?"—an ironic remark considering the extent to which Acker would mine that particular vein). "I think you understand the work very well in many ways," he began, "the unfulfillingness of the sex, the lack of motivation, etc. All that is there and intentional." Recently, he says, his focus has been on "figuring out ways to convey immediacy and gesture as significant in themselves and as relatives to the feelings I was writing about and conveying." Of particular importance has been his study of Bresson because "he does exactly some of the things you point out in my work."[36] Cooper's subsequent discussion of Bresson's films and their overlap with his concerns illuminates his debt to the filmmaker, whom he names "the greatest artist of all."

> While [Bresson] never works with sexuality except in the most removed possible fashion, he is interested in monochromatic movement, very little variation from moment to moment, and presenting people as unmotivated, even slightly vacant beings drifting through their existence, sometimes twisted and pushed in incorrect ways by his concept of God or the religious concept by which the characters rule their lives. To me this is the best way of creating a mode of deepest conveyance. The people are, as much as people could be, blank canvasses, stick [figures] in a way, sometimes weighted down with urges and emotions they don't necessarily understand. I'm very interested in people incapable of saying what they mean or feel and instead forced to act in unsatisfying broad gestures which satisfy no one but give them what they must have in the only way they know how to get it. This idea and aesthetic is, by its nature, I guess pretty depressing. But it feels appropriate to what I want to convey about people and things, and appropriate to the lives and feelings I see around me now. That perception is, of course, all subjective, and to take on a somewhat extreme mode of conveyance and style is a risk.

It can seem, in the case of my work, overly depressing, so much so that the reader is repelled in some way. But it is, I firmly believe, the best way I can, within my particular skills, do what I want to do best.[37]

Cooper's interest in distance and disconnection, especially in terms of emotions—between emotion and understanding, between how people feel and how they express those feelings in voice and gesture—thus finds its corollary in Bresson's "monochromatic movement, very little variation from moment to moment, and presenting people as unmotivated, even slightly vacant beings drifting through their existence." Similarly, those Bressonian protagonists who appear to be blank canvases and stick figures, who cannot permit themselves to be understood in the usual ways, and who are ordinarily young people (at least in the case of Monnier's Charles or Bresson's other protagonists like Joan of Arc), could also be said to populate the worlds of Cooper's California.

The novella *Safe* is clearly indebted to Bresson and Cooper's reading of him. Although hardly an homage to him in the same way as *Antoine Monnier* was, like the earlier piece, *Safe* improvises upon Bresson's asceticism, incorporating features absent from his work (including explicit sex) and giving it a distinctly American setting. The Bressonian influence is nonetheless very much there, most obviously in Cooper's approach to character. Like the subjects of *The Missing Men* who Acker complained lacked faces or features, a kind of anonymity also surrounds the characters in *Safe*. We are told, for instance, that Mark's appearance is unremarkable and that his clothes usually consist of "dyed black jeans, black coat, and a black T-shirt, his typical nonregalia."[38] He also believes that his worst facial features are "oversized ears, a too turned-up nose," but without an agreed-upon measure of size or upturn, this reveals little specific detail: How much is "oversized"? How turned up is "too turned-up"?[39] The overall impression of Mark is "shiftiness," a vagueness that even the camera cannot counteract: his boyfriend Rob has a framed photo of him sitting on his desk, "in it Mark's camping, lips puckered, eyes crossed," his beauty a "smear."[40]

The pervasive sense of Mark's vagueness or lack of specificity is not alleviated by his circulation in a world of gay signs. In the first section, Los Angeles's gay culture circumscribes the environment through which

Mark moves. The reader attempts to locate him through the intersection of his character and certain scenes and locations: Mark reads the *Advocate*, cruises the Santa Monica strip, drops into a gay porn theatre, and so on. We are led to believe that these scenarios exemplify the life of an urban gay man. Yet such is the ubiquity of the generic gay context in which he is submerged that distinguishing Mark's individual features from these archetypal ones is a difficult task. What differentiates Mark from another gay man who might read the *Advocate* at the time or have someone give him a rim job or dolefully recall a scene of childhood homophobia? The facets of a typical gay lifestyle that are repeatedly attributed to his character only exacerbate Mark's "shiftiness," rendering his portrait still more elusive. In contrast to the New Narrativists, Cooper's contemporaries who, as we will see in the next chapter, employ elements of gay culture to establish a connection with the reader, for Cooper these tropes mean only uniformity and blandness, further eroding Mark's specificity.

Overall, the imprecision of Cooper's descriptions ensures that it's almost impossible for the reader to identify Mark—or identify with him: without distinguishing features, he hovers, a half person, distanced from our understanding and empathy. But this vagueness is amplified in the text by the way characters are depicted as various types of automata like dolls and dummies. A smudged portrait of Mark as he gets "dolled up," for instance, finds that "in theory [his efforts] should make him about as alluring as one of the mannequins in these display windows."[41] We are told that Jeff Hunter, Rob's favorite porn star, looks like "a Ken-doll with orifices."[42] When he's being fisted, Mark's friend Carl thinks that "this is a shit-load of pain but he'd like to embrace it like a dummy does its ventriloquist."[43] He imagines himself "like a statue in the Hollywood Wax Museum."[44]

These correlations, subtle but insistent, turn the work into a kind of Bressonian tableau where characters are uncannily impassive or blank, making them present as untrained amateurs in a scenario not of their choosing. *Safe*'s Bressonian mood is made more explicit later when Doug meets a group of teenage punks: "Their flailing used to bug Doug, particularly at parties. Now he's met several and found an attractive naiveté in their voices, as misplaced as a ventriloquist's behind the wooden expressions."[45]

These stylistic features—anonymity, vacancy, automatism—are used by Cooper in order to produce his aesthetics of distance, where characters are separated not only from one another but from their bodies and emotions too. As Bellamy remarks (and Acker complains), this also affects the reader's relationship with the characters, making it difficult to sympathize with them. This is the crux of *Safe*'s effect: if the production of empathy lies in our mapping of our own experience, our emotions, our perspective onto another person in order to better comprehend how they are feeling, Cooper's characters *elude* our empathy and avoid a situation in which their difference might be reduced to the relative sameness of our worldview.

Regarding the distancing effects of Bresson's films (models, the elimination of psychology, a temporally unspecific voice-over, etc.), Céline Scemama argues that "the spectator of a film by Bresson goes through the living experience of someone else without ever being put in his place: he may feel very close to him while remaining an absolute stranger." Consequently, she states, "the 'I' of the viewer can never become an incarnation of the character's 'you.'"[46] Likewise we could argue that Cooper, after Bresson, attempts to create a literary work where the reader's "I" has difficulty subsuming the character's "you"—and herein lies the larger gambit of a Bressonian work like *Safe*. An aesthetics of distance impedes our ability to identify with a character, but it does so in order to bring about the semblance of a higher understanding of the world as one populated by others who are not merely an extension of ourselves. Scemama says that "Bresson imposes an unusual experience upon his viewer: perceiving the inner experience of another without sharing it. This impossible identification paradoxically gives birth to the greatest expression of an inner life, but it is someone else's."[47] A similarly "impossible identification" occurs in *Safe*, which encourages our apprehension of the strangeness of these characters, their otherness. In this way, we might say that an *ethics* of distance inheres in Cooper's *aesthetics* of distance: Cooper's universe may be one in which things do not connect, but it is also one where everything, in Bob Flanagan's words, is a "unit" with its own integrity and difference that resists being subsumed by another.

"If There Actually *Is* Such a Thing as New Narrative . . ."

6   *SAFE WAS GENERALLY* well received by the critics, especially those who liked Cooper's poetry. Writing in the *Village Voice*, sometime *Little Caesar* contributor (and *New Yorker* art critic) Peter Schjeldahl acclaimed its publication as "a literary event of a kind not seen since the '60s . . . *Safe* is a work of ambitious scope, moral seriousness, and innovative style, the sort that galvanizes a literary generation."[1] Robert Prager's review in the *San Diego Gayzette* also found the novella to be a generation-defining work and picked up on its less-than-laudatory representation of gay male culture. Cooper, he wrote, "represents the new generation of gay writers—a generation that takes being gay for granted and sees no reason to write endless coming out novels. . . . His characters—far too young to remember the Stonewall Riot and the euphoria of liberation that it triggered—are pitted not against a hostile straight world so much as against a complicated, all-consuming gay subculture."[2] In the *San Francisco Sentinel*, meanwhile, fellow *Rolling Stock* AIDS Award–winner Steve Abbott composed a profile of Cooper under the headline "Gay Lit's Bad Boy" and championed his style over more conservative examples popular in gay literature at the time (David Leavitt, for instance, was treated to a withering appraisal). *Safe* was an example of "serious" writing, he said, "socially disturbing but spiritually transformative."[3] Abbott's article, which claimed that in the early 1980s "a whole New Narrative movement was taking shape and Dennis Cooper, among others, was in the forefront," was also one of the first to associate Cooper's prose work with New Narrative.[4]

While Cooper and his punk poet friends were carving out a niche for themselves at Beyond Baroque and bringing a new writing scene to life in Los Angeles, up the coast in San Francisco another scene was elbowing its way into existence. Launched by Robert Glück and Bruce Boone in the late 1970s as a reaction both to the increased commodification of gay identity and the marginalization of homosexuality in the progressive politics of the Bay Area, New Narrative would ultimately have profound implications for experimental prose writing across the United States. Boone's and Glück's novels and short stories and their writing workshops at Small Press Traffic bookstore influenced a group of innovative prose writers that included the likes of Mike Amnasan, Dodie Bellamy, Kevin Killian, and Camille Roy, whose smart, sex-radical works updated New York School chattiness for the 1980s.

The origins of the name "New Narrative" are somewhat obscure. According to Earl Jackson Jr., one of the first scholars to be tuned into the new queer writing of the 1980s, it began as a kind of joke. Sometime in the early 1970s, Boone and Glück met at the San Francisco Art Institute. Both gay writers, they soon discovered they also shared a love for Frank O'Hara's poetry and quickly became friends—and, as it would turn out, lifelong colleagues and collaborators. Glück was twenty-three or twenty-four and Boone was older than him by seven years, but both writers were similarly concerned with the future of gay community in the aftermath of Gay Liberation and with the role played by writing in how that future would unfold. By 1980, they were both writing similarly homoerotic, Marxist-inflected mixes of fiction and autobiography and felt they needed a name to distinguish themselves from their antagonists, the Language poets, who were also active in San Francisco at the time. "How about New Narrative?" Boone suggested. "What a stupid name."[5]

If the name was something of a joke between friends (intended to ruffle the feathers of the Language poets, who famously despised narrative forms), the work undertaken by Boone, Glück, and their friend and comrade Abbott was serious, vital, and politically engaged. Surveying the subaltern status of homosexual men and women at the beginning of the 1980s and the spectrum of violence and intimidation that continued to target them, the newly minted New Narrativists considered the project of Gay Liberation to be incomplete. Even in San Francisco, a hub of the gay civil rights movement, gays and lesbians were still routinely abused, discriminated against, beaten, harassed, and murdered; with the assassination of Harvey Milk in 1978, the 1980s began on a distinctly bleaker note than the previous decade had.

New Narrative writing was created as a continuation of Gay Liberation activism and consciousness-raising by other means. As indicated by Glück's *Elements of a Coffee Service* (1982), one of the first books in the burgeoning New Narrative canon, homophobia would be addressed head-on. In one scene, Glück's narrator flees a Chevy pickup full of abusive homophobes and, hiding from them, recalls a litany of antigay aggression endured by himself and his friends, from "Kevin's bashed-in teeth" to "Bruce getting rousted and then rousted again by the police," not to forget "the Halloween when a man yelling 'queer' charged Ed and me with a metal pipe" and the friend "murdered by someone he brought home."[6]

Writing these moments into their stories was part of Boone and Glück's broader strategy of using writing to support gay community-building efforts. Making legible the details of modern life that other gay men would be familiar with and had also experienced (incidents of homophobia, for instance, which were rarely reported by the mainstream news) allowed readers to see themselves as participating in an imagined gay community that included others with the same experiences they had. Theoretically, the implied relationship between writer and reader could transfer to the world outside the text and strengthen connections between gay people, gay neighborhoods, and gay communities. As Abbott writes in the introduction to the second issue of his literary magazine, *SOUP*, "New Narrative is language conscious but arises out of specific social and political concerns of specific communities," and the writing of Boone and Glück fed back recursively into the gay community it arose out of, reinforcing its bonds and presenting it with a vision of itself.[7]

That vision, however, was a critical one—or rather, community was presented not as a fait accompli but as a question. If New Narrative novels and collections like Glück's *Elements of a Coffee Service* and Boone's *My Walk With Bob* (1979) and *Century of Clouds* (1980) offered the reader ample opportunity to identify with the narrator and elide the differences between their respective experiences, these were not the kind of easily marketable gay male coming-out stories that were big business at the time, which also contained lots of moments that the gay reader could identify with. Boone and Glück differentiated their work from conventional gay literature of this sort and called on the reader to think critically about community, identity, and the power of stories like the one they were reading. They tried not just to represent and affirm gay experience but also, and more importantly, to encourage in their gay readers a critical awareness of late capitalism. Boone's *Century of Clouds*, which in the intervening years has become a kind of New Narrative urtext, exemplifies this approach, presenting an autobiographical account framed by a recurring critique of narrative, writing, and community.

Boone's short work packs a lot into its hundred or so pages. It is, first and foremost, an abbreviated memoir that describes his experience at the Marxist Literary Group's Summer Institute where "Fred" (aka Fredric Jameson, the Marxist academic) holds court. Most of the other Marxist attendees are heterosexual and, even in these radical circles, mostly oblivious to the matter of gay rights; some are even hostile to the idea, viewing gays as "a tertiary concern."[8] In reaction Boone stages an intervention, interrupting an afternoon volleyball game and symbolically challenging the oppressively straight male world of the Institute: "I wanted to speak as a socialist to other socialists about the necessity of making the liberation of gays a goal integral to socialist liberation and revolution," he writes.[9]

Memories of this time fade in and out of focus in a meandering account that is frequently interrupted by long Proustian digressions on Boone's education as a Christian Brother at Mont La Salle monastery and his life in San Francisco after he abandoned his novitiate training. While it can be difficult to orient oneself in a story that's so fragmentary and interruptive, the theme of community—its construction, how it's maintained, the conditions that allow it to survive—is ever present. In a narrative preoccupied by gossip and brimming with references to pop culture (from *Sesame Street* to *I Love Lucy*), overarching social and political concerns also loom large.

[Orlando] Letelier is being blown up in his car by the agents of Chilean reaction. The sound of nearly silent bullets—and 9 black men are dead in Oakland from police assassination. Racism; poverty. Lives of women and gays oppressed in patriarchy. Daily violence done to workers. A workers' movement now bloody and sundered with wounds.[10]

"These thoughts large and public, how to relate them to my life?" Boone writes. "How to link with experiences and touches—only rarely—my past? To tell about desiring too. Perhaps beginning to tell you stories."[11] *Century of Clouds* is full of moments like these, where the narrator directly addresses the reader and reflects on the narrative as it's in the process of being composed. One sequence lays bare Boone's intentions for the story and his yearning to simultaneously educate and interest the reader. He says, "By writing this story I want to make you think about certain political matters—a praiseworthy objective, no? But I also want to amuse and entertain you, and more. In what I write I would like you to feel pleasure, even joy."[12]

Boone and Glück referred to this running commentary on the story, which would become characteristic of New Narrative practice, as their text-metatext approach. In Glück's words, "The metatext cuts naturalistic illusion. It includes the reader, it asks questions, asks for critical response, makes claims on the reader, elicits comments."[13] As Kaplan Harris would have it, "For the writer, the trick is to embrace the narrative while at the same time exercising a critically reflexive distance. This balance is always at risk of being dismissed as postmodern irony but what New Narrative ultimately seeks is a textual performance that can recognize itself as a cultural construct and simultaneously affirm the political value of a life-changing story."[14]

A memoir that both uses narrative and undermines its conventions, that shows its workings and subverts readers' expectations, that mixes pop culture and gossip with a commitment to global political issues, above all that creates *connections* (between the author and the friends they name in the story, between the narrator and the reader, and between a community of readers): Boone's *Century of Clouds* set the standard for New Narrative works that would follow.

Although much more experimental and surreal (and certainly much more graphic in its treatment of sex), Glück's *Jack the Modernist* (1985) shares many of the same features. A pornographic gay picaresque that portrays the author's tortuous relationship with a lover named Jack in a New Narrative style, the work is obviously autobiographical and draws on the author's life and his relationships with a number of named, real-life friends like "Bruce" (Boone) and "Kathy" (Acker). The narrator even mentions the writing workshops Glück conducted at Small Press Traffic bookstore. As in Boone's work, the practice of storytelling is regularly remarked upon and examples of text-metatext abound, portraying the narrator's story itself as an innovative approach to an age-old form: "Society wants its stories," the narrator says at one point; "I want to return to society the story it has made—if unhappy, as a revenge, critique."[15] Pop culture like Minnie and Mickey Mouse, *West Side Story*, and werewolf movies is a recurring feature, and gossip proliferates ("Jack, I trust gossip," Bob says).[16] The narrator also goes to great lengths to situate his story and his personal concerns within what Boone might call "thoughts large and public":

> Nuclear catastrophe, destitution, famine, additives, melanomas, losing face, U.S. involvement in El Salvador and Nicaragua, Puerto Rico, South Korea, Chile, Lebanon and Argentina, war in the Middle East, genocide of Guatemalan Indians and extermination of the native peoples of Brazil, Philippines, Australia, answering the telephone, resurgence of the Nazis, the KKK, auctioning of the U.S. wilderness, toxic waste, snipers, wrinkles, cult murderers, my car, Jack's safety, queer bashers, South Africa, being unloved, considered second rate, considered stupid . . .[17]

"I write for gay men the same as La Fontaine wrote for the court of Louis XIV," Bob says, and the experience of community and its implication in the practice of storytelling is as ever present a theme in *Jack the Modernist* as it is in *Century of Clouds*.[18] Connection is too: even though the text is made up of fragments from sources like Bataille, Baudelaire, Ovid, and the "Porn Corner" of the *Bay Area Reporter*, our attention as readers is drawn not so much to their disjunctive relationship with one another as to the resonances between them when they're placed side by side on the page. As Glück writes in a note that concludes the work, "Mine is an art of collage," and his art lies in producing *connections* between different collaged elements, just as his narrator Bob sees the fetishistic parts of bathhouse bodies reconstituted in a communal encounter of "ecstatic sexuality."[19]

: a waist arching calls attention to the nipples and sends the smooth
ass backward giving access—someone slowly kneels
Two mouths, four nipples, four hands, two cocks, two
: the shifting of buttocks
scrotums, two assholes, two hundred and sixteen possi
: one excited man excites others to a circle of masturbation—hands
and cocks group and regroup like a sudden wind shifting in a garden,
or like a story: when a cock comes it withdraws from the plot
bilities and then another man joins you—an orgy in the
: someone is fucking a face he can't see, slow rhythmical ass that
opens up and then clenches, its dreamtime logic has a unity that can't
be dismissed or broken into parts.[20]

In American avant-garde circles at the time, especially in the Bay Area,
New Narrativists' commitment to the progressive politics of storytelling
was a controversial position, one that was not shared by the contemporary
yet far-better-known Language movement. Poets like Charles Bernstein,
Ron Silliman, and Barrett Watten thought that narrative was a bourgeois,
content-oriented, ideologically complicit mode of literary composition
that had nothing to do with the practice of politically engaged writing. In
his summary of Language poetry, Jerome McGann writes, "Narrativity is
an especially problematic feature of discourse to these writers, because its
structures lay down 'stories' that serve to limit and order the field of experience, in particular the field of social and historical experience. Narrativity is, in this view, an inherently conservative feature of discourse, and
hence it is undermined at every point."[21] In their work, Language writers therefore used nonnarrative and antinarrative strategies designed, in
Harris's words, "to facilitate a more autonomous, less consumer-oriented
reading practice . . . narrative structure was discarded in favor of a liber-
ating discontinuity at the level of sound and syntax."[22]

This produced Language works that were highly regarded at the time
but haven't aged especially well, their antinarrative experiments sugges-
tive of a particular period of poststructuralist fervor in the United States,
which is difficult to translate into a contemporary context. This includes
works like Ron Silliman's *TJANTING* (1981), where, according to Bernstein, "detail is cast upon detail, minute particular upon minute particular, adding up to an impossibility of commensurable narrative."[23]

Not this.
What then?
I started over & over. Not this.
Last week I wrote "the muscles in my palm are so sore from halving the rump roast I cld barely grip the pen." What then? This morning my lip is blisterd.[24]

For Boone and Glück, however, dispensing with narrative wholesale was a privilege Silliman and his kind could afford: historically, straight white male subjects had ample opportunity to narrate their stories. But it presented more of a danger for those groups who traditionally found themselves the *objects* of history, who had found their attempts to write their own stories stymied and censored. In his critique of Language poetry, published in Abbott's *SOUP*, Boone wrote, "If you take away people's emotions, their ability to tell stories and their capability to deal generally with the outside world, you are really not going to have much of an appeal to several significant groups. Blacks, Latins, and other racial minorities for instance. Most feminists and politically oriented gay men for instance."[25] Boone saw that narrative and storytelling were essential in the post–Gay Liberation era, allowing the community to come together and presenting an opportunity for queer people to openly tell their stories and see themselves and their concerns reflected in public. In Rob Halpern's précis: "Although New Narrative evolved together with late twentieth-century avant-garde poetries, it pushed against Language writing's privileging of poetic form, stressing instead the value of storytelling—in both verse and prose—as the means by which to deepen the convergence of writing and politics, while aligning that convergence with the work of gay community building."[26]

The New Narrativists weren't blind to the ideological bias of narrative or to its traditionally conservative form, but they chose to offset these issues with the introduction of a text-metatext technique. It was hoped that laying bare the structure of their narratives—and assessing the problems of narrative more generally—would encourage the reader to critically reflect on the presumed transparency of stories and the subjectivities that were constructed through them: "The storyteller thus emerges as a composite of stories, the many faults and fissures of which draw attention to the constructed dimensions of our social world, as well as to the way the self itself is tangled in artifice."[27]

TALKING UP THE MOVEMENT whenever he could, Steve Abbott emerged as a kind of mouthpiece of New Narrative and even seemed on occasion to have more invested in its success as a movement than either Boone or Glück. ("I was reluctant to promote a literary school that endured even ten minutes, much less a few years," Glück said in 2000).[28] Abbott's 1985 clarion call "Notes on Boundaries/New Narrative" was an attempt to present a coherent portrait of New Narrative as he saw it and outlined the principal stakes of New Narrative writing—which for him included not just the work of Boone, Glück, and their students Dodie Bellamy and Mike Amnasan, but Kathy Acker and Dennis Cooper too.

New Narrative, Abbott said, was like the graffiti he saw scrawled on subway cars when he visited New York—it spelled danger with its "sprayed names, attempts of the powerless to assert individual or gang identity. Graffitists can be run down by trains, mauled by guard dogs, killed by police. They stray at the edges, talking to death."[29] Like graffiti artists, New Narrativists were cutting edge and underground—their work was transgressive and exuded a Bataillean obsession with "ecstasy, death, love, terror."[30] Still more important than its transgression, New Narrative was also about subculture and community; like graffiti, it was forged in the margins, one group's resistance to linguistic-political oppression by the status quo. "'It's an affront to our community,' Mayor Koch gripes about subway graffiti. Yes, but it *represents* community more deeply than the mayor," Abbott says. "New Narrative explodes, speaking to and creating community."[31]

To a tourist like Abbott, all New York graffiti might very well seem the same. Clacking noisily by on defaced subway carriages, all those jagged, luminous ciphers in a strange urban tongue can appear monolithic in their unintelligibility. Graffiti, as Abbott's piece shows, is a space of projections: *delinquency* to Mayor Koch and his forces of law and order, *subcultural community* to people like Abbott (to both: *transgression*). But when the trains slow down and you start to pay attention, you can see graffiti is in fact richly variegated, expressing different ideas and states;

assertions of individual identity and group allegiance jostle for space with inanities and obscene scribbles. Before the train departs again, distinctive artistic styles surface and diverge. In short, graffiti artists, taken together, might not have any more in common than the same spray paint, and (before the analogy is strained any further) Abbott is a little hasty when he groups all these writers together under the same name.

His taxonomy is useful to a degree: Bellamy and Killian claim that the essay helped them to understand that they shared certain attributes with some of their contemporaries, namely a preoccupation with boundaries (and their transgression). But New Narrative was never a movement in the same way as, say, the French Nouveau Roman was a movement, with the manifestos of people like Alain Robbe-Grillet and Nathalie Sarraute to codify its aims and working practices. New Narrative had no manifesto. Cooper wasn't even sure what it was—or if it existed at all. At an OutWrite conference in 1990 he opened his talk by saying, "If there actually *is* such a thing as New Narrative writing (and it's possible, but the title's weird) . . ."[32] According to its soi-disant practitioners, Bellamy and Killian, it was somewhere between a genre and a sensibility—"New Narrative was like porn . . . you know it when you see it."[33]

Abbott's efforts to have the various kinds of writing he discusses cohere as New Narrative thus rides roughshod over some crucial differences. This isn't a major problem in itself: suppression of nuance is sometimes the curse of the critic, especially one with the laudable aim of wanting to draw attention to his friends' work. But it misses out on the opportunity to show just how varied New Narrative writing actually was; how New Narrative named something dynamic and radically porous that addressed itself differently in response to different conditions and influences; how, most of all, the aesthetic Boone and Glück pioneered was modified and updated as it was passed on to another generation of writers who had their own ideas about the best way to intervene in their contemporary moment.

It should be clear that Cooper's *Safe* contrasts markedly with the New Narrative work of Boone and Glück. His novella approaches Robert Bresson's films in its evocation of distance and disconnection, bringing about a kind of writing that denies his readers a satisfying identification with his characters or at least makes that difficult. Boone and Glück, on the other hand, write about the experiences that gay men share to create a sense of solidarity and connection between the reader and the narrator. The writers themselves remarked on these characteristics: In his blurb for *Jack the Modernist*, Cooper remarked on the "startlingly complicit relationship between [Glück] and his readers"; meanwhile, reviewing *The Tenderness of the Wolves* in November 1982, Boone exclaimed, "Cooper's feelings are so incredibly distant!"[34]

As we've seen, both Cooper and the New Narrativists also employ the signifiers of a gay male lifestyle at the beginning of the 1980s drawn from the worlds of gay media and social life, but Cooper seems to take a more cynical view of that world than either Boone or Glück. Gay cultural signifiers exacerbate the pervasive anonymity of *Safe*'s context and its characters. There's no sense, for instance, that one could build on them to create Glück's community of "ecstatic sexuality." Finally, Boone's "large and public thoughts" (global crises and political issues within which his and Glück's narrators try to situate their personal thoughts and concerns) rarely feature in Cooper's novella: it would be rather incongruous to explicitly connect the self with these larger issues in a work determined by disconnection.

Although they may seem somewhat incidental, these differences in fact constitute a fault line that divides Cooper from Boone and Glück and their version of New Narrative writing. It shows that the associations Abbott and others have made between Cooper and New Narrative have been too simplistic. More importantly, it also helps us understand how a New Narrative aesthetic changes when it's taken up by the writers who attended Boone and Glück's Small Press Traffic workshops. While they were obviously indebted to their mentors, who were hugely influential and encouraging, younger writers on the scene like Mike Amnasan, Dodie Bellamy, and Kevin Killian also wrote novels and stories that departed significantly from them in both style and politics. These departures dovetail in certain respects with the work of Cooper, who was held in high esteem by the younger New Narrativists: "He towered high like some symbolic building in modernist biography—like the Martello Tower," Bellamy and Killian write.[35] In short, Cooper's work foreshadows a shift in New Narrative writing that saw the next generation of writers move away from the global concerns of their teachers and become noticeably more focused on the individual than the community.

BELLAMY AND KILLIAN, by their own admission, came to the Bay Area just after the first era of New Narrative had ended; as they write in the introduction to their 2017 anthology, *Writers Who Love Too Much: New Narrative 1977–1997*, "The heroic age of New Narrative had already come and gone by the time that the two of us arrived in San Francisco."[36] With their participation and under their influence, however, a new era of New Narrative would begin.

Bellamy hailed from Chicago, Killian from Long Island, and both had come West "looking for something else—something rarefied."[37] Around 1981 they wandered into Small Press Traffic bookstore in the Noe Valley neighborhood of San Francisco and soon found themselves attending Glück's California Arts Council–funded writing workshops with a group of other writers that included Camille Roy and Mike Amnasan. The effect of the workshops was as radical as it was all encompassing, and their encounter with Small Press Traffic would reshape their writing and social lives forever. "As soon as we joined, we entered a bustling world of continuous education," Bellamy and Killian recall. "Everyone went to the same readings and parties and lectures and the same movies. Poets Bruce Boone and Steve Abbott informally mentored young writers outside of the workshop system, and we soon recognized them as the second and third members of the troika that was eternally formulating 'New Narrative.'"[38] Remembering the parental influence of Boone and Glück in particular, they write that "any student of Bob and Bruce had the exhilaration of participating, on the one hand, at the cutting edge of something entirely new, and also the sheer comfort of the oldest cradle in the world, that of a mother and father creating a world for their young ones."[39]

But the kids were all right—building up a scene for themselves in much the same way as the punk poets of Los Angeles had done by putting together reading series and starting up magazines that featured writing by themselves and their contemporaries. Roberto Bedoya, a queer California Chicano whom Bellamy and Killian call "the quiet genius of the Bay Area writing scene of the 1980s," headed up the literary program and reading series at the nonprofit arts space Intersection for the Arts from the early 1980s until 1988.[40] Bedoya was passionate about a broad range of literature, and he offered lots of little-known writers the chance to read their work to a smart and receptive Intersection audience. "I was committed to presenting the most innovative/fresh/probing voices for the public," he recalls, and his reminiscences of the time attest to an almost vocational commitment to experimental writing. "I understood my curatorial responsibility along the lines of contributing to the aesthetic education of the public," he says, adding, "I often thought of my job at Intersection as a connector. And, to use some popular jargon, to be a contributor to a 'tipping point' moment in an artist's career or a publisher's effort to establish themselves or expand their audience."[41]

As for magazines, in 1981 the heroic age of New Narrative might have just ended, but the golden age of New Narrative print culture had just begun. Abbott's *SOUP*, which started in 1980, had already established itself as the go-to venue for New Narrative writing. In his introduction to the second issue of the magazine in 1981, he wrote that "the first *SOUP* was intended as a mini-anthology, a cross-section of current work emphasizing new directions. It won approval. One consistent recommendation: *SOUP* should clarify its focus. Gradually I realized my main interest was toward 'New Narrative' writing."[42]

SOUP was followed by Bryan Monte's more streamlined, even chic *No Apologies: A Magazine of Gay Writing*, first published in 1983. Monte, a younger friend of Abbott who had also participated in Glück's writing workshops, put out the magazine with the assistance of Kevin Killian and Dodie Bellamy. He remembers that "Killian volunteered to do the typesetting for the magazine on his word processor at work. He, in turn, introduced me to graphic designer and writer Dodie Bellamy (who would later become his partner), and she introduced me to her colleague Mike Belt, who donated his time to create a one-color magazine cover for *No Apologies* to save expenses."[43] Monte went on to publish many Small Press Traffic alumni—the second issue in particular reads like a who's who of New Narrative and includes contributions by Abbott, Bedoya, Bellamy, Boone, Glück, and Killian along with associated figures like Gabrielle Daniels and Lew Ellingham.

Drawing on his experience of editing *No Apologies*, Killian later set up his own magazine: "When Bryan began a MFA program at Brown, he left San Francisco, and took *No Apologies* with him," says Killian. "The materials I had left over, gathered for *No Apologies*, I used to start up a new magazine, *Mirage*, which was the name of our neighborhood bar in the Mission District of San Francisco."[44] *Mirage* ran for four issues between 1985 and 1989. Bellamy came on board as a guest editor for the fourth issue and stayed on as a coeditor of the magazine, which changed its name to *Mirage #4/Period[ical]* and ran for 155 xeroxed issues from 1992 right up to 2009.

Mike Amnasan, meanwhile, launched his own more sober, perfect-bound literary magazine, *Ottotole*. Named after a misread sign for a turn-pike toll ("auto-toll"), Amnasan's editorial approach was mobile in its allegiances, and the magazine included the work of New Narrative writers alongside that of Language poets. The first issue, edited with poet Gail Sher and published in the fall of 1985, included contributions by Glück and Amnasan in addition to essays by Language writers Carla Harryman and Steve Benson. It also included a long, wide-ranging telephone conversation between Bruce Boone (in San Francisco) and Charles Bernstein (in New York), which was emblematic of the editor's broader attempt to have the magazine stage a dialogue between the two sides of the narrative/antinarrative divide. Amnasan recalls that "I wouldn't align myself with any group at the time and started the first magazine (that I knew of) that included Language writers and New Narrative writers."[45] Later issues would bear out his intention, publishing the work of Bellamy and Killian beside Language pieces by the likes of Ron Silliman and Bruce Andrews.

Amnasan's writing itself doubles down on the refusal of his magazine to declare loyalty to one group or another. In his compact but lapidary oeuvre that includes *I Can't Distinguish Opposites* (1983), *Beyond the Safety of Dreams* (2000), and *Liar* (written in the '90s but published in 2007), group loyalty and belonging, in addition to overarching concepts of community and friendship, are routinely scrutinized and found wanting. Whereas Boone and Glück sought out community in their New Narrative pieces, in Amnasan's work it is something that one might wish to hold more at arm's length. He, like Cooper, is far more skeptical than they are of the demands that community makes on a person, and his work is in general protective of solitude and difference.

In the novella *I Can't Distinguish Opposites*, Amnasan takes the measure of intimacy and weighs the expectations people have of one another in order to enter into relationships. His protagonist, Tom, like all of his protagonists, feels acutely the restrictions of friendship and relationships with other people. He is told by his girlfriend, Joan, that she thinks of him as her brother. "I don't want to be your brother," he replies. The narrator explains, "[Tom] didn't like that expression of similarity. He felt that she associated him with her like that because of a lack of interest in him. He realized that he was trying to share her feelings, trying to become like her. He should have made a difference."[46] In other words, Tom sees the flip side of Joan's apparently innocuous expression of intimacy—how, within her identification resides a yearning for sameness, a desire to reduce Tom's otherness, his absolute difference from her as another human being, to something that is instead predictable and familiar to her. What's worse, he sees this propensity in himself, too. An otherwise unremarkable statement ("I feel close to you like a brother") whose ostensible aim is to communicate closeness is therefore reconfigured in Amnasan's deceptively simple prose into something altogether more suspect. Joan's clichéd phrase comes across more as an involuntary expression of the systemic demands of society and groupthink—where sameness is a prerequisite— than a yearning for authentic attachment.

If his approach to community distinguishes him from his teachers, Amnasan's style nonetheless marks him out as a New Narrativist. Text-metatext is regularly employed in his writing, with the narrator frequently addressing readers directly and putting questions to them. All of Amnasan's works are also, for all intents and purposes, memoirs (even if the narrator and his lovers are given pseudonyms), and, as in earlier New Narrative works, the author's real-life friends and acquaintances often surface in the text—figures like "Ron" (Silliman) and "Leslie" (Scalapino), for instance, appear in *Liar* as themselves. Robin Tremblay-McGaw sees New Narrative practice come through most explicitly in Amnasan's work in his refusal to dispose of the subject (and narrative) as the Language poets had done:

> Like the work of many of the New Narrative writers . . . Amnasan's writing is shaped in part by his engagement with and critique of the ideas and practices of the Language Writers, including Bruce Andrews and Ron Silliman. Amnasan does not jettison the subject, a subject who is a subject of discourse but also of feeling, experience, community and discontinuity; he opts for expenditure and risk, exposing the negativity that constitutes experience with its blind spots and in all of its confusion, humiliation, frustration.[47]

Boone and Glück's enormous impact on Amnasan's work is thus plainly evident, even if Amnasan seems more willing to explore the negative aspects of community building and is more wary than they are of the impulse to connect.

While not as extreme as Amnasan in the criticisms they bring to bear on community and relationality, Bellamy and Killian also diverge from Boone and Glück in significant ways while still operating in a New Narrative mode. In its offbeat approach to memoir, Killian's *Bedrooms Have Windows* (1989), for instance, situates itself firmly within the New Narrative canon, but it's also reticent to confront political issues head-on. The work begins in the usual way of memoirs ("I grew up in Smithtown, a suburb of New York . . .") and goes on to describe the narrator's early sexual experiences as a teen, but examples of text-metatext clog the progression of a narrative that otherwise resembles a generic coming-out story.[48] For instance, when the narrator seems to falter in his depiction of his older boyfriend, he turns to the reader for help:

> What is the trick of description, that writers must use? How do I make him more clear, vivid, real—or even imaginary? You know the film actress Rosanna Arquette? He had the sulky, pouting look of a male Rosanna Arquette. But what happens if you don't know her? I could say: Pia Zadora; Brigitte Bardot: but at each remove the similarity fades a bit more so you don't get my picture. Shall I stick to Rosanna?[49]

As in Glück and Boone's work, pop culture is also a recurring feature, and Killian's writing in the book is as preoccupied with stars of the silver screen and TV shows like *I Love Lucy* and *The Golden Girls* as it is with Milton and Proust.

But where are Boone's "large and public" thoughts? Killian's memoir evades any obvious political engagement, and none of the issues explicitly raised in earlier New Narrative works—homophobia, gay community, anti-consumerism, global events and catastrophes that demand to be set right—are addressed here. AIDS is mentioned briefly, but it's coupled with other acronyms characteristic of the 1980s in a way that dulls its effect and precludes any deeper treatment:

> How do I explain it further? We boys lived in time, in a seething jungle the vines and contours of which, while never as gruesome as,

say, Vietnam, have now vanished with progress and OPEC and MTV and AIDS. When something happened we could place it real quick, just the way it happened for us. Now there's no time . . .[50]

When he *does* talk about broader political issues, Killian seems to put them at a distance from the narrative—the narrator recalls, for instance, "I was in New York having an awful kind of sex on the night of the Stonewall Riots in 1969 . . . I didn't hear any police sirens or drag queens crying, only the familiar Manhattan rumble of ironwork and street noise."[51] This creeping sense of distance in *Bedrooms Have Windows* aligns Killian's writing more with Cooper than with Boone and Glück, and, as in Cooper's *Safe*, this distance seems to influence the way the story treats emotions. Recalling a night of hot sex with someone he hated, the narrator muses, "I wonder if the kind of sex people have when they love each other feels equally disconnected, related only inconsequentially to their emotions. Maybe."[52]

Bellamy also parts with aspects of an early New Narrative aesthetic in her cult classic *The Letters of Mina Harker*, which was published in sections in different venues throughout the 1990s and came out in its entirety in 1998. Rereading the plot of Stoker's *Dracula* from the perspective of Mina Harker and relocating characters from that story into her own memoir, Bellamy draws on many techniques learned in the workshops of Glück, who makes an appearance in the text as Dr. Van Helsing, a mentor who guides Mina/Dodie's writing: "Dr. Van Helsing pokes a craggy finger at my manuscript, says, 'You can always perk up your Readers' attention by asking them a question no matter how shallow, *can't you?*'"[53] Mina/Dodie duly obliges, and she piles other New Narrative techniques on top of it—naming her friends directly (in the case of Sam D'Allesandro) and indirectly ("KK" is Kevin Killian), referencing specific streets in San Francisco, even referring to the Small Press Traffic bookstore itself, its parties, and its regulars. Like the narrator of *Jack the Modernist*, Mina/Bellamy also "trusts" gossip, and her letters teem with the sexual life of the New Narrative community.

KK smirks, "Sam picked up that guy from the Patti Smith Group and I had that affair with that Hitchcock star *remember* in the elevator at the MLA and Felice Picano had sex with JOE ORTON—but Mina you've never slept with anyone famous!" I elbow his ribs, "I want to be the famous one that others have sex with—like when I read with Richard Hell . . ."[54]

But like Killian, Bellamy seems to skirt the matter of larger political issues—of explicitly situating her long, polyvocal ruminations within a context of political activism. Glück's litanies of cataclysmic events peppered with relationship problems and emotional foibles are plainly not for her. There's also little effort made by Mina/Dodie to deal in a sustained way with the question of community: gossip may be relayed in an attempt to replicate the chatter that circulates in the New Narrative group, but it can often feel cliquish and, combined with the admittedly shallow direct addresses, sometimes results in ostracizing readers rather than making them feel connected to the narrator and implicated in their story.

Mina/Dodie's tale thus seems to run contrary to the activist orientation of Boone and Glück's version of New Narrative. What it offers instead is an unflinchingly candid anatomization of the self. The narrator's relationship with her body, her interior life, her thoughts and desires, her vulnerability and abjection—these are Bellamy's principal concerns. All of this is to say that the politics of Bellamy's work is a *feminist* politics and her raunchy, gossipy, embodied narrative is radical because her writing is coded as female. "I like to talk dirty too," Mina/Dodie writes to Sam. "But sometimes it's such a yawn since all the cards are stacked on my side—being female anything I do is automatically twice as scandalous as anything you do. . . ."[55] Consequently Bellamy covers many subjects left unexplored by her gay male teachers—the injunction to reproduce, for instance, and its connection to literary production is treated in one letter with virulent contempt.

> Sam, who'd been eavesdropping, stepped into the foreground and snickered, "Mina are you planning to have a baby?" I stomped my satin feet like Sylvia Plath did the night she met Ted Hughes, "Who? Me? No! NO BABIES!" Then you, Dr. Van Helsing, of all people, warned me not to underestimate my biological drives *an author on autopilot, motherhood bound . . . she sits before a hand-painted antique mirror, pink and blue flowers frame a blonde organism that others seem to recognize . . . who . . . she drops her pen leans forward*

pores enlarge and open, eyes merge into a single greenish corona, all this mindless duplication I might as well be a Xerox machine.[56]

Taking these differences into account—Amnasan's suspicion of connection, Killian's placing "large and public" thoughts at a remove, Bellamy's turn toward her embodied experience as a woman—it's clear that the second generation of New Narrativists was hardly a Xerox copy of the first. These younger writers (along with other members of the Small Press Traffic workshops not considered here, like Camille Roy and Sam D'Allesandro) evidently absorbed the teachings of Boone and Glück (and Abbott, too, who ran an important series of workshops on literary theory). They were greatly influenced by their style and the way they breathed a new relevance into the practice of narrative. But read in the light of Cooper's *Safe*, their writing also seems to embody or at least resonate closely with a number of his work's attributes, namely his reluctance to engage with broader political issues and the aesthetics of distance that characterizes his writing—attributes that distinguish his work from the first generation of New Narrativists. New Narrative's second generation, in other words, seems to straddle the divide between Cooper on one side and Boone and Glück on the other. It channels these separate but sympathetic influences in many ways, resulting in work that is by turns distant but also intimate, wary of association with others but searching nonetheless for an authentic connection with them.

"Fuck Sexual Conformity" |
Anarcho-Homo Radicalism in the 1980s

7 IN JUNE 1983, the same month as the AIDS Awards were announced, Cooper received a short, handwritten letter from his friend Bernard Welt. A poet and critic, Welt was a younger member of the Mass Transit group of poets based in Washington, DC, from 1972 to 1974, which centered on the Community Bookstore on P Street and included figures like Donald Britton, Tim Dlugos, Michael Lally, Diane Ward, and Terence Winch. At one time the group also included Karen Allen, later star of George Lucas's 1981 blockbuster *Indiana Jones and the Raiders of the Lost Ark*, who also appeared alongside Jeff Bridges in John Carpenter's *Starman* (1984) and Bill Murray in the Christmas classic *Scrooged* (1988).

Welt and the Mass Transit poets first came to Cooper's attention through the endeavors of Dlugos, who saw that Cooper and the DC writers shared an interest in New York School poetry. In her retrospective appraisal of the scene, Patricia Griffith found Mass Transit work "accessible, fresh, and funny without sacrificing seriousness. They were closest to the New York poets, Frank O'Hara, who was already dead, Kenneth Koch, and John Ashbery but with a freshness all their own."[1] Echoing similar descriptions of Cooper's later Beyond Baroque reading series and its integration of Los Angeles's writing and art scenes—not to mention its aversion to hippie communalism—Welt comments that Mass Transit's weekly poetry readings "communicated to you this tremendous enthusiasm of a very serious kind, I mean there were some very well read people there. It wasn't just a lot of hippie nonsense. I think a lot of them might have had a better background in visual arts and what's being said about aesthetics than you might find among most writers, so I got exposed to that through Mass Transit."[2]

The subject of Welt's letter in June 1983 was his upcoming participation in Gay Pride Day in Washington, DC, and the six-page tract he and a couple of friends had produced for the occasion, which he had enclosed. "We're supposed to sit at a little table and pass these out and argue with people," Welt says, before adding with notable apprehension: "I cannot remember how I got into this."[3] Given the pamphlet's subject matter and the site of its impending distribution, it's not hard to understand Welt's concern. Calling themselves the Gay Anarchist Circle (GAC), Welt and his friends had put together a xeroxed A5 leaflet comprising text, stock illustration, and playfully doctored cartoon strips in the style of Joe Brainard and containing a number of incendiary pieces that promoted an anarchist take on American society. In his lead article, "Silent Radio," Welt writes, "We subscribe to the ridiculous notion that people know how to run their own lives; that they value freedom and diversity over authority and homogeneity; that they are willing to work to make a better world. We are crackpots. We are anarchists. And we're coming to get you."

Briefly citing the influence of writers like Emma Goldman and Henry David Thoreau, Welt's position in this opening salvo is explicitly indebted to Paul Goodman, whom he names "the outstanding gay anarchist thinker of recent times." Goodman's 1966 tract, "Reflections on the Anarchist Principle," which foresees the anarchistic coming together of disparate political positions around a shared critique of authority, offered Welt a suitably broad concept of anarchism to present to his gay readers. He declares:

> Anarchists do not accept a particular class analysis of society; they have been communist and radically individualist, religious and atheistic, revolutionary and evolutionary. Yet, as Goodman says, "despite these differences, anarchists seldom fail to recognize one another, and they do not consider the differences to be incompatibilities." This is because it is basic to anarchism that no body of authority should

Nancy and Sluggo collage in the *Gay Anarchist Circle* (June 1983). Used by permission of Bernard Welt. Source: Dennis Cooper papers, box 22, folder 94, Fales Library and Special Collections, New York University Libraries.

be imagined to speak for all of us, and no abstract set of principles allowed to stand in place of complex human realities.[4]

Anticipating a hostile reaction to his piece in the seat of US government—but evidently not from his correspondent Cooper—Welt may have been most concerned about the reaction of Gay Pride Day attendees to the pamphlet's angry mix of anarchist thought and sexual dissidence. Radically resistant to the United States' authoritarian regime and all extant forms of progressive politics, the GAC also vehemently opposed the reformist agenda of contemporary gay politics. According to Welt and his collaborators, the gay politics of the day was simply not radical enough. They demanded not merely piecemeal reform but an overhaul of the entire system of state domination that divided heterosexual from homosexual, men from women, and white from black. For Welt, such binary logic set social groups against one another and obscured the fact that "*All* people, of whatever class, race, gender, or religious or political persuasion, are oppressed in authoritarian society; all are bullied or bribed into placing the welfare of the state before their own."[5] Welt and the GAC condemned all forms of activism that appeared to participate in "the system": "Stay outside it and work against it," Welt concludes. "If we do that, we have a chance of forming our own personal ethical goals, instead of accepting the ones imposed on us by authority."[6]

The GAC pamphlet would almost certainly have provoked debate on Washington's Gay Pride Day in 1983. Suggesting that those who supported reformism were complicit in their own subordination and indicting gay politics for its collectivism on a day dedicated to gay solidarity was a bold move; also, as indicated by Welt's evident anxiety, it was surely not a popular one. Nevertheless, the intermingling of anarchism and sexual radicalism the GAC proposed had a number of important precursors in the United States, and even if their position was out of sync with the prevailing reformism of Gay Pride Day, it was also part of a long-standing tradition of sex-radical anarchism in the United States.

American anarchist and free-love advocate Ezra Heywood, for instance, was a prominent nineteenth-century exponent of sexual liberation, and his defenses of sexual nonconformity in his magazine the *Word* (1872–90, 1892–93) and in publications like *Cupid's Yokes* (1877) frequently got him charged with obscenity. Other well-known American anarchists such as Emma Goldman, Benjamin R. Tucker, and Alexander Berkman also addressed same-sex concerns in their lectures and writings. Historian of sex radicalism Terence Kissack even goes so far as to argue that the discussion of homosexuality in the United States was initiated only through the work of the growing anarchist movement. America didn't have the prominent same-sex intellectuals, reformers, and sex-radical advocacy groups that Europe had, and in the US in the 1800s same-sex intimacy was a topic that only anarchists would dare to broach. "The first sustained US-based consideration of the social, ethical, and cultural place of homosexuality took place within the English-language anarchist movement," Kissack states. "From the mid-1890s through the 1920s, key English-speaking figures of the anarchist movement debated the subject of same-sex passion and its place in the social order."[7]

Same-sex advocacy was therefore a strong current in American anarchist thought, and Welt and his friends could draw upon a radical tradition that stretched back more than a hundred years. But the GAC also gave voice to a contemporary anger and disappointment felt by certain parts of the gay community—that Gay Liberation had somehow turned out badly and gay politics was increasingly conservative at a time when it should have been more radical. It was a concern shared by Cooper, who wrote that in the years following Gay Liberation's explosion of radical queer politics, "the gay community at large, giddied and a little spooked by its growing political power, seemed to meet calls for anarchy with a collective finger to the lips . . . many gays in the early '80s had gotten as lazy as the heterosexual mainstream who sought to oppress them. 'Problem children' (punks, activists, women in general) were marginalized via an unspoken but entrenched class structure that effectively alienated all but the most 'privileged.'"[8]

Cooper and the GAC weren't the only ones to take umbrage at the creeping conservatism of the gay movement, and Cooper's remarks preface his article for the *Village Voice* in September 1990 that reflected on the emergence of an anarchistic queer movement in the 1980s that was as critical of the gay politics of the day as it was of the heterosexual mainstream. Cooper was talking about Queercore (or Homocore, as it was also known)—a dynamic, irreverent movement made up of mostly young, mostly queer activists and artists who hated establishment politics as much as they loved punk rock. The Queercore music and zines that flourished across North America in the 1980s and 1990s loudly affirmed a version of the GAC anarchist ideology while overloading its aesthetics with the adrenaline shot of punk. If the GAC pamphlet introduced Cooper to the intersection of sexual dissidence and a tradition of American anarchism, Queercore radicalized his politics and turned his thought irrevocably toward anarchist ideas.

QUEERCORE STARTED AROUND 1985 in the dilapidated downtown Toronto apartment of two friends, G. B. (Gloria) Jones and Bruce LaBruce. Jones was an artist, filmmaker, and musician who founded Fifth Column, a band that exploded onto the Toronto scene in the early '80s. Post-punk, all female, and almost all queer, the band would later be recognized as one of the main inspirations behind Riot Grrrl, the famous grassroots feminist rock and zine scene that came to prominence a decade later and launched the careers of people like Carrie Brownstein and Kathleen Hanna and bands like Bikini Kill, Sleater-Kinney, and Huggy Bear. But if Riot Grrrl was at times a little po-faced, its precursor Fifth Column loved to be transgressive and had a wicked sense of humor: their first album, released in 1985, was titled *To Sir With Hate*, their most famous track was "All Women Are Bitches," and when asked by a TV presenter in 1982 if they were feminists, they responded that they were in fact "bull dykes from Transylvania."[9] The band was made up of a rotating cast but most regularly featured Jones, Caroline Azar, and Beverly Breckenridge—all young Toronto-based artists and filmmakers who supported each other's work, collaborated, and performed in one another's films.

Jones had a day job she hated at a restaurant called Just Desserts, where she worked with a gay artist and film student named Bryan Bruce, whom Azar described as "a wild crazy guy that had hair like John Sex."[10] When Jones turned up for Fifth Column's gig supporting the Jesus and Mary Chain, she announced that they were going to have a male go-go dancer. Reversing the usual male/female, band/go-go dancer dynamic, Bryan Bruce—whom Jones renamed Bruce LaBruce—danced provocatively around the stage as Jones and her bandmates thrashed out tracks like "Boy, Girl," "Incident Prone," and "The Fairview Mall Story."

Jones and LaBruce became closer and started collaborating. He recalls that "when G. B. Jones—or Gloria, at the time—and I became friends, we had an intense relationship. For six years, it was almost like lovers, but without sex. It was romantic and intense. She's a brilliant artist. She mentored me, basically."[11] Both were into punk music and style, but they also saw that, in spite of the rather queer roots of punk where androgyny, for instance, was affirmed, the punk scene had become more and more straight, male, and homophobic. They also saw that gay life and art had become increasingly commercial and mainstream. Vehemently reject-ing both, in a polemical piece typical of their style called "Don't Be Gay, Or, How I Learned to Stop Worrying and Fuck Punk Up the Ass," they declared:

> The gay "movement" as it exists now is a big farce, and we have nothing else to say about it, so we won't say anything at all, except that, ironi-cally, it fails most miserably where it should be the most progressive— in its sexual politics. Specifically, there is a segregation of the sexes

Dennis Cooper (left) at Queercore zine fest Spew 2, held in Los Angeles in 1992. Courtesy of Larry-bob Roberts.

where unity should exist, a veiled misogyny which privileges fag culture over dyke, and a fear of the expression of femininity which has lead [*sic*] to the gruesome phenomenon of the "straight-acting" gay male.[12]

Lampooning conservative ideations of homosexuality in a typically punk assumption of the abject, they continued: "The New Lavender Panthers (male contingent) would like it to be known that not only do they consider themselves butt-rangers, but also bum-chums, turd-burglars, knob-gobblers, cocksuckers, and gaylords, while the girls are well-known diesel-dykes, baby butches and lezbo killer whores. In other words, fuck sexual conformity."[13] Out of this resistance to mainstream gay politics and homophobic punk culture came Jones and LaBruce's zine, *J.D.s*— according to Cooper, "the zine whose style of combustible romanticism triggered the onslaught."[14]

Named for juvenile delinquents, James Dean, or J. D. Salinger, depending on whom you ask, *J.D.s* was charged with the task of "putting the gay back in punk and the punk back in gay."[15] It ran for six years and eight issues, full of comic strips, Sapphic illustrations, tell-all porno memoirs, and photo stories starring Bruce LaBruce as a character they named "The Prince of the Homosexuals." Mixed in with this original content Jones and LaBruce also pasted naked or revealing photos of ostensibly straight punk band members and pictures cut out of porn mags. *J.D.s* also had a Top Ten Hits of what they started calling "homocore" that featured punk bands like Nip Drivers and Gay Cowboys in Bondage who weren't actually gay but had tracks like "Quentin Crisp" and "Cowboys Are Gay" (a band called Aryan Disgrace had one called "Faggot in the Family").

The DIY mingling of disparate types of material that characterized *J.D.s* wasn't a radical departure from the punk aesthetic that had emerged a decade earlier with the likes of *Sniffin' Glue*, which of course Cooper had tried to emulate in his *Little Caesar*. But Jones and LaBruce's zine was also emphatically queer and emphatically sexual; by comparison, other punk zines could have been considered positively coy. Curran Nault's recent study of Queercore, for instance, finds that "across the eight issues [of *J.D.s*], sex does not simply function as a turn on—although it often is that—but as a favored tool to challenge hetero- and homo-normativity, serving to queer the presumed-to-be-straight punk and trouble conventional, safe representations of gay and lesbian desire."[16]

What also distinguishes *J.D.s* from previous punk zines was that Jones and LaBruce weren't so much documenting a scene as actually *inventing* it. There were, in fact, hardly any punk bands at the time that were openly gay, and in the world beyond the pages of the zine there certainly wasn't any queer punk scene per se. But the growing readership of *J.D.s* believed there was. LaBruce remembers that "we borrowed from The Situationists quite heavily—this idea of creating a spectacle and propping it up in the media, even though it was fiction."[17] So convincing was the zine's fiction of a Queercore community that people across North America started reading *J.D.s* and assuming that an incredibly vibrant queer punk scene *actually existed* in Toronto. In places like California, Texas, and Florida, young punks and disenfranchised queers wanted to add their own voices to the hubbub, and *J.D.s* was quickly followed by a slew of Queercore zines.

One of the most notable was Tom Jennings's *HOMOCORE*. Although now better known as the controversial cocreator of FidoNet, a popular networking hack for bulletin board systems (proto-LISTSERVS widely used in the '80s and '90s), Jennings was also a major figure in the emergent Queercore scene. Cooper characterized him as the "unofficial conscience of the movement": "His pronouncements, even when couched in who-the-fuck-am-I-to-say-ism, give the zine the hyper-earnest tone of classic punk periodicals like *Flipside* and *Maximumrocknroll*."[18] Jennings identified as anarcho-homo or homopunk and stamped the pages of his zine with his anarcho-homo logo that depicted a circle-A (an anarchist icon) superimposed on an inverted pink triangle. In the editorial to the second issue, "What the Fuck Is *HOMOCORE?*," Jennings channels Jones and LaBruce in his resistance to normative labels: "You don't have to be a homo to read or have stuff published in *HOMOCORE*. One thing everyone in here has in common is that we're all *social mutants*; we've outgrown or never were part of any of the socially acceptable categories."[19] Like *J.D.s*, *HOMO-CORE*'s newsprint pages were filled with altered photographs and illustrations, letters, interviews, erotic stories, manifestos, and the occasional poem, cut up and pasted together in sumptuous, erratic arrangements.

Published in Los Angeles by the intersex African American artist Vaginal (Creme) Davis, the delirious *Fertile La Toyah Jackson Magazine* was named after Davis's drag queen muse and took the same approach to gender as *J.D.s* took to sexuality—in other words, it gleefully reviled and parodied convention. With a punk taste for controversy and a disregard for fallout, it also ratcheted up Jones and LaBruce's trick of documenting sexual fantasies starring straight celebrities. As Davis told Adam Block, "After I ran that story 'Inside Rob Lowe's Booty Hole,' I got a call from his lawyer threatening to sue! I told him, 'Go ahead, sue a black drag queen. I haven't got anything. All you're gonna win is some used wigs and makeup!'"[20] Regarding her approach to punk and her "fit" with the California gay and punk scenes, Davis remembers, "I was basing my [drag] persona on Angela Davis, the radical black feminist. I sexualized her name! The only people who got the outsiderness of it were the people who went to punk rock clubs. I started opening for a lot of punk rock bands in the late 1970s and early 1980s. I didn't fit in with those scenes either but I fit in better there than I did with the gay scenes."[21]

Larry-bob Roberts's *Holy Titclamps*, Rex Boy and Johnny Noxzema's *Bimbox*, Steve LaFreniere's *Gentlewomen of California*, Donna Dresch's *Chainsaw* . . . regarding this avalanche of Queercore zines, Cooper wrote,

"Mutually supportive for the most part but individualistic in outlook and design, these zines share a hatred for political correctness, yuppification, and all things bourgeois, especially within gay culture . . . in classic anarchist fashion, they just invent a world for themselves in and around the givens of the big fucked-up one, and say, 'Join or leave it alone.'"[22] This exciting network of zines spawned punk bands like Pansy Division and Tribe 8. As Jon Ginoli of Pansy Division recalls, "I formed Pansy Division, with Chris Freeman, because there were no other gay bands. As it turned out, a few others formed around the same time. At the second Pansy Division show, we were on a bill with Tribe 8—we hadn't heard of them. I thought, 'Great, we have comrades!'"[23] With bands and zines spreading across North America, constituting an anarchistic and radically nonmainstream queer culture in music and print, the Queercore scene that Jones and LaBruce had imagined and dramatized in the pages of *J.D.s* had finally become a reality.

AS HIS ENTHUSIASM for its zines shows, Cooper was excited about the rise of Queercore, which not only tapped into his long-standing love of punk but also affirmed his feelings about remaining outside the gay mainstream. Seeing his interests reflected back at him from the pages of *J.D.s* and other zines, he soon considered himself part of the Queercore movement, writing that he was "a giddy and awestruck participant in this anything but settled scene." In the same piece, he continues, "Up until a few years ago we were quirky outcasts—punk rockers, film buffs, artists, bookworms, etc. Now there's an intense if scattered community (ugh!) interconnected by zines like *J.D.s*, *HOMOCORE*, *Holy Titclamps*, *My comrade*, and *Fertile LaToyah Jackson Magazine*—obsessive, personal little Xeroxed rags some of us make and circulate as a way of formalizing our offbeat tastes and seeing if other like-minded people are out there."[24]

If Cooper was happy to be part of a growing network of misfit creatives who were somewhat like-minded—a curiously "anti-assimilationist and anti-separatist" group he cautiously refers to as a "community (ugh!)"— Queercore artists and writers also found a lot to enjoy in Cooper's writing.[25] He was welcomed into the scene and asked to read his work at Queercore's inaugural convention, Spew, held in Chicago in May 1991, which also included film screenings and performances by G. B. Jones, Bruce LaBruce, Fifth Column, Vaginal Davis, and others.

In a more literal enfolding of Cooper's work into Queercore, Jones and LaBruce also took one of his stories, "Introducing Horror Hospital," and pasted parts of it into *J.D.s*—without permission, of course. A short piece that had previously appeared in *He Cried*, a 1984 chapbook published in Robert Glück and Bruce Boone's Black Star Series (and that would later be the basis for Cooper's 1996 comic-book collaboration with artist Keith Mayerson, *Horror Hospital Unplugged*), the story foreshadowed Queercore's heady mix of homoeroticism and punk rock by a few years and, in setting and characterization, included a number of elements that would later be identified as quintessentially Queercore.

The main character in "Introducing Horror Hospital" is Trevor Machine, a Los Angeles teenager with a charmingly overinflated sense of his own talent and originality who fronts a young punk band called Horror Hospital. We first glimpse the band through the eyes of two stoned high school students standing at the back of the Undo Club in North Hollywood: "To sparse applause, four scrawny teenagers hooked in their instruments. One stepped to the microphone, running a hand through his spew of blue hair. He stared blankly at the audience for a couple of seconds. 'Oh, hi,' he yawned. They began their first number."[26] The stoners, Frank and Doug, aren't overawed. But even here, in the story's opening lines, punk's potential to stoke the homoerotic desire of those in the pit stands out over its other attributes. We're told that Doug in particular "watched the band carefully, hot for the singer . . . as a rule Doug thought punk rockers were sex gods. He'd always liked the last-legs look."[27]

The day after the gig, Trevor, in a ragged purple ensemble with the slogan "Beat Up Your Child" printed across his chest, drops into a music store called Rotten Records, eyeing the Cramps display in the window and thumbing through the 45s before picking up "one single each by Swans, Coil, and Big Black."[28] Next door to the record store is a gay bar, which after some thought Trevor decides to check out: "Sometimes his friends and he went to gay bars and let men try to pick them up. The lines gays used were hilarious."[29] The way Cooper places these two spaces side by side—an edgy neighborhood record store frequented by punk kids and a gay bar whose clientele are regarded with some derision—and has his protagonist move back and forth across the thresholds of each represents the larger intermingling of punk and queer scenes in the story. It declares from the outset Cooper's intention to transgress the boundaries between both and, as G. B. Jones and Bruce LaBruce might say, put "the gay back in punk and the punk back in gay."

At the bar Trevor meets a gay high schooler named Tim. They start hanging out and soon fall for each other. Tim writes to his friend, "I'm in love with a guy I met. His name's Trevor," while Trevor's bandmates worry among themselves that his newfound happiness is affecting their carefully cultivated nihilism.[30] Given the story's proto-Queercore combination of queer sexuality and punk rock, naturally when Tim and Trevor have sex it takes place backstage in a dingy rock club, right after Horror Hospital has finished its set: "The place smelled of barf. 'Let me undress you,' Tim whispered, unzipping Trevor's black jacket, sliding the heavy thing over his hands. He undid his friend's sneakers, unsnapped the jeans, and peeled them with his shorts to his ankles. Trevor stepped out of the wad. His cock was partially hard. His skin was as cold as the sink that he rested against."[31]

Relocated into an issue of *J.D.s*, there's little to distinguish this scene from other erotic homopunk fictions found in the magazine, like La-Bruce's recurring "Butch" stories (subtitled "The Adventures of a Teenage J. D. and His Young, Eager to Please Punk") or readers' erotic memoirs submitted to the editors and pasted in between sexy cartoons and lists of favorite Queercore zines.[32] A reader named Mark Dreher, for instance, contributed an account of his late-night encounter with a swarthy teen in downtown San Diego: "'O.K.,' he said, and undid his pants to reveal a virgin jockstrap. Underneath that was his perfect cock, stiff and straight as a rocket; thick and juicy and hard. I sucked it hungrily without hesitation. His cock filled my mouth and went down my throat. He moaned low. People passed us by, even a military patrol, but we didn't care."[33]

Taken together, scenes like these characterize what Curran Nault calls "the power of the pornographic" mobilized by Queercore zines such as *J.D.s* in order to mount an assault on sexual repression, emanating at the time from both the heterosexual mainstream *and* conservative wings of the gay community. "The sexually explicit is one of the defining characteristics of Queercore," he writes. "This insistence on the power of the pornographic builds on legacies of the sexual revolution and reacts against the forces of sexual repression that were in a heightened state in the 1980s/90s years of HIV/AIDS panic and anti-sex discourse, both inside and outside the LGBTQ+ community. Queercore's sexual representations thus contribute an unseemly danger to the subculture's efforts to unseat hetero- and homo-normativity."[34] But in contrast to the uninhibited sex-radical fantasies that filled the pages of *J.D.s*, which generally went out on a high (Dreher's story concludes by exclaiming, "Fuck what the people think or say—Fuck in the streets and be happy"),[35] Cooper's story ends on a somber note, with Trevor receiving news of Tim's death in a traffic accident moments before an important Horror Hospital show. Taking to the stage, he loses it, drops to his knees midsong and blubbers, "I'm the one who should die. All you fucking assholes know it. I want to *die. . . .*"[36]

QUEERCORE WOULD ITSELF suffer an untimely end, brought about through the demise of *J.D.s* and the implosion of its editors' friendship. In 1991 LaBruce released his debut film, *No Skin Off My Ass*, a low-budget black-and-white movie best described as a "tender love story of a punk ex-hairdresser obsessed with a young, silent, baby-faced skinhead" that featured LaBruce in the role of the hairdresser and Jones as his sister.[37] The film received a relatively large amount of attention when it was released—Kurt Cobain, front man of Seattle grunge band Nirvana, called it his favorite film—and LaBruce started to get grouped together with other directors like Todd Haynes and Gregg Araki as part of what the film critic B. Ruby Rich would call the "New Queer Cinema," acquiring a certain renown as a result.[38] This led Cooper to reflect on the "gentrification within its own ranks" that Queercore was experiencing. He wrote, "A current burning question goes: when exactly has one crossed the assimilationist line? It's thought that Bruce LaBruce, one of the earliest proponents of a punk/queer aesthetics via the seminal *J.D.s*, might've sold out last year when his film *No Skin Off My Ass* met with a moderate underground success. Ever since, he's been careering with a Jayne Mansfieldian blatancy that many in the scene find cringeworthy."[39]

Cringes quickly turned to snarls as many Queercore punks felt that when it came down to it, LaBruce simply didn't give Jones enough recognition as his longtime collaborator. As well as acting in *No Skin Off My*

Ass, she had also cowritten the script but received no on-screen credit. Led by Johnny Noxzema—widely regarded as the most toxic commentator on the scene—a vicious backlash against LaBruce ensued, and he was roundly condemned in a proliferation of Queercore zines. One diatribe ran: "Mr. LaBruce has made an art of appropriating the ideas of his female friends (now, understandably, ex-friends) and basking, alone, in the glory they bring him."[40] Under the weight of this acrimonious split, the Queercore zine scene soon fell apart: *J.D.s* folded and was quickly followed by *Homocore*, *Holy Titclamps*, and others that wound up operations in the early '90s.

But if Queercore was rather short lived, its broader effect was hardly negligible. Apart from its construction of real-life and in-print networks of young alienated nonmainstream queer people and its palpable effect on Riot Grrrl, some commentators also credit the movement with the reclamation of the term "queer" as a site of radical resistance—or at least catalyzing certain tendencies within the LGBTQ+ activism.[41] In terms of Cooper's personal outlook, his encounter with Queercore's version of anarchism also gave him the opportunity to situate his previous beliefs and convictions (his individualism, for instance, and his suspicion of community) within a larger conceptual framework. In an interview with Robert Glück, he says:

> I rediscovered anarchism through my love of punk rock. It was referenced [by] a lot of punk artists and by people writing about punk so I read a number of books about it. It just made absolute sense to me, especially as articulated by Emma Goldman. The impracticality of revising society into an ideal anarchist state was obvious, so it appealed to me more as a philosophy, although if there's ever a viable revolution I'll definitely join the front lines, and anarchist action groups have my heart. (2006)[42]

As "Introducing Horror Hospital" shows, by the time Queercore came around Cooper's work was already investigating the intersection of queer and punk concerns that would become a Queercore hallmark. Queercore's network of bands and zines amplified this queer–punk connection and yoked it to a political radicalism that noisily challenged a despised status quo and the integrationist gay politics of the 1980s. But as Bakunin wrote, "The passion for destruction is a creative passion too!,"[43] and in addition to its negative or critical aspect, Queercore was also hugely creative—generating a large, cross-continental community ("ugh!") that was itself musically and artistically creative. This was the kind of anarchism that Cooper would later champion when asked to identify the most important political event in the history of homosexuality. Framing his response in explicitly anarchistic terms, he responded,

> I have to split my vote between 1) the formation of ACT-UP [AIDS Coalition to Unleash Power] and 2) the emergence of the Queer zine movement. My hope is that we stop buying so mindlessly into the notion of collective identity. Our attraction to members of our own sex gives us something in common but it doesn't make us inherently responsible to each other. We're not a family. We're not a religious sect.[44]

Cooper's attachment to anarchism, forged through his participation in the Queercore movement, would become more and more evident in his life and work. In interviews he would more regularly describe himself as an anarchist and, as we shall see, from the 1990s his writing, including the George Miles Cycle of novels for which he is best known, would more explicitly bear the traces of an anarchist's interrogation of contemporary society.

The George Miles Cycle

New York, New York

8 "WRONG," A SHORT STORY that appeared in 1986, powerfully evokes Cooper's disenchantment with New York City. It opens with a brief account of a gay serial killer named Mike, who goes around Lower Manhattan picking up young men, taking them home, and murdering them. He finds his first victim, Keith, at the Ninth Circle, then one of the city's most famous gay bars. At Mike's place, Keith is beaten and whipped before being stomped to death: "Mike kicked Keith's skull in before he came to. Brains or whatever it was gushed out. 'That's that.'"[1] José, a cross-dressing junkie from Dallas, is the next to fall afoul of Mike's homicidal rampage, thrown from a window in a pink satin ankle-length dress: "Mike fisted 'her' on the window ledge. 'She' dangled over the edge. Mike shook 'her' off his wrist. 'She' fell four stories, broke 'her' neck."[2] Steve, a blond with chapped lips, and Will, an underweight hustler with blue eyes, are Mike's last victims—tied up, bludgeoned, and strangled to death before Mike finally does himself in, looking out across the Hudson River.

> Mike walked from Will's place on West Tenth to Battery Park, chains clinking each step. He stared out at the Hudson. He put a handgun to his head. 'Fuck this shit.' His body splashed in the river, drifted off.[3]

The next morning police drag Mike's body from the river, observed by a group of tourists from Los Angeles, "abuzz with the idea of death, in grim

127

or joking tones."[4] The remainder of the story follows one of the tourists, a gay teenager named George, as he wanders around the city taking in the sights, underwhelmed by what he sees: "The World Trade Center was not what he'd hoped. It wasn't like he could fall off"; "Wall Street was packed with gray business suits. . . . It was like watching a film about some other time and place, very far back and relegated to books."[5] Lecherous eyes follow him as he walks through the West Village: "'I'm tired of sleeping with *that*,' a man sneered as they crossed paths."[6] Sitting in a park, he dashes off a postcard to his friend Philippe and notes the destitution around him, writing that he's "sitting under a bunch of trees. They'd be great if bums weren't dying all over the place."[7]

Later, at the Ninth Circle, George gets picked up by a rich older guy named Fred and they go back to his trendy Downtown loft. Unluckily for George, Fred is also a serial killer, who performs some sadistic feats on his ass before brutally beating him to death. In the final sections of the story, George returns as a ghost, drifting through Christopher Street and the decrepit Hudson piers, gliding by bars on West Street, haunting the West Village with a bored indifference before evaporating into the afternoon.

First published in the celebrated Lower East Side literary magazine *Between C & D*, "Wrong" is noteworthy for a couple of reasons. Not only does it mark the first sustained appearance in prose of George Miles, the inspiration for Cooper's famous George Miles Cycle of novels, it is also one of Cooper's only pieces that's set exclusively in New York City. Despite his avowed attachment to New York and the impact of its writing, music, and art on him, never before in his work has the city's influence been so evident in such a manifest way—or, it must be said, in such wholly negative terms. In "Wrong," Cooper combines *Safe*'s cynical take on the vanity and exploitation prevalent in gay life with the gay serial-killer trope found in "A Herd" in a kind of tranquilized riff on *Cruising*, the 1980 William Friedkin film that caused such outrage in the gay community. His bleak envisioning of metropolitan gay culture in the story is therefore hardly new, but here the space of New York is fundamental to this bleakness. The city is depicted in such a way that it appears as an environment that is singularly hospitable to the misery felt by the story's serial killers and their young victims alike. Lower Manhattan in this account is marked by hostility, deprivation, disappointment, and death. It's boring too.

Cooper hadn't always felt this way about being in New York. Arriving in the city in 1983, he was glad to be free of Beyond Baroque and what he bitterly referred to as Los Angeles's "small-minded, lax, windbag of a poetry scene" (1983).[8] His apartment on East Twelfth Street placed him at the heart of Downtown, an area south of Fourteenth Street that had served as New York's countercultural, artistic, and literary hub since the early 1920s. By the 1970s, Downtown artists, writers, musicians, and activists lived together with poor immigrant families in cheap, closely packed tenement buildings, largely ignored or neglected by forces of law and order. In *Blood and Guts in High School* (1978), Kathy Acker, a regular Downtown resident whose early works were written and published there, paints a vivid portrait of the area that echoes other recollections of the scene.

> A racially mixed group of people live in these slums. Welfare and lower-middle class Puerto Ricans, mainly families, a few white students, a few white artists who haven't made it and are still struggling, and those semi-artists who, due to their professions, will never make it: poets and musicians, black and white musicians who're into all kinds of music, mainly jazz and punk rock. In the nicer parts of the slums: Ukrainian and Polish families. Down by the river that borders on the eastern edge of these slums: Chinese and middle-middle class Puerto Rican families. Avenues of junkies, pimps, and hookers form the northern border; the southern border drifts off into even poorer sections, sections too burnt out to be anything but war zones; and the western border is the Avenue of Bums.[9]

Downtown was an exciting and politically fertile environment for the creative imagination that had captured Cooper's young dreams as a site of infinite, varied artistic possibility—down its streets had walked Frank O'Hara and the New York School poets, Andy Warhol flanked by his Factory superstars, and punks like Patti Smith. "Growing up in LA and being heavily influenced by poets and musicians and performance artists associated with Downtown New York, the scene there seemed like a dream situation for me," he recalls (2006).[10] From 1983 until 1985, Cooper lived at 232 East Twelfth Street, which stood within easy reach of the landmarks of this artistic dreamscape: St. Mark's Church-in-the-Bowery, the site of the famous Poetry Project, was a couple of blocks south; performance art space PS122 was three blocks east; the unofficial nerve center of punk and No Wave, CBGB, was a ten-minute walk to the Bowery.

Cooper's first few months in New York appear to have exceeded his expectations, and Downtown offered the vibrant, challenging social scene he craved and worked hard to create in Los Angeles. In an *Advocate* feature in 1983, Cooper claimed to feel very much at home in New York, among "so many writers whom I admire, who are my friends, and whom I feel very close to aesthetically." "I knew I'd be happy here," he told Rudy Kikel.[11] Years later, in conversation with Eileen Myles, another fixture of the Downtown scene whose poetry collection *Sappho's Boat* was published by Little Caesar Press, he recalled his excitement about coming to New York and finally finding a community of artists and writers that was "multigenerational and just thrilling": "I'd go to a party with Tim [Dlugos], Donald [Britton] and Brad [Gooch], and there would be slightly older writers like Joe Brainard, and Kenward Elmslie and Ron Padgett, and then the established greats like Ashbery and Schuyler and Edwin Denby and nonpoets like Donald Barthelme and Alex Katz and Roy Lichtenstein and just an incredibly multigenerational group of artists, gay and straight" (2006).[12]

Diary entries from the time of his arrival in New York also reveal Cooper's continued interaction with older and younger members of the Downtown scene and describe, for instance, intimate dinners with Downtown editor and publisher Raymond Foye, lunches with Dlugos, and late-night phone conversations with Elmslie. The guest list for *Safe's* launch party, carefully noted by Cooper in his diary on May 6, 1984, similarly attests to his growing visibility and participation in Lower Manhattan's cultural scene, listing such notable attendees as poet and punk rocker Richard Hell and pop artist Keith Haring. The party also drew a sizeable number of established writers like Edmund White (who wrote the introduction to *The Tenderness of the Wolves*), poet and critic Marjorie Welish, doyen of Language poetry Charles Bernstein, and Anne Waldman, the artistic director of the Poetry Project from 1968 to 1978. A younger generation of writers and artists was also well represented, including Carl Apfelschnitt, the abstract artist, novelist and art critic Lynne Tillman, and Peter Lamborn Wilson, whose anarchist poetry and philosophy were later published under the name Hakim Bey.[13]

Cooper also became engaged with Downtown's performance scene, collaborating with musician Chris Cochrane and choreographer Ishmael Houston-Jones on *THEM*, an improvisational dance piece first performed at PS122. Cooper's text accompanied Cochrane's droning, feedback-heavy score and Houston-Jones's contact improv in an aggressive, sexually charged work that, for audience members like the *Village Voice*'s Burt Supree, obliquely addressed the AIDS crisis: "*THEM* isn't a piece about AIDS but AIDS constricts its view and casts a considerable pall," he wrote.[14] In an article for the *Advocate*, Cooper described Houston-Jones as "a powerfully built black man whose work concerns his race and sexual preference in a general way [and] concentrates on the issue of repression"—his 1984 solo piece *f/i/s/s/i/o/n/i/n/g* in particular "suggested how difficult it is to be an individual in our uncertain world, implying that all men and women are potential victims, whatever their subculture."[15] Unsurprisingly, given this shared interest in individuality and subcultural identity, Houston-Jones and Cooper continued to work together, producing pieces like *Knife/Tape/Rope* in 1989 and *The Undead*, which premiered at the Los Angeles Olympic Arts Festival in 1990.

Despite his increasing involvement in Downtown culture, ultimately the move to Manhattan was an anticlimax for Cooper, leading him to remember that "I did feel disappointed that the real Downtown New York wasn't exactly what I'd foreseen and dreamed."[16] Alienated by a poetry scene that had become predominantly straight and had turned from his beloved New York School poetry to that of the Naropa Institute, Cooper rarely visited the Poetry Project at St. Mark's Church. On the rare occasion that he did, he found the space itself—gutted by fire in 1978 and rebuilt in a stark, minimalist style—as conservative and forbidding as the scene that surrounded it: "By the time I went to a reading at St. Mark's, the church was this big empty sterile white space," he recalls. "It wasn't intimate or pleasurable to be in there at least for a poetry reading. I just felt, like: wow, this isn't what I thought it was going to be like at all. . . . I definitely got the feeling that I had missed the great period of the Poetry Project" (2006).[17]

Somewhat unexpectedly, given that it was the promise of a community of like-minded artists and writers that had led to his move from Los Angeles, Cooper also became aware of his growing discomfort with the intense sociability demanded of the Downtown scene. Early on, he had remarked to Rudy Kikel, "I've done more drugs in New York than I did in LA, and drunk more. Everyone seems to be an alcoholic or about to become one at any minute" (1983); indeed, the interviewer noted that "Cooper looked a little heavier than I'd seen him in Los Angeles and perhaps a little groggy from the night's festivities."[18] While plainly enamored of New York's exciting artistic community, the constant expectation of immersion in it appears to have been ill suited to Cooper's temperament, which, looking back, he considers more West Coast in character: "The heavily social aspect of life in New York wore me out," he says. "I grew up in LA, which is an asocial city unless you make a big effort to be social and I think that suits me" (2006).[19]

But of the factors that caused Cooper's uneasiness with his situation and that finally contributed to his decision to leave New York, the most significant was the tightening grip of the AIDS epidemic. Even at the time of his arrival, he says, it "was casting its darkness over the group of gay writers [he] was close with," and in the following months things would only get worse. "My group of artist friends was decimated by AIDS," he says. "I mean, Tim Dlugos tested positive and then Donald Britton and the filmmaker Howard Brookner and the performance artist John Bernd, and it was just bam, bam, bam . . . one after another in really quick succession. We were almost all gay, and we got hit particularly hard" (2006).[20] Having been inseparable from Dlugos and Britton during his first few months in New York, their HIV-positive diagnosis suddenly indicated the plague's worrying proximity: "AIDS was starting to happen, people were getting sick and it was just so terrible that I just wanted to get away" (2001).[21] Offered the opportunity to move to the Netherlands with his new Dutch boyfriend, Cooper assented without hesitation and fled for Amsterdam in 1985.

"WRONG" THEREFORE READS like an embittered breakup letter to the city Cooper once loved, now associated in his mind with disillusionment and death. Living in New York had also badly affected his writing. Collaborations with Houston-Jones notwithstanding, his creative output during those years was negligible: the social demands of the scene and frequent drug binges seem to have eventually taken their toll on his work. He was also broke and, to make ends meet, spent his time and energy drafting paid book reviews or features for newspapers and magazines.

In Amsterdam, on the other hand, far from the rush of Downtown society and its attendant pressures, Cooper's focus would soon come back to his writing projects. They became, in fact, his only means of moral and financial support during his two and a half years there. Within days of his arrival, his relationship with his boyfriend fell apart, and he found himself living in almost complete isolation, with no friends and no money to return to the US. Writing to Lynne Tillman, he lamented, "I have no money to move, no job prospects, etcetera. Kind of grim. It just seems increasingly foolish to be here. I do get a lot of work done, but that doesn't disguise my loneliness and the general lack of stimulation."[22] In loneliness and privation, however, he devised his most ambitious project to date: the series of works that would come to be known as the George Miles Cycle.

Cooper had thought seriously about creating a large, elaborate work of literary fiction since he was a teenager but didn't feel at the time that he had the skills necessary to achieve all that he envisaged. Years went by, and gradually, with more confidence in his abilities, his thoughts returned to it. George Miles became the heart of the project, its lodestar: "Other people had written books about their beloved, their muse, and used the muse's name, and the muse became a source of great interest and fascination like Robbe-Grillet's Angélique or Dante's Beatrice'" (2011).[23] The George Miles Cycle would take fifteen years to complete and would include the novels *Closer* (1989), *Frisk* (1991), *Try* (1994), *Guide* (1997), and *Period* (2000).

CLOSER

The first book in the series, *Closer*, was written entirely in Amsterdam—most of it while Cooper was bedbound for two months with a bad case of German measles. A thematically bold but formally conventional text, the book is made up of eight interlinked accounts of teenage boys who attend the same suburban high school (and one anomalous section about an older man, Philippe). Written alternately in third and first person with occasional segues into diary entries, each character's story inhabits the same terrain of adolescent gay sex, punk, pop music, and high school art classes that served as the setting for Cooper's *Idols*.

All of the narratives turn around the body of a cute, insecure sophomore named George Miles: *Closer*'s characters are irresistibly drawn to him and obsessed by him. This circling of protagonists around a shared object of affection obviously owes much to the writing of *Safe*; as in that work, the other characters' desire to control or understand him is constantly frustrated. As in the earlier novella, in *Closer* there are also many references to mannequins, dolls, and ventriloquism, especially where George is concerned. When Philippe imagines George expressing a feeling, we're told, "he saw pretend pain, the look that would creep over dolls' faces when children left them alone in the dark."[24] George's own fondness for "empty things normally filled up with people," like "abandoned houses, parking lot structures on Sunday nights, holograms, telephone booths," extends the sense of hollowness and automatism that suffuses the text and gives the interactions between characters—and the George Miles character above all—a Bressonian quality.[25] Cooper called the novel "a stylized version of a really boring world where nothing ever happens. There's no momentum in the book at all except for the meeting of these different people. Just like a drift . . . like drifting" (1989).[26]

To begin with, *Closer* had a hard time finding a publisher. Felice Picano told Cooper he would be happy to put it out under his SeaHorse imprint for Gay Presses of New York, as he had *Safe* and *Idols*, but Cooper was eager "to get away from the gay presses" and try what he called "the majors."[27] Unfortunately, as he admitted to his friends Joel Rose and Catherine Texier, the editors of *Between C & D*, it was "rejected all over the place" (1987).[28] Weidenfeld, for instance, told him they admired his writing but *Closer* was too experimental for their list.[29] At Farrar, Straus and Giroux, editor Jonathan Galassi passed on the manuscript, taking issue with Cooper's aesthetics of distance. In terms that recall Kathy Acker's in her letter to Cooper years earlier, Galassi wrote:

> The trouble I had with *Closer*, primarily, comes down, I think, to a lack of affect in the relations among the characters as you portray them—there is something terribly untouchable and untouched about the characters as you present them and I think that is the core of my problem with the piece, much more than the subject matter. I know from your last book that this is far from being the whole story with you and I think that if you were to find your way into the heart of the

connections between your characters you would have something very real and strong.[30]

Realism was, of course, beside the point in a text populated by quasi-automata, and Cooper hoped that the editors at Grove Press might have a better idea of what he was trying to do. Legendary champions of avant-garde writers like William S. Burroughs and Henry Miller, Grove was used to publishing transgressive work like Cooper's, so it was unlikely to be put off by the underage gay sex, violence, and scatological scenes in the book. In earlier decades, under the direction of the charismatic and pugnacious Barney Rosset, the press had been involved in a number of high-profile obscenity cases like the trial of D. H. Lawrence's *Lady Chatterley's Lover* in 1959, which forever changed the literary landscape of the United States (and almost bankrupted the press). Before he was ousted by the new owners of the press, Rosset had signed Kathy Acker in 1984.

In early 1987 Cooper wrote to Rose and Texier that Grove was his "last big chance": "[*Closer*'s] at Grove right now and I have my fingers crossed, as I think that would be the perfect press for this book, and I wouldn't mind being stablemates with Kathy. We'll see."[31] He had to wait, but at the end of July—eight long months after he submitted the manuscript to them—Cooper received a reply from Grove editor Walt Bode: he was interested in the book. *Closer* was published in 1989 to widespread acclaim, winning the inaugural Ferro-Grumley Award for gay fiction and launching a relationship with Grove that would last over a decade and see the publication of some of Cooper's best-known works, including the four other books in the George Miles Cycle.

FRISK

Even before *Closer* was picked up by Grove, while still in Amsterdam Cooper started working on *Frisk*, the second novel in the series, published in 1991. Cooper called it his "revenge on Holland for the unpleasant time [he] had there" (2001).[32] Bleaker and more claustrophobic than the previous work, *Frisk* takes the form of a memoir written from Amsterdam, its narrator Dennis describing at length his interest in understanding his sexual partners inside and out. "I want to know everything about you," he confesses to a hustler he meets in a hotel room, "but to really do that, I'd have to kill you, as bizarre as that sounds."[33] His often homicidal ruminations are interrupted here and there by scattered pieces of fiction that are similarly obsessed with the young male body, compelled to represent its processes and functions—before and after death.

The fictional space established by *Closer* is greatly expanded, and scenes take place in Amsterdam, New York, and Los Angeles, in homes and hotels, with a greatly enlarged cast of characters; the time covered by the narrative is also extended, now spanning two decades from 1969 to 1989. In spite of this capacious fictional time and territory, *Frisk*'s range of thematic concerns is greatly restricted, focusing almost exclusively on themes of sex, death, and corporeal investigation that it worries over with an attentiveness bordering on the psychotic.

An early draft of the novel in Cooper's papers at New York University's Fales Library and Special Collections includes a Xerox of Charles-Amédée-Philippe Van Loo's famous portrait of a young Marquis de Sade, and *Frisk*'s style, more than any of Cooper's other works, seems to have been inspired by Sade's coldly mechanical forays into depravity and death. "Numb, 1989," a section of the book that takes the form of a letter from Dennis to a childhood friend, is especially Sadean in its representation of the methodically planned and executed scenes of violence that Dennis is supposed to have perpetrated on young Dutch men. At the close of the novel, however, the letter is revealed as pure fantasy, as Cooper explains:

> The novel is about the differences between what is possible in one's fantasy life, and what is possible in one's real life. It tries, in various ways, to seduce readers into believing a series of murders are real, then announces itself as a fiction, hopefully leaving readers responsible for whatever pleasure they took in believing the murders were real. I mean it to challenge readers around issues of morality, and to make them wonder why the novel's ending leaves them feeling disappointed or relieved.[34]

Frisk has the distinction of being the only novel by Cooper to be made into a feature film. Director Todd Verow, sometimes associated with New Queer Cinema along with the likes of Gregg Araki and Bruce LaBruce, and producer Marcus Hu, who worked on Araki's *The Living End* (1992) and LaBruce's *Super 8 1/2* (1994), tried to translate the work to screen in 1995. The results were decidedly mixed. First to go was the moral reflexivity Cooper describes—the director opting to leave open-ended the question of whether or not Dennis had in fact committed the crimes he details in his letter. Cooper wasn't happy with the change: "I question very strongly the decision to leave the question of whether the murders are real or not up in the air," he wrote to Hu around the time of the film's release. "This is not to say *Frisk* is a bad film. . . . But I do wonder if, in eroticizing sadistic sexual acts against innocent people in an uncomplex way, the film doesn't perpetuate a common, simplistic misreading of my work, and that concerns me."[35]

The film's principal actors—handsome, muscular hunks of a type that graced the pages of *Mandate*—also located its aesthetic close to the mainstream of gay culture, whereas the novel was written more in its margins. It wasn't clear whom the film was for and what it represented—an ambiguity that provoked many gay spectators who saw the film premiere in June 1995 at Frameline, the international lesbian and gay film festival in San Francisco. Kevin Killian, who attended the screening and witnessed the walkouts and cries of "SICK! SICK!," would later report to Cooper that "people were very angry": "Now I don't know exactly why they were angry. But basically it was, I believe, because the film was not showing some uplifting light little coming out two girls in love type message picture. That's all. . . . Either people don't like 'negativity' or they don't like the 'avant-garde'—and this Todd Verow film had both galore."[36] If the novel's meditations on violence and perversion had generally been well received—lauded by Edmund White in the *New York Times* for instance, for representing "the very stuff of Jesse Helms's worst nightmares"—the film, on the other hand, was lambasted in the letters columns.[37] One San Francisco resident called it "one of the most virulently anti-gay movies I have seen," which tried "to prove that there actually are gays who are as sick and perverted as Jesse Helms, Pat Robertson, and Fred Phelps claim us to be."[38]

In 1991, before *Frisk* had been optioned by Marcus Hu, Cooper foresaw the difficulties his novels would have making the transition to film. When asked by the editor of *Holy Titclamps*, Larry-bob Roberts, what he thought about someone making a movie out of one of his books, he replied, "My books are so much about language and writing it seems like it'd be weird to make movies out of them," but he added, "You know what I'd rather do? I'd rather write a movie for somebody . . . it'd be fun to write a movie."[39] Almost twenty-five years later, his wish would be granted when he met his collaborator, Zac Farley, and began working with him on a series of feature films including *Like Cattle Towards Glow* (2016) and *Permanent Green Light* (2018).

TRY

With *Try*, the third book in the Cycle (published in 1994), Cooper moved away from *Frisk*'s psychotic interest in the body to create a work that was more engaged with the emotional lives of his protagonists. This shift was particularly obvious to his friend Catherine Texier, who wrote in a review for the *New York Times* that "*Try* ventures, sometimes precariously, into what must feel like dangerous terrain, especially for Mr. Cooper, because this time his dizzy teen-agers are trying to connect emotionally and to express their craving for love."[40]

The longest and most conservatively plotted of the Cycle's five novels, *Try* returns Cooper to a California setting. Centered once more on inarticulate and excitable adolescent boys and the men who love them, it follows the traumatized teenager Ziggy McCauley, his heroin-addicted writer friend Calhoun, and Ziggy's sexually abusive family, including his adoptive gay fathers, Brice and Roger, as well as a pedophilic Uncle Ken. Just as Ziggy occasionally appears to be a regular sixteen-year-old (in passages where, for example, he is pasting together the latest issue of his zine or neurotically obsessing about his looks), *Try*, with its linear plot and abundant dialogue, sometimes looks like a conventional novel. Both Ziggy and the work itself are infused with a recurring trauma, however, which lurks, ticking, beneath the surface.

The attempts at emotional connection identified by Texier in her review largely center on Ziggy's relationship with Calhoun. Ziggy's affection for his stoned friend is overwhelming, as is his desperate desire to have his love affirmed and reciprocated. Their conversations are marked by his anxious efforts to restrain himself from constantly declaring his devotion: "'You mean so much to me, Calhoun,' Ziggy whispers . . . 'You really do. But now I'll shut up. And, uh . . . we can talk about something else.'"[41] Meanwhile, amplified by the heroin he takes in regular shots throughout the story, Calhoun's solipsism and emotional reticence mean that Ziggy's needs will never be fully met.

"Yeah," says Calhoun. His eyes seem like they're aimed through Ziggy's chest at some infinite point. "I don't know . . . I guess I don't want to be that close to people."

Ziggy nods, but it feels really stiff. "Don't you think maybe you do like how close we are now, you just can't think about it too much, like you said?"

"I don't know." Calhoun's still staring way out . . . wherever. "I hate talking about this."[42]

Ziggy and Calhoun's relationship works, to an extent, but both characters are locked into a lopsided emotional dynamic, where Ziggy's adoration stimulates the narcissistic parts of Calhoun's personality, which makes it even more difficult for him to reciprocate. This in turn ensures that Ziggy, unsatisfied, must continue his doomed pursuit of reciprocity. Nonetheless, as Sean Grattan argues, the friendship between Ziggy and Calhoun offers a precious modicum of hope in a nightmarish fictional world: "*Try* ends with two friends grappling with what it means to exist in a space of intimacy with one another . . . [with] the possibility of friendship to offer succor and hope for a better tomorrow, even when that friendship is risky, fraught, and dangerous."[43]

Calling *Try* Cooper's most autobiographical work would be an overstatement: many of his writings explicitly bring parts of his life into play and employ memoir reflexively as the New York School poets did—and indeed the entire Cycle was intended as a monument to his friend George Miles. Nevertheless, the emotional dynamic at the heart of the book that characterizes Ziggy and Calhoun's relationship draws directly on Cooper's firsthand experience of heroin addiction and his friendship with Casey McKinney, a talented eighteen-year-old writer he met in 1991.

Cooper had left Amsterdam by that point; after a short, ill-advised move back to New York, he returned to Los Angeles. When McKinney moved out West, he and Cooper started hanging out and quickly became close friends. Writing fueled their friendship. They both adored Rimbaud, for instance, and, as he wrote to Ira Silverberg in May 1992, Cooper was in awe of McKinney's work: "I consider Casey the most original and talented writer I've come across in a very long time, probably since first reading Amy Gerstler's work in the late seventies."[44] Assuming the role of "guide, encourager, and critical reader," Cooper told Silverberg, "I'm going to do everything I can to clue people in to [Casey's] greatness, from helping secure a publisher if possible to writing on Casey's work and vision whenever possible for the *Voice*, the *Weekly*, and elsewhere."[45] True to his word, Cooper sought out opportunities for McKinney, and the two collaborated on pieces about artists Lari Pittman for *Artforum* and Mike Kelley for the catalogue of Kelley's *Catholic Tastes* show.

But McKinney's heroin habit soon became a problem. Cooper had experienced the devastating effects of heroin addiction before (he had an intense affair with an ex-boyfriend, Chris Lemmerhirt, who was a violent addict), but his relationship with McKinney was different, and Cooper was determined to stick around and help him get clean. It was emotionally taxing, to say the least. In mid-1992 he wrote to Elizabeth Young, a British critic and journalist whom he'd recently become friendly with, that he felt "crazed and depressed" by the situation: "Really, all I do is see him, reasearch [*sic*] what he might need to help get off, and worry about him these days. It's sort of driving me . . . crazy, but I don't see as I have any other choice, and, obviously, I love him and will do anything to help."[46] McKinney finally quit for good in 1993.

Speaking with Steve Lafreniere in 1994, Cooper admits that "the conversations between Ziggy and Calhoun . . . the tone of them is very much my relationship with Casey. Me trying to help him, me giving him all this love and him wanting it and needing it and being afraid to ask for it and freaking out about it. This whole code thing that develops, all that."[47] While hardly a roman à clef in the traditional sense, Cooper's intense and fraught friendship with McKinney is nevertheless the central dynamic of *Try*, routed through the relationship between the novel's two central characters.

GUIDE

In the mid-1990s, when Cooper wrote *Guide*, the world had changed somewhat from the hellscape of the 1980s that had spawned *Closer* and its successor, *Frisk*. Comparatively, things were looking up. The election of Bill Clinton in 1993 put an end to twelve long years of AIDS-denying, war-mongering Republican presidents. Toni Morrison declared Clinton "the first Black president," and for many, the arrival in the White House of this "single-parent household, born poor, working-class, saxophone-playing, McDonald's-and-junk-food-loving boy from Arkansas" heralded the emergence of a new, more progressive, more compassionate style of government.[48]

AIDS activists were wise to Clinton's shtick, however. On the campaign trail when heckled by a member of ACT UP, he famously declared "I feel your pain" and promised a "Manhattan Project for AIDS."[49] Yet once in office, the epidemic was way down his list of priorities, and in December 1993, further humiliating his LGBT supporters, he signed off on "Don't Ask, Don't Tell," which barred openly homosexual men and women from serving in the American military. Nonetheless, in spite of Clinton's heel dragging, the work of AIDS activists and scientists finally paid off: in early 1996 combination therapy, the single largest breakthrough in HIV/AIDS research, was announced. Finally, people with AIDS had hope that they would live to see the new millennium.

After the demise of grunge in 1994 with the unexpected suicide of Nirvana's Kurt Cobain, in the mid-1990s youth culture also found renewed hope in the emergence of techno and rave. Fueled by the ubiquity of ecstasy, a psychedelic that produces a sense of euphoria and connection with others (thus its odious nickname, the "love drug"), rave culture offered a chemically controlled hedonism where, in contrast to pop and rock scenes, the performer or performers were rarely the focus. "The audience was the star," Simon Reynolds wrote in his landmark *Energy Flash: A Journey Through Rave Music and Culture* (1998), and on the dance floor young ravers found a release from their solitude and loneliness, and perhaps even the tyranny of selfhood.[50] Reynolds remembers:

> Dance moves spread through the crowd like superfast viruses. I was instantly entrained in a new kind of dancing—tics and spasms, twitches and jerks, the agitation of bodies broken down into separate components, then reintegrated at the level of the dance floor as a whole. Each sub-individual part (a limb, a hand cocked like a pistol) was a cog in a collective "desiring machine," interlocking with the sound system's bass-throbs and sequencer riffs. Unity and self-expression fused in a forcefield of pulsating, undulating euphoria.[51]

When its virtues were explained to him by his young friend Joel Westendorf, Cooper admitted that rave music gave him "a rumble of countercultural hope."[52] Cooper and Westendorf met in Chicago in 1994 and, despite differences of age and musical taste, struck up an intimate friendship that deeply affected the writing of *Guide*, which was published in 1997. Composed of fragments of autobiography, long drug-trip sequences, and sex scenes staged on pornographic film sets, the novel could be described as *Frisk*'s more thoughtful sibling. Like *Frisk*, it contains memoir and ruminates on the fantasy/reality divide; unlike the earlier work, whose concern is primarily libidinal, *Guide* is psychological and analytic. "I live in my head, as you're aware, and reality doesn't necessarily impinge on my wishes," says the narrator, Dennis.[53]

But *Guide* also includes digressions on rave culture and music, prompted by the narrator's friendship with twenty-five-year-old Luke (standing in for Westendorf), a raver who's into "trippy, computer-built, danceable soundscapes."[54] Luke introduces Dennis to techno music like British electronic outfit the Black Dog—and the sense of quasi-mystical connectedness rave culture represents for him.

> Like every CD Luke loves, it has no lyrics, emotions, or intellectual ideas. If you buy into the Black Dog's mystique, their music connects listeners to some sort of ineffable energy source in the collective unconscious or something. It causes one to dance around in a particular way, and the resulting motion effects some temporary biological change whose spiritual benefits outweigh the mere emotional support and/or visceral kick that you get from alternative rock bands like Sebadoh, Guided by Voices, et al.[55]

Although the narrator is far from persuaded by notions of connectivity (he cynically refers to the Black Dog as "Muzak"), these ideas nonetheless share space in the narrative with the narrator's own self-absorbed reflections on his ethics of distance: "Luke will always be tantalizingly separate from me. He'll never dissolve into all my imaginative bullshit. Whatever happens to me from now on, good or bad, he'll be safe. That's love, right? Anyway, that's love to me."[56]

While he never fully convinces Dennis to let go of his obsession with "people's specialized needs for one another," Luke's belief in rave culture and the connection it offers, coupled with Dennis's abiding respect for him, encourages the narrative to countenance these notions more readily.[57] In Cooper and Westendorf's laudatory review of rave culture for *Spin* magazine, "A Raver Runs Through It," they write that "rave is not about destroying corrupt power structures; it's about general things like self-belief, open-mindedness, and faith. It's about seeking the limit-less."[58] Despite the appearance in the book of predictably bleak themes (i.e., sexual abuse, child pornography, violent murder), by allowing for the possibility of connection—in mysticism or in friendship—*Guide* is also, weirdly, about hope.

PERIOD

The Cycle's fifth and final novel, *Period*, did little to extend *Guide*'s tenta-tive optimism. A bewildering, skeletal work so slight that its effect almost dissipates in the description, it opens on a remote, rural landscape dotted with dark woods and spooky cabins, through which shuffle horny teen-agers Leon and Nate, a mute boy called Dagger, and a grief-stricken art-ist named Bob. Chapter by chapter a second, mirror narrative slowly in-trudes upon the first, featuring an artist named Bob, a disabled boy called George, and randy adolescents Etan and Noel. Both of these stories are veined by a perpendicular story that presents a warped version of Cooper himself and the motivations behind the George Miles Cycle: here we find a cult writer named Walter Crane, who writes a popular book also called *Period* in tribute to George, his now-deceased friend and sometime lover.

Written after Cooper had learned that Miles, from whom he had been estranged for a number of years, had shot himself in 1987 before the Cycle had even begun, *Period* reflects the wordless grief that affected Cooper for months afterward and a sense of agonized futility that the George Miles Cycle should exist when his friend did not. Walter Crane's elegies for his dead lover in the section titled "Cycle" gesture toward Cooper's mourning for Miles and, in their brutal simplicity denuded of artifice, underscore the grim pointlessness of art when faced with a beloved's tragic death.

It's great you lived
at all, though maybe
not toward the end.
I loved your weird
mind, your easy
going face, deep
eyes, your long hair,
how it swished on
your shoulders, your

skin as tight as a
tree's, though your
life was shorter and
more exciting than
its. When you were
here, I thought only
of you, and went to
bed with any boy
who resembled you,
I was so haunted. So
I forgot who you were,
and you wanted me
to know. You're the
one who fired a gun
at his head, so high
on whatever, and so
depressed by my lack
of whatever that you
were afraid you might
otherwise not hit
the target, wherever
I was at the time. Not
with you, I guess. It's
finally hitting me now.[59]

The publication of *Period* was marked in March 2000 by a special two-day event at NYU's Fales Library, which also launched an exhibition of Cooper's manuscripts, diaries, books, and correspondence called *Beautiful: The Writing of Dennis Cooper*. The Fales had recently acquired Cooper's papers as part of their Downtown Collection, which documents SoHo and the Lower East Side arts scene and includes the archives of a number of cultural figures who lived and worked south of Fourteenth Street from the 1970s to the 1990s, like Richard Hell, Lynne Tillman, David Wojnarowicz, and the Guerrilla Girls collective. Although he didn't live in New York for long, Cooper's inclusion in the Downtown Collection was testament both to the tangible effect of New York on his poetry and prose since the 1970s and the impact he in turn had on the emergence of a distinctively Downtown aesthetic.

Featuring academics, novelists, artists, and filmmakers, the list of participants at the Fales event on the second and third of March also indicated Cooper's massive influence across a wide range of cultural fields. The first day included contributions by prominent queer theorist Michael Warner, art critic Bruce Hainley, and academic Leora Lev, who would later put together the first collection of critical essays on Cooper's work, *Enter at Your Own Risk: The Dangerous Art of Dennis Cooper* (2006). Philosopher Avital Ronell also presented a disquisition on the act of rimming in Cooper's novels and spoke about how, in his work, "Cooper tends to conflate the beloved ass in his works with the production of meaning, and, irreversibly, with the act itself of writing."[60] The next day a group of famous fans read Cooper's work—Thurston Moore from Sonic Youth and Stephen Malkmus from Pavement joined novelists Tillman and Bret Easton Ellis and sculptor Robert Gober in reading parts of Cooper's novels to a large crowd that had taken over the Fales reading room. A late addition to the lineup, filmmaker John Waters brought the house down by reading a single line, his favorite from *Try*: "'If you really loved me . . .'— Ziggy slugs—'you wouldn't *rim* me while I'm *crying*.'"[61]

By all accounts the event was a huge success. Feted in the pages of the *New York Times* and the *Village Voice*, it marked Cooper's triumphant return to New York, a city that he had such an ambivalent relationship with in the past. But the Fales event is haunted by memories of *Safe*'s book launch sixteen years earlier, which announced Cooper's arrival on the Downtown scene. As star-studded as the list of contributors to the more recent event is, when compared with *Safe*'s guest list it's also decimated—just as the final book in the George Miles Cycle, when compared with the first, is decimated, ravaged and haunted by the violence of the intervening years.

Putting the list of participants at the Fales side by side with the guest list for *Safe*'s party, the devastating effect of AIDS on Cooper's group of friends and on the wider culture of New York is immediately clear. Of the many prominent cultural figures who came to the Limelight to celebrate Cooper's achievement in 1984, were it not for AIDS how many would have been there in 2000 to mark the high point of his thirty-five-year career? Carl Apfelschnitt, John Bernd, Keith Haring, James Merrill, Larry Stanton—how many of these men lost to AIDS might have read alongside Moore and Malkmus? Would Christopher Cox, Stan Leventhal, or Howard Brookner have taken part in the 2000 event? Taking to the stage from where they sat on either side of their old friend, would Tim Dlugos and Donald Britton have shared an anecdote or two about the young Cooper and his time in New York, before, perhaps, opening their copies of *Period* and reading excerpts for the assembled audience?

> Well, I'm living in two worlds. I'm here like this, and I'm somewhere else, too. In there. A place really different from here. I'm pretty sure one of them only exists in my mind, but I can't tell which one anymore. Because they're both foreign now.
>
> Look, you really shouldn't do drugs.
>
> No, it's not like that. I knew you were going to say that. I can make it come and go. I could open the other dimension right now if I wanted. Or I could stay here with you. I'm kind of like a god.
>
> Go on, then. Here, I'll hold your hand if you're worried. I want to see something.[62]

The Subject and the System

Gay pornography, pedophilia, serial murder, underage sex, drugs, death, heavy metal: given the Cycle's range of themes, it's not surprising that it attracted a lot of press as it appeared. Most influentially, Michael Silverblatt would term the kind of literature represented by Cooper's Cycle "transgressive writing"; it was the "new new thing," he claimed, which in the '90s was delighting young readers and writers (especially those with "very modern hair" and "piercings and/or tattoos").[63] A regular of Beyond Baroque during Cooper's time there and current host of KCRW's popular radio show *Bookworm*, Silverblatt distinguished transgressive writing from minimalist and postmodernist literature, connecting it instead with a contemporary appetite for cultures of sadomasochism and shocking body art. "Exploring the sexual frontiers implicit in Mapplethorpe's photographs or Karen Finley's performances, transgressive writing has violation at its core," Silverblatt wrote, "violation of norms, of humanistic enterprise, of the body. Really, it's the Marquis de Sade who officiates at the American orgy."[64]

Silverblatt's rather simplistic label turned out to have quite an impact at the time. Many started to think about transgressive writing as something like a genre or a movement—albeit a rather ill-defined one that came to include writers as diverse as Cooper, Acker, Ellis, Mary Gaitskill, and later Chuck Palahniuk—and it found plenty of support among critics and readers in the United States and abroad. In the style section of the *New York Times*, of all places, transgressive writing was hailed as a hip new thing for young readers (presumably these hypothetical readers also had very modern hair). Alongside a piece welcoming the arrival of the Bi-Bop wireless telephone, Rene Chun's article of April 23, 1995 declared that "Stephen King and Tom Clancy may not be losing sleep over book sales that can be charted with four figures, but the transgressive market is clearly growing."[65] Cooper was naturally skeptical of the term, and he's quoted by Chun as saying, "I understand all the marketing things that are happening, and it makes me nervous. If there isn't a transgressive Harlequin romance novel out yet, there will be soon."[66]

Not all critics were happy about the arrival of transgressive writing. In the *National Review*, James Gardner trashed books like Cooper's *Try* for their assault on decency and the status quo. Taking aim at Cooper, Ellis, and A. M. Homes, he wrote, "One senses that their gaze is always steadily fixed on the reader, as though asking, 'Are you revolted yet? Are you shocked?' If this work were marketed as pornography, the term being used not in reproach but simply for the purposes of description, we should be forced to acknowledge its usefulness to those whose fantasy life comprises the sodomizing of children, necrophilia, and coprophilia."[67] But if transgressive writing's subjects were unfit for publication, its suggestions of moral relativism were even more obscene to Gardner who, writing in William F. Buckley's conservative rag, could be counted on to defend the *true* and the *good* against this "literature of self-defined immorality, anguish, and degradation."[68]

With an established tradition of alternative culture, Britain seemed to welcome the influx of transgressive writing pouring in from the United States via Serpent's Tail, Pete Ayrton's independent press and Cooper's UK publisher. Roger Clarke claimed in the *Observer* that reading Cooper's novels was "like having ECT treatment when you're well. He nauseates and enthralls." Cooper was the real deal, Clarke wrote, "a genuine *enfant terrible*, that makes you wonder how you took those other *enfants terribles*—Tim Willock, say, or Will Self—so seriously."[69] The High Risk imprint of Serpent's Tail, set up by Ira Silverberg and Amy Scholder in 1993 and run from New York, turned many British readers on to transgressive writing from the States, publishing Acker, Robert Glück, Gary Indiana, Tillman, and others before it closed in 1997. In his column in the *Independent* in March 1996, John Walsh lauded Serpent's Tail—then at the height of its popularity—saying its list of writers "has always been ultra-modern, international, avant-garde and tough as nails, especially writers promoted under the 'High Risk' label."[70]

In 1992 Serpent's Tail published Elizabeth Young and Graham Caveney's *Shopping in Space: Essays on American "Blank Generation" Fiction*, a collection of critical articles on Cooper and his contemporaries. Written by two British critics for a British audience they felt was underserved in terms of smart criticism of contemporary American writing, the book primarily focused on New York–based authors, including Indiana, Jay McInerney, Tillman, and Wojnarowicz. For many of these, it was the first time they had been written about in a sustained, scholarly way (although the authors didn't consider themselves academics and held that "no one should feel excluded from a passionate engagement with modern fiction; it does not belong to academia").[71] This was the case with Young's essay on Cooper, which could be read as a kind of blueprint for much of the criticism of his work that would follow.

Her essay, "Death in Disneyland: The Work of Dennis Cooper," situates the concerns of Cooper's fiction squarely within a context marked by psychoanalytically oriented studies of sexuality and a tradition of French theory. Drawing heavily on Lacan, for instance, she argues that an extended sequence where George visits his dying mother in hospital corresponds to a developmental stage in Lacanian psychoanalysis. With the death of his mother, Young says, "George now enters human culture and society, that is the Symbolic Order that is dominated by the Law of the Father," and "in a textbook case of Oedipal crisis, George has at last grown up and entered the signifying circles, the marriage of Heaven and Hell that comprises language and desire."[72]

Psychoanalysis also underpins Earl Jackson Jr.'s assessment of *Closer* from 1993, and his critique bears the influence of Julia Kristeva's *Powers of Horror* (1982) and her theories of abjection. Of George's probing, scatological sex with the older Frenchman Philippe and George's almost-homicide at the hands of the shadowy Tom, Jackson writes, "Philippe and Tom sought the secret of George through literal invasions and excavations of George's body. George (like the other boys) confused his inner self with his 'innards,' in a detour of abjection, which according to Kristeva is an attempt to individuate the self by demarcating the divisions of inside and outside."[73] A testament to the influence of critical theory, Jackson, like Young, also draws many of his insights from French writers like Maurice Blanchot and Guy Debord.

THIS LENS OF psychoanalysis and poststructuralist theory was employed in many subsequent assessments of the George Miles novels. Such notable critics as Hal Foster, Gregory Bredbeck, and Michele Aaron conjoined Cooper's work with interpretive frameworks borrowed from the likes of Lacan, Barthes, Derrida, and Paul Virilio.[74] Somewhat apart from this pattern of criticism, however, lies the work of Marvin Taylor, who acquired Cooper's archive while he was the director of the Fales Library; though influenced by poststructuralism, Taylor's critical readings of Cooper display an attentiveness to the *form* of the George Miles Cycle that is missing from almost all other appraisals. His is the only critical perspective that tries to combine theory with a detailed examination of the Cycle's meticulous construction, the structure of which he has called "geometric."[75] In his essay on *Closer*, for instance, Taylor's exploration of Cooper's unsuccessful attempt to "represent the unrepresentable, those things that lie outside of the systems of signification" derives in large part from a detailed exposition of *Closer*'s range of formal systems.[76] Surveying the text's bipartite schema that, he argues, are embodied by the characters of John, David, George, Cliff, Alex, Philippe, and Steve, Taylor writes:

> Each chapter employs a different symbolic system reflecting the
> titular character's attempts to explain the world around him. Each
> world is structured around a dyadic relationship: John: art/life; David:

imagination/reality; George: words/his body; Cliff: pornography/ experience; Alex: film/life; Philippe: beauty/death; and finally Steve: words/love. In each system there is an attempt to make sense out of experience, especially the experience of male-male desire, and to give meaning to life. That each system fails and leads to fragmentation is symptomatic of the text.[77]

Taylor's presentation at the opening of "Closer: The Dennis Cooper Papers," an exhibition of material from Cooper's archive that took place in Amsterdam in 2012, gave another fascinating overview of the numerous structures and systems at work in the George Miles Cycle "at both the macro and the micro levels."[78] "For several years I had been analyzing the geometric structures that underlie each of the novels and the entire structure of the cycle itself," he said; taking the text of *Guide* as one example, he suggested that the structure of that text is star-shaped.[79] This form is replicated in the text by the recurrence of a star-shaped sigil—a magical sign imbued with a supernatural power by its creator whose purpose must remain a secret.

> Cooper played his hand on purpose by titling one of the chapters "Star-shaped" and by having the starlike body on the cover. . . . The structure is a six-pointed star with a character associated specifically with each point. Each of the male/male relationships in the novel also constitutes a part of the structure. Dennis/Luke, Mason/Drew, Chris/ the dwarf represent differing modes of attraction. Dennis and Luke are platonic lovers. Luke is also the maker of sigils. At one point he paces out a six-pointed star in the living room of the house he and Dennis share.[80]

Taylor's talk also covered the form of *Frisk*, which corresponds to an infinity symbol, and *Period*, which consists of four concentric circles "set around a central moment when everything in the novel goes retrograde."[81]

While Taylor's work differs greatly from other criticism, Cooper's own comments seem to endorse his ideas about the various recurring, quasi-geometric forms of the George Miles Cycle. In interviews and commentaries, Cooper has been keen to foreground the Cycle's structure and explain its detailed architecture. In a 2011 interview he is explicit about the systems that structure the project and the patterns and diagrams used to plan each novel:

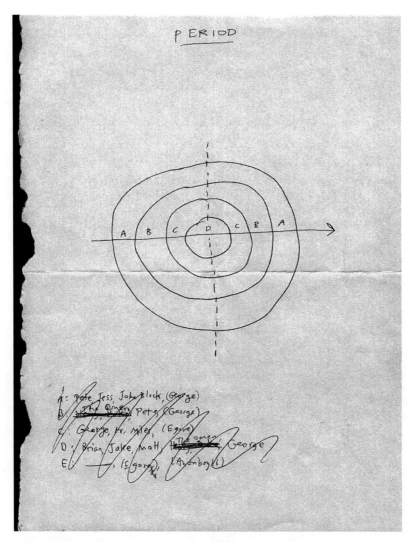

Period diagram (undated). Used by permission of Dennis Cooper. Source: Dennis Cooper papers, Accretion 2002, box 20, folder 30, Fales Library and Special Collections, New York University Libraries.

I made two dozen or so graphs and equations and formulas. The most
general one shows an overall formal structure, and each of the five
novels has the same structure as the cycle itself. *Closer* and *Period*,
which are the first and last books, have a strong correspondence
to each other, as do *Frisk* and *Guide*, the second and fourth novels.
The middle novel, *Try*, is built in such a way as to unify the group by
whatever means necessary, but it doesn't have a strict formal relationship to the others, and it functions as a kind of oasis. Each of the five
novels shares or replicates the cycle's physique, with the chapters or
sections within the novels strictly corresponding. Structurally, each
of the novels and the cycle itself are identical. That's the skeleton. . . .
Those systems, and a lot of other, more intricate schematics, were
already in place before I wrote the cycle, and my goal was to work
within those rules and to enliven, disguise, or reveal the blueprint
using the novels' content.[82]

This description is accompanied by a diagram that charts the complex
architecture of the Cycle and illustrates the interaction between the different systems or structures that dictated the rules within which Cooper
chose to write.

In spite of their emphasis on the structure of the Cycle and their careful explanation of its systems and forms, neither Cooper nor Taylor suggests *why* such a structure is employed. Where does this adherence to
elaborate structures and strictly defined patterns and rules come from? In
Cooper's and Taylor's foregrounding of structure, they also fail to address
an apparent contradiction between Cooper's anarchism and the rigorous
systematicity and control employed by him at the level of chapter, novel,
and cycle. Put it this way: If we take a basic definition of anarchism to be
a resistance to coercive methods of control, how can an anarchist like
Cooper conduct his texts through such strict, plainly coercive structures?
How could he apply them so obsessively, pouring his protagonists' slacker
talk into these rigid forms?

One resolution to this apparent paradox might be to think about Cooper's works as microcosmic representations or reflections of the world
from an anarchist perspective. By setting his wayward characters against
rigorous structures, Cooper dramatizes the predicament of modern society. Quite simply, the Cycle depicts an ongoing struggle between the

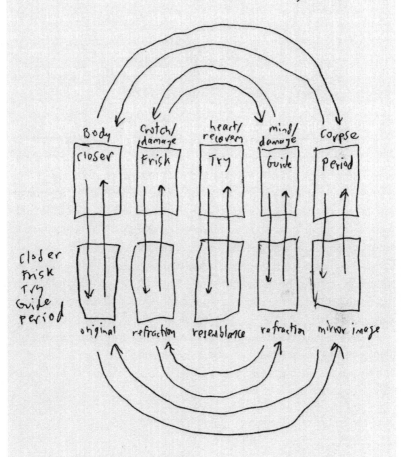

George Miles Cycle diagram. Used by permission of Dennis Cooper. Source: *Paris Review* 198 (Fall 2011).

subject and the system. This is implied throughout the series but is made particularly obvious when characters themselves sense that their actions are observed, constrained, or somehow manipulated by forces beyond their control. In the opening lines of *Closer*'s second section, "David: Inside Out," the titular character confesses, "I have the feeling that someone is watching me."

> I use the term loosely because I have few feelings, and even they're too simple, like primary colors. Fear is the basic one lately, no thanks to my nemesis (it could be male, female, imaginary, ghost—I'm not big on subtleties) poring over my every move, whether I watch TV, eat breakfast, ride a bike, sleep, shower, go to school . . .[83]

Its title a thinly veiled reference to the 1980 Diana Ross pop single "Upside Down," whose lyrics famously run, "Upside down / boy, you turn me / inside out / and round and round," David's section turns Ross's lines macabre, insisting upon the presence of a shadowy but intrusive force hell-bent on controlling him: "It's hard to describe the sensation. Maybe rape or demonic possession come close."[84] Later, in a sequence that could be taken from Wes Craven's *Nightmare on Elm Street* (1984), this invisible menace seems to seep into David's daydreams, embodied by an older man who turns David's body grotesquely inside out: "Before I can step back he's slashed at my face. Blood splatters onto his shirt. He carves, and uses his fingers to pull back the loose skin, until my whole skull is exposed to the air, and flesh hangs in waves around my neck like a Shakespearean collar."[85]

Period's teenagers also suffer the intrusion upon their world of a malevolent and manipulating force. Nate and Leon make the mistake of invoking it in a rudimentary Satanic ritual using a dead cat and a cassette tape of a goth band.

- Fuck, that's him. Look at that. It's like a smudge. On the cat.
- Oh, shit.
- What?
- I think he's screwing me. Ow.
- Relax, let him. It's his thing, man. Uh. . . . Welcome Master of Darkness. We want to ask you for something. We want you to give Leon that deaf boy. What's his name?
- Dagger. Ow, ow.

- We want Dagger to be Leon's sex slave, so he can do what he wants. Can you do that for us?
- Ow, ow.[86]

Their wish is later granted when Dagger is suddenly possessed: "He writes down that he's scared, then, boom, he starts looking real weird, and you can see Satan's taking him over, then, sure enough, he writes down that he'd really, really like to suck dick, with about ten exclamation marks."[87] The lack of autonomy in his sexual partner is not a turn-on, however, and Leon laments that while they fuck, "I start thinking, Why am I doing this? Not like, This is dumb. More like, This boy deserves better. Or I deserve better, or both of us do."[88] Haunting the rest of the work, the unseen power they unleash makes its presence felt not just in the actions of the characters but also, it would seem, in the novel's weird refractions of time, space, and characterization.

In these examples, Cooper draws the reader's attention to the struggle between his adolescent protagonists, imbued with a semblance of autonomy, and each novel's system, to which they are obliged to relinquish their control. We see elsewhere in the Cycle that these systems are implicitly considered in parallel with larger social systems and that the demands Cooper's fictional structures make upon his characters mirror social demands. To take one example, *Try*'s Ziggy thinks about what might be called heteronormativity—presumptive heterosexuality—in terms like those used by David and Leon to describe the invisible menace that stalks them.

> With Nicole, make that with every girl so far, sex ends up being so . . . planned in advance, not by him obviously, but by history or whatever. So no matter how wild sex gets, he's still following this preset, like, outline, point by point, and when an experience is over, such as now with Nicole, it sort of gradually dilutes into a zillion other people's identical experiences, until Ziggy feels . . . used in a way? Or maybe it's just his rebelliousness problem. Still, gay sex seems to have this great scariness quotient, whereby no two situations are ever alike, as far as he can tell.[89]

Ziggy's reflections on the difference between straight sex (prescribed, normative, "planned in advance") and gay sex (aberrant, singular, "scary") echo theorist Gayle Rubin's discussion of heteronormativity in her influential 1984 essay, "Thinking Sex: Notes for a Radical Theory of the Politics of Sexuality." According to Rubin, unproductive (that is, unreproductive) sex acts, including gay sex, masturbation, sadomasochism, and so on, were historically considered threats to the social order whose hierarchy was founded on a reproductive ideology. As a result, in Western societies such acts were excluded from the interior of what Rubin calls the "charmed circle" of sexuality, and the boundary that separated normative sex (inside) from nonnormative sex (outside) was constantly, anxiously policed. Rubin accompanies this Foucauldian analysis with a diagram plotting the "charmed circle" that divides normal (or, in Ziggy's words, "preset") sex from abnormal ("scary") sex, which, coming full circle, is itself reminiscent of the diagram for *Period*. Cooper is obviously not the only one thinking about the social order in geometric terms.

An important part of Rubin's study is her attempt to critique the submerged beliefs that underpin sexuality's "charmed circle"—assumptions that, she says, "are so pervasive in Western culture that they are rarely questioned."[90] Sexual essentialism, for instance, "the idea that sex is a natural force that exists prior to social life and shapes institutions," is an "embedded" belief system that seems so normal and is apparently so obvious it is, to all intents and purposes, invisible: it is as if "sexuality has no history and no significant social determinants."[91] The systems and forms that structure Cooper's Cycle are as subtle as these normative systems of thought: although Cooper carefully details and diagrams the form of the Cycle in his paratextual comments, his characters seem to feel its presence less explicitly. They sense only that their behavior is being observed or manipulated by invisible powers, which occasionally manifest as demons or Freddy Krueger-ish figures in dark rituals or dreams.

By representing the struggle between individuals and the invisible systems they circulate in, Cooper's Cycle can be read productively alongside Rubin's work. She traces the development of normative systems of thought and questions the unquestioned; he, in a less determinate way, also makes systems of control palpable by portraying their effects on his characters. Of course, his purpose is more diffuse than hers and not primarily sexual: for Cooper, constraints placed on sexual liberty are symptomatic of deeper, more pervasive regimes of control. As an anarchist, he doesn't just want to show us that heteronormative thinking is problematic; he wants to show us that a society that produces heteronormative thinking, that is predisposed to generating groupthink, that interferes with how all individuals conduct their lives—a society like that is *itself* the problem. In this way, the George Miles Cycle acts as a kind of diorama where we see free individuals competing with the influence of various invisible systems that stand for wider social constraints. Reflected and elucidated in what Cooper elsewhere calls the Cycle's "dual qualities of excessive form and improvisational looseness," this is "the central contradiction in the work."[92]

THIS CYCLE-AS-DIORAMA represents an elegant critique of modern society from an anarchist standpoint, but Cooper's interest in devising premade forms for his fiction arguably extends much further than their capacity to evoke the effects of social control. Zooming out a little, it's possible to see that their employment also indicates a more profound engagement with anarchist thought at the level of the work's *composition*. Speaking with Robert Glück in 2006 about *Safe* and the limitations of writing, Cooper commented:

> I wanted the work to be about the cruel, self-defeating nature of aestheticism itself and how art could only short-circuit in relationship to experiences that were too deep or frightening or complex to be represented by language. I felt, and still feel, that when language tries to encompass those kinds of experiences, it becomes overly infected with the consciousness of the artist who tries to represent them and, as a result, it flatters the artist and lies to the audience.[93]

Previously we saw that Cooper's poetry describes a life of anguished isolation: although he takes Sade's belief in subjective solitude and nonrelationality as his own, he desperately tries to resist it, "reaching for" some kind of intersubjective communion. His efforts are in vain, however, and *Idols* underscores the sad fact that to encounter another is merely to sense more of oneself, as all experience is refracted through consciousness. His remarks to Glück frame *Safe* as the obverse of this. Not only does consciousness inflect the artist's experience of another, all attempts at objectivity by the artist are "infected" by consciousness. The representation of experience in language and consequently in writing is for him necessarily subjective, misleading, and coercive.

John, one of *Closer*'s disillusioned teens, repeats Cooper's statements about *Safe* almost verbatim. When asked by a teacher to speak to his classmates about his art (vaguely described in the book as quasi-realistic portraits that look like police sketches), John writes, "What you seem to like in my drawings is how they reveal the dark underside, or whatever it's called, of people you wouldn't think were particularly screwed up. But you should know the real goal of my work is a Dorian Gray type of thing. I make you look awful, and I start to look really good."[94] In other words, art is a kind of trick that appears to reveal weighty truths that are in fact artistically contrived, brewed in the consciousness of the artist himself. This idea is echoed throughout Cooper's work, which constantly struggles with the inescapably subjective nature of experience.

But these kinds of ideas raise some serious problems for the anarchist writer. If the communication of experience in literature lies to its readers, how can that be reconciled with a political and social philosophy like anarchism that in its many iterations renounces subtle coercion like this? Furthermore, can an artistic representation ever be anarchistic that wheedles and cajoles its audience into affirming the subjective vision of an artist over their own, when anarchism takes as its basic premise the autonomy of the individual—and, in this case, *reading*—subject?

In general, anarchist writers haven't raised these questions, nor have they sought to problematize the coercive effect of literature to any great degree. In the preface to her collected essays, Emma Goldman, for instance, praises the power of the written word and champions written over verbal communication. "My great faith in the wonder worker, the spoken word, is no more," she says. "The speaker, though ever so eloquent, cannot escape the restlessness of the crowd, with the inevitable result that he will fail to strike root."[95] Conversely, "the relation between the writer and the reader is more intimate": the experience of reading creates a one-to-one bond, the better to persuade the reader of the writer's position and allow the writer's thoughts to "strike root" in the reader's mind.[96]

Goldman doesn't address the inherent contradictions her comments raise from the standpoint of anarchism's resistance to authority as that

which corrupts the mind and controls the behavior of the otherwise autonomous individual. Cooper's comments, on the other hand, demonstrate far more sensitivity to the problem writing poses for the committed anarchist. He is keenly aware that the writer–reader relationship is
dogged by hierarchical associations and—given anarchism's suspicion of
the corrupting influence of authority—what he calls the "infection" of
authorial consciousness may even make the idea of an anarchist literature
hypocritical.

Following the logic of this formulation, however, it may be argued conversely that if writers' subjective interference were minimized and the
coercive effect of their expression somehow curbed, then literature might
be better aligned with anarchist ideas. If authorial intention could be sub-
tracted—the coercive effect curbed—then perhaps a literature could become more appropriately anarchistic. Within this context it's possible to
reflect on Cooper's use of concentric circles, six-pointed stars, and other
elaborate structures and systems. These arbitrary forms are part of the
author's attempt to efface a part of his subjectivity from the project by
handing over its composition to a formal procedure. This might seem like
an unusual idea, but it's been done before; John Cage's and Jackson Mac
Low's procedural poetry in particular blends compositional constraint
with anarchist thinking in ways that foreshadow Cooper's work.

Cage's Dada-inspired derivative poetics and his application of "chance
operations" to works such as James Joyce's *Finnegans Wake* or Emma
Goldman's autobiography are underpinned by Cage's anarchist beliefs.[97]
Scanning source texts and selecting words or phrases beginning with
the letters of the title or a name, Cage produced mesostics, or writings
through the middle, freeing canonical works from their old syntactical
arrangements and dissolving the voice of the artist into the operation of
nonintentionality. "The political correlative to Cage's aesthetic practices
is anarchy," N. Katherine Hayles claims. "He believes that anarchy, like
linguistic strategies that overwhelm intentionality without annihilating
it, can dissolve the coercive bonds of social regulation while still fostering
individual responsibility."[98] Andy Weaver agrees with Hayles, pointing
out that these poetic procedures "worked against the commonly held notion of the individual genius, the writing subject who brings forth great
texts through his or her own solitary, unique brilliance. Instead, [he]

created texts that show the importance of anarchic communities, texts that show the importance of non-hierarchical giving to and taking from others in a radically free exchange of ideas."[99]

Jackson Mac Low's procedural poems in *Stanzas for Iris Lezak* (1971) take a similar tack, and the work is made up of a number of "diastic reading-through nonintentional text-selection procedures" (or simply, diastics)—one example of Mac Low's many attempts "to develop artistic forms that advance and encourage freedom."[100] A sometime student of Cage at the New School for Social Research, Mac Low improvised on his teacher's methods by selecting words from a source text and arranging them on the page using a series of constraints determined in advance. These kinds of procedures impose an algorithm onto how a poem is made and produce a kind of machine writing (indeed, like Cage, Mac Low used computer programs to automatically select his texts in the 1980s). As Brian McHale points out, this represents Mac Low's endeavor to create a non-egoic poetry by withdrawing subjectivity from the work: "At the extreme of self-effacement occur practices like Mac Low's, in which all local decisions are left to the operation of the machine."[101]

What's remarkable in the work of both of these anarchist artists, then, is a commitment to diminishing subjective interference by transferring the responsibility for how a piece of writing is made to an arbitrarily selected procedure or algorithm. Their process anticipates Cooper's project, which finds its own procedural constraints in the systems and geometric structures that undergird the George Miles Cycle.

But Cooper's procedural prose also differs from Cage's and Mac Low's work in crucial ways. Although elaborate structures function as constraints in his writing (determining, for example, the placement and activity of characters, chapters, and novels in the series), Cooper does not appear to believe, as Cage and Mac Low do, in the *salvation* of these constraints, even going so far as to state rather emphatically that "all structures created to impose order of any kind are inherently corrupt" (2006)[102]—that is, their forms are never perfect and their effect will always be somewhat unpredictable. Cooper therefore seems to be attentive to the conspicuous tension haunting an anarchist art that would defer responsibility to an artificial form and attempt to subdue the individual voice. He exploits this tension to produce his work's distinctive combination of stasis and motility, blankness and vehemence, but, as a careful reading of *Frisk* shows, for better or worse he ultimately affirms the sovereignty of the subject.

MARVIN TAYLOR SAYS that *Frisk*'s corresponding form is an infinity symbol, examples of which stand at the beginning and end of the novel as titles for the opening and closing chapters. These chapters mirror one another, each composed of five paragraphs of similar length that describe five photos of an adolescent boy, naked, recumbent as if dead, a rope tied around his neck. Small details differ between the two chapters, however, indicating their relationship to one another is more refraction than reflection. In one, the subject's eyes "could be parts of a doll," while in another they are "alert, antsy"; in the first, "his ass sports a squarish blotch, resembling ones that hide hard-core sexual acts, but more sloppily drawn," while in the last, "his asscrack is covered with something that vaguely resembles a wound when you squint."[103]

Although uncannily similar in their staging, these are evidently not the same photographs, and, more importantly, they are not described in the same way. The figurative passages that open the work—oblique, imaginative, thick with detail that segues into simile—are in the end demystified and resigned to a plain, unadorned account of the scene. It is as if the opening lines travel through the cleansing fire of the work and endure its ordeals only to emerge again slighter, older, more distant, disenchanted.

While Taylor describes the form that underlies *Frisk* as an infinity symbol, it might be more accurate to describe the structure as that of a Möbius strip: despite the illusion of alterity, *Frisk*'s narrative traverses just one surface and, though looping, the path Cooper has his protagonist tread does not deviate. Hemmed in both by the strip's form and the other systems that dictate the work's thematic concerns (i.e., the libidinal imperative), Dennis is made to depart from these photographs and at length returns, the Escherian epic antihero, to find them a little unfamiliar and himself much changed. In structuring *Frisk* this way, the range of authorial decisions available to Cooper is much reduced, as his choices must produce the textual arrangement demanded of the strip. Like Cage's procedural poetics, the Möbius strip imposes a structure that introduces subjective constraint by limiting the author's actions. But unlike Cage, Cooper is not resolved to excising the subject from his work; putting the lie to its procedural limitations, *Frisk* turns out to be a work that is in fact determinedly subjective.

In the novel Cooper traces a linear developmental narrative, told in the first person by the narrator, Dennis, a writer who includes sections of his novel-in-progress in his ostensible memoir. At least in its opening chapters, the work carefully differentiates between its autobiographical and fictional parts by insisting on the truthfulness of Dennis's autobiography. The section "Tense, 1969–1986," presents the reader with a clear chronology of Dennis's life ("When I was thirteen...," "When I was seventeen...," "When I was eighteen...," etc.), which plots a credible and conservatively plotted story of his psychological development.[104] As a traumatic consequence of seeing some pornographic photos at the age of thirteen, the reader is told that Dennis's psychosexual growth was fundamentally altered, prompting a lifelong quest for the satisfaction of a (sometimes violent) desire to explore his sexual partners. He later says,

> Maybe... if I hadn't seen this... snuff. Photographs. Back when I was a kid. I thought the boy in them was actually dead for years, and by the time I found out they were posed photographs, it was too late. I already wanted to live in a world where some boy I didn't personally know could be killed and his corpse made available to the public, or to me anyway. I felt so... enlightened?[105]

In these passages Dennis confides in the reader; recounted in an informal register, his testimony appears all the more truthful for its minor lapses and failures. Dennis tells us that when he was twenty-eight he paid a hustler named Finn to spend the night with him but confesses that he cannot recall how much he paid or how Finn's voice may have sounded: "He named his price (I forget)... I'm trying to remember his voice. I just can't."[106] Dennis may be an unreliable narrator, but in the imperfection of his account he nonetheless comes across as sympathetic and sincere.

Elsewhere the text distinguishes these autobiographical sequences from its fictional ones by clearly introducing them as such: Dennis states that he spent several months working on "an artsy murder-mystery novel, some salvageable fragments of which are interspersed through the following section."[107] The next section then maintains this distinction by dividing the "artsy murder-mystery" taking place on the ground from the journal entries Dennis scribbles in a plane en route to New York.

Having firmly distinguished Dennis's disarmingly honest memoir from his fictional interludes, the next chapter then unveils a harrowing and nightmarish tale of rape, murder, and mutilation in Amsterdam in the form of a letter written by Dennis to his childhood friend Julian. Assisted by a couple of amoral German henchmen, Dennis has finally realized his desire for death and destruction by indiscriminately fucking, killing, and dismembering helpless adolescent boys. In their death, we are told, he has found "this major transcendence or answer."[108] "I feel strong, powerful, clear all the time. Nothing bothers me anymore. I'm telling you Julian, this is some kind of ultimate truth."[109]

Yet as the story winds up, truth is revealed as a ruse. Julian and his brother Kevin visit Dennis in Amsterdam and find no bodies. The room on the third floor of the windmill that was supposedly filled with rotting corpses doesn't even exist: "'I knew it,' Kevin said, gazing up. 'Rooms like that exist only in books.'"[110] With this revelation the entire edifice of autobiographical truth constructed and meticulously maintained in the preceding pages all at once fractures and crumbles, and the entirety of the work is shown to be "infected by the consciousness of the artist." In this way *Frisk* returns us to familiar territory, where we find subjective solitude triumphant and Cooper's work once again caught in a recursive feedback loop that admits no other. Here, once more, there is only subjective representation: no outside the narrator's subjectivity; no truth. It all forms the one fictional fabric or what, following Paul Hegarty, might be termed a textual epidermis, replete with alluring hollows, folds, and apparent depths but all constituting the same surface: "Cooper's fictions seem to offer surface only, however convoluted and twisted that surface, but it is vital to recognize that depth is always in play, even though there is no depth that does not come to be shown as only surface."[111]

Frisk's bathetic conclusion extends Cooper's theme of subjective isolation, but in doing so it effectively contradicts the procedures designed to limit individual expression. The Möbius strip even comes to reinforce the solitude of the subject: the text's premise, that subjectivity is proscribed and ineluctable, is amplified by its unfolding across a single, enclosed surface. Not only does the system fail, therefore, but it also comes to serve the subjectivity it was designed to master. There is a familiar sense of tragedy to this state of subjective isolation, especially when we find that in the case of *Frisk* it is we, the reader, whom the narrator is now "reaching for"; we whom he confides in; we whom he wishes to experience an inter-subjective encounter with.

A kind of political optimism can nonetheless be drawn from the text. Hypothetically, if the writer of *Frisk*, like the characters in his Cycle, is limited by certain procedures and finds his actions determined by pre-made structures that separate him from what he can do, the failure of these procedures demonstrates the resources of the individual and the individual's capacity to overcome constraints. "I'm a super optimist and idealist," Cooper says. "If you're an anarchist, you have to believe that people are essentially good and the corruptions and distortions all come from power structures and things that overly organize people" (2014).[112] In the George Miles Cycle, systems and overbearing structures vie with the free individual, corrupting and distorting the behavior of author and protagonist alike. In the end, however, systems are turned inside out, corrupted, repurposed, made to short-circuit; in the end, the individual overcomes.

JT LeRoy and *My Loose Thread* |
"I Had No Other Choice"

9 ONE WAY TO PLOT the progress of Dennis Cooper's life and work is by looking at the acknowledgments sections of his books. Inside the front cover are the names of a few people Cooper wishes to thank: lovers, allies, editors, agents—all friends he was close to while writing the book, whose appearance here indicates something of the personal and professional conditions under which the book was made. *The Tenderness of the Wolves*, for instance, attests to his total immersion in Beyond Baroque and his enthusiasm for the scene that he created with Amy Gerstler. In addition to dedicating the book to Gerstler, he extends his thanks to Tim Dlugos, Michael Silverblatt, and Jack Skelley—friends and supporters from the Beyond Baroque era. *Closer*'s list of thank-yous, on the other hand, is a portrait of a writer in transition, as Cooper gives credit to those who helped him in the past while nonetheless looking forward to the future of his career. He thanks his previous publisher, Felice Picano, in addition to his current Grove Press editor, Walt Bode; Christopher Cox, his agent who sent around the manuscript of *Closer*, is thanked along with Ira Silverberg, his agent from 1990 onward. Not only do these lists of names help to position each book in terms of Cooper's career trajectory, like the contents pages of *Little Caesar* magazine they also offer a glimpse of who was important to Cooper at the time.

An unusual name surfaces for the first time in the acknowledgments of *Guide*, showing up again to preface the text of *Period* before vanishing forever from Cooper's oeuvre: Terminator. The alias of a teen writer and sometime hustler who contacted Cooper in 1995 and was friends with him for seven or eight years after that, the appearance of Terminator in *Guide*'s acknowledgments marks the beginning of one of the strangest and most controversial episodes in Cooper's career. The encounter between Cooper and this young teenage fan set in motion a series of events that would see the latter gain a cult following among devotees of transgressive writing and eventually propel him to international superstardom as the transgressive novelist JT LeRoy. Before it was over, Cooper, his writer friends, and innumerable others who were similarly touched by the inspiring story of a poor, abused teen's triumphant survival would be involuntarily implicated in one of the most successful literary hoaxes in a generation.

It started in 1995, when Ira Silverberg received a phone call at his office from a fifteen-year-old calling himself the Terminator. He told Silverberg he was a huge admirer of Dennis Cooper's work and asked if he could be put in touch with his hero. Silverberg gave him Cooper's fax number, and before long the two were speaking with each other over the phone. Cooper remembers that "I got a phone call from this person. . . . He was saying how much he worshipped my work and all—and that he wrote. We had a long conversation and he was just a peculiar and interesting kid. He ended up calling me all the time, almost every day."[1] As Terminator revealed his tragic backstory to Cooper with breathless monologues in a high-pitched Southern drawl, it seemed like he had walked off the pages of one of Cooper's novels. Indeed, Terminator admitted that when he read *Try*—given to him, he said, by one of his more benevolent tricks—it was a revelation. He identified so closely with the abused and emotionally dependent protagonist that for a while he called himself Ziggy.

Terminator liked pseudonyms. His given name, he said, was Jeremiah. Born in West Virginia to a teenage mother from a Christian family, he was soon given up for adoption. After a few years in the care of a loving foster family, for some unfathomable reason he was returned to the custody of his birth mother, Sarah, a mean drunk and a meth addict who had been abused by her evangelical father as a child. Abuse runs in families, they say, and Jeremy was thus subjected to years of emotional, physical, and sexual violence at the hands of Sarah, her parents, her many boyfriends, and sundry other pedophiles who, Jeremy told Cooper, variously fucked him till he hemorrhaged, burned his little boy penis with a cigarette lighter, bathed him in bleach, or mutilated his genitals.

As a result of this torture and neglect, Jeremy was an extremely disturbed young man who often seemed to experience psychotic breaks in the middle of his phone conversations with Cooper—speaking in different voices, for instance, or declaring his intention to commit suicide. These episodes only subsided when Cooper heaped comfort and consolation on him, spending hours on the phone trying to calm him down. At one point Jeremy revealed that after years of unprotected sex with innumerable men, he had contracted AIDS and wasn't expected to live long. Many of Cooper's friends had tested positive for HIV in the '80s and '90s and had passed away soon afterward, so this was devastating news for him. That a mere teenager should have to experience the ravages of AIDS was beyond heartbreaking.

Jeremy had first called Cooper from San Francisco. Homeless, turning tricks in the Tenderloin district, and addicted to drugs, in 1993 he contacted a child psychiatrist at St. Mary's Medical Center in San Francisco, who counseled him over the phone and encouraged him to write about his experiences as a form of therapy. Jeremy had always composed stories in his head and said that writing had become a lifeline for him; he asked Cooper to look at some of his stories and Cooper agreed. What he read impressed him: for a fifteen-year-old without a high school education, Jeremy could really write. Which is not to say that the work was flawless, but as Cooper would later recall, "The fact that his books had serious weaknesses—rampant sentimentality, clichéd characters and storylines, uneven writing, etc.—was forgiven due to 'his' youth, the fact that 'he' supposedly had never attended school in 'his' life, 'his' emotional problems, 'his' precarious health, and so on" (2005).[2] Cooper readily admits that his personality tends toward caregiving, that he's "someone who tries to help people, kind of a big brother figure," so he and Jeremy quickly became close (2001).[3] Speaking with Marjorie Sturm, director of *The Cult of JT LeRoy* (2015), he said, "If this person just calls up and they're completely like the kind of characters in your books that, you know. . . . You're *interested* in this kind of person and you have a caretaker side like I do, and this person lays one thing after another, like: 'I'm going to kill myself,' 'I have AIDS,' 'I'm dying,' it builds this intense relationship."[4] As evidenced by his friendship with Casey McKinney, Cooper was especially disposed to nurturing the talents of promising young writers (particularly those who were in need of emotional as well as creative support), so in addition to managing Jeremy's unpredictable moods, Cooper also encouraged him to develop his writing skills and sent him books he thought might help him.

One of these was *User: A Novel* (1994) by Cooper's friend Bruce Benderson, a writer and translator who was well known on the Downtown New York scene. Weaving together the lives of drug addicts, hustlers, and transgender sex workers, Benderson's "cosmology of Times Square" anatomizes the city's rampant sensuality and the derangement of the senses that could be acquired there.[5] Most importantly, *User* conveyed an impression of America's underclass from the inside; the novel expressed what Benderson, in his literary manifesto "Toward the New Degenerate Narrative," called his "extreme and perverse point of view" that the "total deprivation" of the American underclass and the immediacy of underclass lives, their appetites and aggressions, were literature's "last fresh 'material.'"[6] Given that Jeremy's writing was similarly set among those who lived in the shadow of the American dream (albeit in West Virginia rather than New York), Cooper figured that Jeremy would connect with Benderson's vision; under its influence Jeremy might try to improve his own work and become the hard-edged, avant-garde author his writing foretold.

Once he'd read the book, Jeremy called up Benderson, as he had previously called up Cooper, raving about how much he loved his work and *User* in particular. Benderson remembers:

> Terminator refused to tell me his birth name, his living situation or anything about his family, only that he was calling from San Francisco ("I got a friend at the phone company who got me a few months of free calls"). He didn't hang up until he was convinced that I wouldn't mind his calling again soon. In the meantime, his first call stayed with me. The voice had been alternately timid and insinuating, breathily distracted and pushy. I hung up intrigued, but found myself anxiously half-hoping that he wouldn't call again.[7]

Jeremy did call again, however, multiple times, and once he had established a rapport with Benderson, he asked if he could share some stories with him. Benderson agreed, and when he read them his reaction was similar to Cooper's: here was a rare young literary talent. In his long, frequent phone calls with Benderson, Jeremy was just as emotionally needy and volatile as he was with Cooper, and they developed a similarly intense relationship. Benderson recalls that "our conversations became more and more intimate on the level of friendship till finally I felt a kind of responsibility to look after him."[8]

With two well-known and highly regarded mentors like Cooper and Benderson behind him, willing to offer support and critique his work over the phone at all hours of the day and night (it would be years before either would meet him in person), Jeremy quickly became connected with a number of other key players in New York's literary set. Cooper reintroduced him to Silverberg, who became his agent; Benderson introduced him to Catherine Texier and Joel Rose, the editors of *Between C & D*; through Rose he got to know Karen Rinaldi, an editor at Crown Publishing Group, who got him his first book deal. Later, with Benderson's help he started working at *New York Press*, and his phone interviews with people like Mary Gaitskill, Michelle Tea, Suzanne Vega, Coldplay, and many others allowed him to extend his network of contacts in the worlds of writing and music. His influence grew exponentially, and soon New York was abuzz with rumors of a teenage author of prodigious talent and scandalous origins poised on the cusp of literary celebrity.

The first piece Jeremy published (as Terminator) came as a result of Benderson's connections. Laurie Stone put together the anthology *Close to the Bone: Memoirs of Hurt, Rage, and Desire* for Grove Press in 1997 and included Jeremy's story "Baby Doll" on Benderson's recommendation. A short memoir about Jeremy's traumatic adolescence living with his mother and her boyfriend in the latter's cramped trailer, the story contains many elements that would become characteristic of the work later published under the name JT LeRoy.

Here Jeremy is a young boy routinely mistaken for a girl (sometimes he encourages this, sometimes he resists it), who is regularly humiliated and abused by his mother, an unhinged racist from whom he learns the art of seduction. A vague Christian religiosity saturates the narrative, which jumps around a lot but orbits three starkly cruel incidents: Jeremy's mother burns his penis with a car's cigarette lighter, his grandparents bathe him in bleach in order to save him from "Hellfire," and his mother's boyfriend rapes him. Each event is graphically portrayed in the text, livid with detail. After he's raped by his mother's boyfriend, he writes, "I wad up some toilet paper and wipe at the sore, throbbing wetness. I bring it back damp with blood and mucus-y stuff."⁹ As his mother sadistically burns his penis, he says, "I see the coils, red and glowing, disappear down to where her fingers hold my thing. I dig my hands, sweaty and cold, under my thighs. I watch the tip of my thing disappear into the lighter. I don't move, I don't scream, I don't cry. I've learned the hard way that lessons are repeated until learned properly, and silently, and Satan is, even temporarily, exorcised."¹⁰

The story is clearly designed to shock. Positioning itself between Silverblatt's idea of transgressive fiction and the emergent, bestselling genre of misery memoir (e.g., Frank McCourt's *Angela's Ashes* [1999]), it's as emotionally manipulative as its narrator and is characterized above all by an overwhelming negativity. There's no respite for Jeremy from the cruelty of adults (even social workers are complicit in his abuse), no escape from the violence he suffers, and, at least within the story itself, there's no redemption for any of the characters. But no reader of this piece—or indeed of any subsequent LeRoy pieces—would have been exclusively focused on the text. Each reader would have come to this story expecting it to illuminate or intersect somehow with the young author's biography, which reviewers and commentators seemed to find endlessly interesting. And herein lies the redemption offered by Jeremy's relentlessly oppressive and tragic stories: their very existence testifies to survival. In her introduction, Stone says, "Terminator writes from inside the battered child who ordinarily does not survive childhood"; Benderson notes that Jeremy's is "a life extraordinary for its gruesome deprivation and triumphant recovery."¹¹ The writer of "Baby Doll" thus masterfully implicated text and paratext in such a way that readers of this sensational work felt they were somehow witness to something great that superseded the mediocrity of the prose: the indomitable nature of the human spirit, the unflagging capacities of the human mind, the power of writing. . . . Shame it turned out to be garbage.

BY THE TIME Jeremy's debut novel *Sarah* came out in May 2000 (under the new pseudonym JT LeRoy), Cooper had started to put distance between himself and his protégé, who lately seemed more interested in growing his list of celebrity contacts than trying to become a better writer. (His famous friends now included Dorothy Allison, Courtney Love, Shirley Manson, and Gus Van Sant.) He'd also started to make extravagant claims that Cooper's characters were inspired by him (rather than the other way around), which Cooper found dishonest. "JT is into doing whatever it takes to get attention," he said at the time. "He likes attention. If it makes him happy it's fine. I am a little sick of it. He's a wonderful guy but I don't want to be part of it anymore. That's enough."[12] With the JT LeRoy celebrity sideshow gaining momentum by the minute, it was time for Cooper to take a step back.

Having just finished the George Miles Cycle, he wanted to try something different—"to rebuild [his] work from the ground up."[13] Silverberg suggested that he might write a nonfiction book that, as it would happen, Cooper had been thinking about doing for years. "I came up with the idea of doing a nonfiction book on the high school shootings phenomenon. But when I started doing research, I realized I didn't have the chops as a nonfiction writer to pull off what I wanted to do. So I proposed to write a nonfiction-like novel on the same subject" (2001).[14] The result was one of Cooper's most popular works, *My Loose Thread* (2002), a short novel set among a group of California high school students and narrated by a teenager named Larry.

The book's first-person narration embeds the reader in Larry's consciousness and, given that our narrator has serious psychological issues and that he lies all the time, it's often difficult to say for sure what's going on. This much is apparent: Larry and his friend Pete murder a kid named Bill at the request of Gilman Crowe, a high school senior who gives them five hundred dollars for the job. Bill's notebook—and whatever he might have written about Crowe in it—has something to do with Crowe wanting him dead. As Larry recounts his tale, he frequently remembers his friend Rand, who died a year earlier of a brain aneurysm after a violent argument with Larry. Rand found out that Larry had sex with his brother, Jim, and confronted him about it. As the story goes on, Larry's psychoses worsen until finally he kills both of his parents while Jim watches. Gilman Crowe, who is also the leader of a pseudo-Nazi group, turns up at the high school the next morning and starts shooting people. "Eventually the shooting just ends. . . . Maybe the last shot was aimed at himself. It sounded like all the others."[15]

Taking California teenagers as its subjects and high school as its focal point, *My Loose Thread* recalls some of the early poems of Cooper's *Idols*. The territory staked out by pieces like "High School Basketball," for instance, with its focus on a group of high school students whose libidinal energy lends its lines a vibrant, impulsive quality, is a prototype for Larry's world, which is similarly occupied almost exclusively by teens who are "too ready" to "stop moving around."[16] *Idols'* interest in teenagers' feelings of isolation is also carried through into the alienation of *My Loose Thread*'s young narrator. Larry hangs out with lots of people from high school, but as his phone calls testify, he fails to communicate properly with any of them, and his life is full of misreadings, misunderstandings, and disconnections.

> "What?" she says, I guess to Pete because I hear him in there. Then she laughs. "I'm not going to tell him. You tell him."
>
> "Tell me what?"
>
> "Pete just made a stupid joke," she says, sounding nervous. Then I guess the phone either gets swiped from her or Pete puts his mouth closer to hers.
>
> "Hey," he says, sounding maybe drunk now on top of being stoned. Whenever I think about him, he's always drunk. But when he's actually drunk, I never know what to say to him. "Larry?"
>
> "Yeah."
>
> "Jude says I should tell you," he says. Then I hear her tell him not to say it. "It's not a joke, Jude." But he laughs.[17]

But *My Loose Thread* is bleaker than any of the poems in *Idols*—and more violent. It's also characterized by an overwhelming confusion, which distinguishes it from the easy legibility of Cooper's early poems. This sense of confusion is everywhere in the narrative, and its effects are felt as much in how Larry expresses himself as in how he perceives the actions of others. His thoughts and feelings are represented in weird convolutions that make no normal sense but seem nonetheless to signify something profound to him. At breakfast, for example, his reflections on his mother have a logic that's not entirely transparent: he says that "something in her is going off about me. I can see it's not the world."[18] After he shoots his parents and leaves their house for Gilman Crowe's place, he later writes, "I guess I stupidly felt like what I did at the house had gone somewhere I couldn't."[19]

Causality is also constantly ruptured and inverted in Larry's account; instead of following a cause through to its effect in a linear way, the reader is generally presented with an event and *then* its circumstances: "'What's wrong?' [Jim] says. 'Nothing.' *I yelled that*, so he looks at the door"; "'Okay.' *I stood up and yelled that*. I didn't plan it."[20] In these examples, Larry doesn't seem to have much control over what he says or does. Violent impulses propel him forward to a point in the future from which he has to then retrospectively figure out what he's done. "I'm really confused," he says.[21] Numerous other elements—non sequiturs, unanswered questions, narrative lacunae, lies and evasions—also contribute to the novel's confusion and undermine any appeal the narrator (or the reader, for that matter) might make to an external reality: "Tell me what was real," Larry's therapist asks; "I don't know. Not much," Larry replies.[22] In short, *My Loose Thread* constructs a world that exists adjacent to the one most of us would recognize; Larry's world is governed by an indecipherable adolescent logic where causality means little and parricide is somehow justified.

If *My Loose Thread* is a take on the phenomenon of school shootings, which has become a distressing fixture of the American cultural landscape since the late 1990s, it's certainly not a typical one. Leora Lev calls it an "authentic and profound exploration of what has now become, tragically, the Columbine-era culture," but the infamous massacre at Columbine High School in 1999, which claimed the lives of thirteen students and teachers, is rarely mentioned in the book; references to it surface only a handful of times and always without much fanfare. At one point Larry says that the Columbine shooters, Eric Harris and Dylan Klebold, are "so boring."[23] Larry's story is also too insular to say much about the broader culture of the United States post-Columbine that Lev speaks of; it doesn't engage, for instance, with America's longstanding obsession with guns, or the ease with which teenagers can acquire high-powered assault weapons in the United States, or how greed, and not a putative belief in Second Amendment rights, underpins the National Rifle Association's lobbying against any form of gun control. The New Narrativist Bruce Boone might have called such issues "large and public thoughts," and Cooper is predictably wary of confronting them head-on. His approach to the school shooting phenomenon is much more modest and sympathetic. *My Loose Thread* attempts to understand such tragedies not by speculating on social or contextual factors but by reconstructing the mind-set of a troubled young killer, drawing on the case of a teenager who shot up his high school a year before Columbine but whose story was quickly eclipsed by that of Harris and Klebold.

On May 21, 1998, Kip Kinkel, a fifteen-year-old student at Thurston High in Springfield, Oregon, walked into his school armed with hunting knives, a rifle, two pistols, and over a thousand rounds of ammunition. He opened fire on his classmates in the schoolyard and cafeteria, killing two people and injuring twenty-five before he was finally subdued. While restrained by police, Kinkel repeatedly screamed "Just kill me!" and lunged at a police officer with a concealed knife in the hope, he later revealed, that he would be fatally shot. Once he was arrested and police searched his house, they found the bodies of his mother and father, each covered with bedsheets, whom he'd murdered the day before the school attack. A note abandoned on the Kinkels' coffee table read:

> I want to die. I want to be gone. But I have to kill people. I don't know why. I am so sorry! Why did God do this to me. I have never been happy. I wish I was happy. I wish I made my mother proud. I am nothing! I tried so hard to find happiness. But you know me I hate everything. I have no other choice. What have I become? I am so sorry[24]

Later, when questioned by police officers, a distraught and overwhelmed Kinkel would claim over and over in between sobs that he *had* to kill his parents and his fellow students because he had "no other choice."

> Detective Al Warthen: So you told me that your mom gets out of the Explorer and starts up the stairs from the garage or basement, is that right?
> Kip Kinkel: Yes.
> AW: Do you say anything to her?
> KK: Yes, I told her I loved her.
> AW: And then you shot—
> KK: Yes. God damn it . . . these voices inside my head.
> AW: Alright, hey, [garbled] Kip . . . Kip, settle down, settle down, it's alright, it's alright . . . Just settle down, okay, just settle down.
> KK: I had no other choice.
> . . .
> AW: I think it goes without saying at least from my perspective but

maybe . . . I want to hear it from your perspective, did you know it
was wrong to shoot your dad, your mom, and the kids at school?
KK: I had no other choice. It was the only thing I could do.
AW: What were the other choices that you didn't have a choice of?
KK: I didn't know I couldn't think I couldn't do anything.[25]

Kinkel's taped confession grabbed Cooper's attention when it was broadcast in January 2000 as part of a PBS *Frontline* documentary on the
Thurston High shooting. Later he would say that the confession was "an
incredibly devastating thing" that "created the book" (2002).[26] It's a heart-
wrenching glimpse into the mind of an emotionally disturbed adolescent
who seems truly devastated by what's happened, but it wasn't simply the
pathos of the confession that interested Cooper; it was also Kinkel's inarticulate attempts to explain what he'd done.

In the wake of Columbine in particular, media commentators were
frantically coming up with reasons why high school shootings were happening, blaming everything from heavy metal music to video games. But
to Cooper it seemed nobody was listening to the teenagers themselves;
to panicked parents and the media, teenagers were simply mindless con-
duits for this or that social anxiety. For Cooper, this reaction exemplified
how teens are "routinely disrespected, objectified, exploited, and disempowered" in a world that dismisses adolescence as "some sort of dark
age between childhood and adulthood, both of which are seen as more
legitimate stages of life."[27] Speaking with Michael Silverblatt in 2002, he
said, "[*My Loose Thread*] came out of the high school shootings phenomenon because I was disgusted at the way teenagers were presented as this
generality: they had no specific consciousness, no emotions. It had to be
bullying, or it had to be *this* cultural phenomenon that was influencing
their actions—but they weren't dealing with the fact that these kids had
very unique reasons for doing it."[28]

Kinkel's confession, however, confronted its listener both with the inescapable fact of his uniquely troubled consciousness *and* the elusive-
ness of any easy explanation for his actions. His claim that he had "no
other choice" couldn't be made sense of in any normal way. Cooper says,
"He was horrified and hysterical, and the police kept asking him why
he'd done it, and all he kept saying over and over was 'I had no choice.'
Somehow, even though I had no idea what he meant, I felt like that was as

deep and truthful an explanation as anyone who wasn't him would ever get."[29] In Kinkel's confusion and impenetrability, Cooper found a way to approach incidents like the Thurston High shooting: "Kip Kinkel's confession made me understand that his emotions held the only answer to why he'd done what he did. It was nowhere else and yet it was incoherent and secret" (2001).[30] As a fictional imitation of Kip Kinkel's confession, made up of the same repetitions, failed explanations, and general confusion, *My Loose Thread* is an acknowledgment of the lethally warped logic of minds like Kinkel's and a refusal to reduce their emotional complexity to easy explanations.

MY LOOSE THREAD was initially sold to Rob Weisbach Books, which was bought by the publishing behemoth HarperCollins, which then refused to publish the book. When the manuscript was finally returned to Cooper, the independent Scottish press Canongate offered to publish it as part of its first season with an American imprint. When the book came out in 2002, Terminator did not appear in its list of thank-yous. Things between Cooper and LeRoy had become tense.

Among other things, Cooper was angry that LeRoy continued to use a picture of George Miles that Cooper took in 1967 as his author photo. LeRoy had begged Cooper to loan it to him before *Sarah* went to print, claiming he needed a publicity shot but was too shy to have one taken for real. Given that Miles was incredibly important to Cooper, this photograph, taken in his parents' backyard when Miles was twelve and Cooper was fifteen, had immense sentimental value; he was initially resistant to the prospect of loaning it to anyone for any purpose whatsoever. LeRoy pestered him, however, and repeatedly promised that he had no intention of doing any publicity photographs in the future, so Cooper reluctantly agreed that he could use it. A thirty-year-old photo of the young Miles thus stood in for the twenty-year-old LeRoy on book jackets and promotional material around the world, further blurring the difference between JT LeRoy and Cooper's characters, many of whom were based on aspects of George Miles.

In spite of his promises, LeRoy did do publicity photographs—tons of them. From 2001 he was, in fact, rarely out of the public eye. In the run-up to the publication of his second book, *The Heart Is Deceitful Above*

All Things, he'd started to make appearances in public, shocking many of the writers who got to know him over the phone as a painfully shy, even agoraphobic kid. Turning up in a blond wig à la Warhol, he was usually attended by a couple named Emily and Astor, whom he credited with getting him off the street, and an entourage of celebrities and hangers-on.

Initially he said he was too nervous to give readings, so scores of his famous fans—Carrie Fisher, Matthew Modine, Jeremy Renner, and Winona Ryder, to name a few—queued up to read for him at fashionable events where a quasi-religious fervor was in the air, prefacing their monologues with declarations of devotion. Later, LeRoy would take to the stage himself, reading into his chest in a mumbled monotone—an affectation that recalled the withdrawn, traumatized young man Cooper, Benderson, and others had once known. *Vanity Fair* was the first to score a photo shoot with him, renowned portrait photographer Mary Ellen Mark snapping him in a mask, wig, and ballet outfit. Many others would soon follow—the *New York Times*, *Rolling Stone*, and the London *Sunday Times* among them. JT LeRoy was on the way to becoming an icon, and Cooper was dismayed by the transformation: "JT LeRoy was a very sweet character at one time. I mean, it went away! As JT started to do the whole fashion and fame thing, he wasn't sweet anymore. He became totally into being famous and [was like] '*fuck everybody.*' He never used to be like that but then he became you know: '*fuck everybody*, I wanna be famous and I wanna be rich'" (2015).[31]

Still the JT juggernaut rolled on. In early 2002, Shirley Manson, front woman of the alternative rock band Garbage, wrote a hit single in tribute to LeRoy called "Cherry Lips (Go Baby Go)." In 2003, LeRoy contributed to the screenplay of *Elephant*, Gus Van Sant's Palme d'Or–winning take on the Columbine shootings, and received an associate producer credit in the final cut of the film. A year later, a film version of *The Heart Is Deceitful Above All Things* came out, Asia Argento adapting the book as a schlocky melodrama with herself in the role of LeRoy's mother. Before the premiere in Cannes, LeRoy was photographed on the red carpet, dressed in trademark wig and sunglasses. In late 2004, LeRoy curated an exhibit at the trendy Deitch Projects gallery in SoHo in anticipation of the release of his third book, *Harold's End*; it included works by Cherry Hood, Danny Hobart, Violet Hopkins, Nick Lowe, Ted Mineo, Paul P., and Lou Reed. The opening reception featured readings of LeRoy's work by Reed,

Shirley Manson, Tatum O'Neal, and Nancy Sinatra. LeRoy's books were translated into twenty languages; his work was known across the world.

But something started to change in 2005, suggesting that people were getting tired of LeRoy's antics. *Harold's End* was put out by Last Gasp press to little commercial success or critical interest; originally published by McSweeney's, even Dave Eggers's help and effusive blurbs couldn't save the novella from being a flop. Roger Clarke's skeptical assessment in the *Independent* of people's tendency to "fall recklessly in love with JT LeRoy" exemplified a shift in the public's mood, as he relayed rumors that LeRoy's new book had been heavily edited by Eggers:

> I have to say, after reading through Eggers's stories and then *Harold's End*, that the latter's opening pages could easily read as an Eggers work. It has a similar rhythm—a similar arterial, self-hugging pump. . . . In Eggers's introduction, he claims LeRoy as an important writer. Perhaps, to be cynical, one could argue that LeRoy is just safe and melodramatic enough for the middle-class audience that Eggers knows so well. He is not a tricky customer like Dennis Cooper. He doesn't frighten the horses.[32]

For his part, an exasperated Cooper finally went public with the truth about the photo that LeRoy kept using, revealing in an interview with Alex Kasavin of Void Books that it was his picture of Miles. According to Cooper, "That started a firestorm that ended up being the end of our friendship. I got these vicious calls: 'You stabbed me in the back you motherfucker!' and all this stuff. [He was] just completely unreasonable about it" (2015).[33]

Cracks in the LeRoy narrative had started to show. By late 2005 they'd become canyons. A few people had always been skeptical about LeRoy: Why did he change his story so often? Wasn't he supposed to have late-stage AIDS? Didn't he say his face was covered in Kaposi's sarcoma scars? Journalist Joy Press raised the possibility of a hoax as early as 2001, writing in the *Village Voice* that LeRoy's "slipperiness" had "led some early supporters to wonder if they've been played."[34] But it wasn't until Stephen Beachy published his article "Who Is the Real JT LeRoy?" in *New York* magazine on October 10, 2005, that the true extent of the scam was revealed and a few dissenting voices became a chorus.

Beachy looked through birth registers in West Virginia; examined phone and financial records; talked to hustlers and johns in San Francisco's Tenderloin, where JT supposedly once tricked; and found no proof that LeRoy ever existed. Yet everywhere he expected to find the twenty-something literary prodigy and former gay hustler, he found a connection to an otherwise unremarkable forty-year-old mother of one from Brooklyn named Laura Albert. Beachy's article offered compelling evidence that Albert, whose previous employment included work as a phone-sex operator and who frequently appeared in public alongside LeRoy as his British friend Emily, was orchestrating the whole LeRoy charade with the help of her partner Geoffrey Knoop (aka Astor). She wrote the books, made the suicidal phone calls in a fake accent, solicited the help of literary mentors, cashed the checks—*and had done so for over a decade.*

Cooper initially wasn't persuaded by Beachy's argument, but as he was presented with more and more evidence that LeRoy wasn't who he claimed to be, the truth finally sank in. Quite simply, he was stunned, and wrote on his blog in October 2005:

> The progression from knowing and caring about a seemingly real 14 year old kid who claimed to have been horribly abused his whole life and was living on the streets and who claimed he was going to die of AIDS any minute and who could nonetheless and quite remarkably write well and honestly and sometimes beautifully about his life to watching this seemingly same kid transform into a fame and fashion-ability and money chasing alternative culture mini–Paris Hilton to discovering that the entire thing was probably a heartless and greedy if rather brilliantly carried out scam has not been fun at all.[35]

LeRoy's other supporters weren't going to be convinced. Benderson and Gaitskill wrote complaint letters to the editors of *New York* magazine; others sent encouraging emails to LeRoy denouncing Beachy's treachery, which LeRoy then published on his blog. By January 2006, however, when Warren St. John of the *New York Times* published an article naming Savannah Knoop, Geoffrey Knoop's sibling, as the public face of JT LeRoy, the jig was finally up.

High-profile literary hoaxes like the Albert/LeRoy one were rife in the opening decade of the twenty-first century. Within days of the final unmasking of JT LeRoy, James Frey's hit memoir *A Million Little Pieces* (2003), a heart-wrenching tale of drug abuse and crime, was revealed as a fiction. In February 2008, Misha Defonseca's bestselling *Misha: A Mémoire of the Holocaust Years* (1997), in which the author claimed to have survived the Holocaust with the help of a pack of wolves, was proved a fake. Later that year, Margaret B. Jones, who wrote *Love and Consequences: A Memoir of Hope and Survival* (2008) about her life as a half-white, half–Native American drug-running gang member in South-Central Los Angeles, was unveiled as one Margaret Seltzer, an all-white woman from the Valley who had attended the same high school as Mary-Kate and Ashley Olsen. "Similar phenomena keep arriving again and again, like the next scheduled train," David Shields wrote.[36]

The Albert/LeRoy hoax therefore wasn't that unusual. It also wasn't that original. Albert's JT LeRoy was likely based on the story of Anthony Godby Johnson, an abused youngster with AIDS who wrote *A Rock and a Hard Place: One Boy's Triumphant Story*, put out in 1993 by Crown (the same publisher that first offered LeRoy a book contract). Like LeRoy, Johnson also had long phone conversations with writers and celebrities—including Maya Angelou, Armistead Maupin, Paul Monette, and Jermaine Jackson—for years before he was finally revealed as the invention of Joanne Victoria Fraginals, a New Jersey schoolteacher in her forties. Maupin's novel *The Night Listener* (2000), a psychological thriller in which a writer strikes up a friendship with a sick young fan over the phone only to sense that all is not what it seems, was based on his experience and his suspicions about Johnson/Fraginals.

Under these circumstances, one might wonder at the susceptibility of Albert's "marks," these savvy writers and editors she fooled over the course of a decade: how did they fall for it? As in the case of Johnson/Fraginals, the key to Albert's deception was her premeditated and malicious use of AIDS and her exploitation of those most affected by the epidemic. Speaking about *The Night Listener* with Keith Olbermann (another of Anthony Godby Johnson's famous friends), Maupin said, "I think I was especially vulnerable because this kid was supposedly dying of AIDS and was going to be dead in six months, and my partner at the time was—and is—HIV positive and my best friend was on the verge of dying, so I was especially compelled."[37]

Most of those targeted by Laura Albert—gay men connected with New York's writing scene or people involved in editing and publishing in New York—were similarly vulnerable to this kind of strategy. Living in

New York in the '90s, all of them, gay or straight, had firsthand experience of AIDS. In 1995, the year Albert made her first call to Silverberg's office as the Terminator, the epidemic had peaked in New York with 8,309 dead from AIDS in the year, the second-highest annual AIDS death toll in the city. (The year before was only fractionally worse with 8,341 deaths.)[38] Looking back, writer and activist Sarah Schulman would equate living in the city at the time to enduring a "mass death experience," "where folks my age watched in horror as our friends, their lovers, cultural heroes, influences, buddies, the people who witnessed our lives as we witnessed theirs, as these folks sickened and died for fifteen years."[39] Laura Albert exploited this experience of mass death in order to prop up the fiction of JT LeRoy and extract attention, contacts, and hours of unpaid labor in editing and mentorship from AIDS survivors like Cooper, Benderson, and Silverberg. For Silverberg, speaking with Warren St. John, this was what he found truly reprehensible: "To present yourself as a person who is dying of AIDS in a culture that has lost so many writers and voices of great meaning, to take advantage of that sympathy and empathy, is the most unfortunate part of all of this. A lot of people believed they were supporting not only a good and innovative and adventurous voice, but that we were supporting a person."[40]

When Margaret Seltzer was shown to have impersonated a Native American and exploited stereotypes around people of color and gang crime, her publisher pulled all the copies of her book and offered refunds to those who had purchased it. When it was proven that James Frey had pretended to be a recovering drug addict, he appeared on *The Oprah Winfrey Show* to apologize and was duly lambasted by the host. When Misha Defonseca (aka Monique de Wael) turned out to have made up her story about being a Jewish Holocaust survivor, her publisher sued her and was awarded $22 million. By contrast, Laura Albert has never apologized for pretending to be a person with AIDS and still benefits from the scam. She republished the JT LeRoy books with Little, Brown in 2016 and retold the hoax from her remarkably self-serving point of view in the 2016 documentary, *Author: The JT LeRoy Story.* Cooper has said, "I'm still truly shocked both by her inability to tell the truth and by some people's readiness to accept the statements of an extremely proven pathological liar to stand unchallenged" (2018).[41]

Albert's books were edited, drafted, redrafted, and published by people who gave their time and expertise to her for free because they thought they were working with a teenager who was dying of AIDS. Why should Albert be permitted to continue making money from this con? Why are those who pretend to be Holocaust survivors or American Indian gang members (or, as in the comparable case of Rachel Dolezal, African American rights activists) shunned in American society while those who pretend to be persons with AIDS are permitted to remain in the public eye—with publishers ready to put out their books and filmmakers eager to tell their "crazy" story?[42] Is the experience of people living with HIV/AIDS and those who survived the AIDS epidemic somehow less important, or is it that cultural amnesia around AIDS and its effects is now so widespread that Laura Albert's grift doesn't utterly disgust and appall?

In his LeRoy exposé, Stephen Beachy acknowledged the usefulness of a hoax—its capacity to reveal the wants and weaknesses of the culture that was duped. "A good hoax is like a good con," he wrote. "Though a con liberates the mark of some of his material things, it also teaches him how easily he was tricked, how ready he was to believe certain stories."[43] As revealing as the JT LeRoy hoax was of the culture LeRoy moved in, the *rehabilitation* of Laura Albert and her continued success perhaps teaches us even more about American society and how a proper reckoning with the devastation and injustice of the plague years is long overdue.

The Automated and the Eerie |
Collaborations with Gisèle Vienne

10 IN JANUARY 2004 Cooper traveled to the south of France for an artist residency at Villa Gillet, a cultural institute in the city of Lyon. His readership in France had been steadily growing as his work had started to appear in translations released by Éditions P.O.L., his French publisher. French editions of *Frisk* in 2002 and *My Loose Thread* (published as *Défaits*) in 2003 were followed in 2004 by translations of *Period* and a collection of his selected poetry, *The Dream Police* (1996). An avowed Francophile, Cooper was excited that his work had started to feed back into a culture from which he'd drawn so much. Indeed, with his trip to Lyon, Cooper embarked on a new phase of his career that would ultimately see him relocate permanently to France and, through his collaborations with French artist Gisèle Vienne, exert a considerable influence on the contemporary French avant-garde.

At the end of his residency at Villa Gillet, Cooper delivered a lecture, subsequently published as *Violence, faits divers, littérature* (Violence, news item, literature), where he spoke about a number of violent memories from his childhood and their connection to his writing. His interest in the conjunction of violence and eroticism was first aroused, he said, while visiting his grandmother in Texas at the age of seven. He remembered observing the guests at a wedding next door making their way to the reception via a trail marked with tiki torches. All at once he was struck by the presence of a young girl about his age, standing on the path dressed in white: "She was dressed in a very frilly, lacey, pure white dress, almost like she was wearing a cloud, and I was mesmerized by her."[1] This radiant image was quickly superseded by one of horrific violence.

> As I stood there in awe of that vision of her, one of the tiki torches lining the walkway suddenly fell over right on top of her, and, I guess because her dress was so insanely flammable, her entire body was instantaneously consumed in flames. I don't remember anything after that until thirty-six hours later when a policeman shined a flashlight in my face. Apparently I had crawled underneath my grandmother's house, gone into shock, and stayed there for a day and a half until one of the search parties combing the city found me.[2]

A number of other troubling memories also surfaced during the course of Cooper's talk: being bludgeoned with an ax as a child; his mother's descent into abusive alcoholism when he was thirteen; his obsession with three adolescents his age who were found murdered in the hills behind his house; being threatened with rape and murder at gunpoint by a group of Hawaiians at the age of fourteen. Taken together, these violent episodes constitute a harrowing portrait of Cooper's childhood and emphasize the importance of writing during his formative years. In the midst of his parents' fractious and prolonged divorce, he says, "I took refuge in writing stories, taking drugs, and obsessing about fantasy worlds that mirrored but created logic out of my own world ruled by irrational, out of control, violent adults."[3]

Continuing *My Loose Thread*'s preoccupation with confession and the (often flawed or calculating) recollection of disturbing events, the Villa Gillet lecture seems to be operating on a couple of levels—in addition to being a straightforward autobiographical account, it's also a formal reflection on memory. Using the conventions of memoir, it attempts to think through how violent or traumatic moments from one's past are remembered, reconstructed, arranged—and presented to an audience. These reflections are central to his theatrical collaborations with Gisèle Vienne, his "longtime collaborator, boss, and friend" whom he first met in Lyon during his residency and with whom he has worked as a playwright and dramaturge since 2004.[4] Cooper's work with Vienne extends his formal interest in violent memory into the fields of contemporary theater, dance, and cutting-edge interdisciplinary art practice—the *pratiques transversales* for which Vienne is best known.[5]

A DIRECTOR, choreographer, and puppeteer, Vienne's compositions range across multiple media, employing styles, scenarios, and tropes gleaned from puppetry, theater, dance, film, and photography. Born in 1976, she studied philosophy and visual art before attending France's foremost academy of puppetry, the École Nationale Supérieure des Arts de la Marionnette in Charleville-Mézières. After graduating, Vienne devised theater pieces with her classmates Etienne Bideau-Rey and Jonathan Capdevielle that put life-size puppets and human performers together on stage in strange experimental tableaux greatly influenced by Polish master Tadeusz Kantor. Her productions from this time drew on avant-garde and erotic literature and included *Splendid's* (2000), which was based on Jean Genet's play of the same name, and *Showroomdummies* (2001), her take on Leopold von Sacher-Masoch's erotic novella *Venus in Furs* (1870), which, she says, focused on "the unsettling eroticism that can emerge from outer appearance and immobility."[6]

Vienne expands on these ideas in her 2003 essay "Érotisme, mort et méchanique" ("Eroticism, death, and the mechanical"), where she talks about bringing together the mediums employed by dance and puppetry: the body and the object. She writes, "The kind of questioning provoked by the confrontation between these two mediums seemed essential to me, having to do with reflections on the imagery, opinions, and actual perceptions we have of the body; the way we transform it into an ideal; the way we dehumanize it or reduce it to the level of an object."[7] Her practice, as she states elsewhere, deals with one idea in particular: "How can a human body become a body-image [*corps image*] like a puppet can?"[8] Embodiment is thus central to Vienne's work; she encourages her audience to consider the ways that contemporary culture makes the living body inanimate (in advertising, for instance) through her use of puppetry and dance and her intermingling of human and artificial bodies.

Vienne's work explores the space between puppetry and dance, animate and inanimate, but she admits in her essay to a fascination with other interstitial spaces. The performers and puppets in her pieces frequently call to mind styles of photography, painting, and statuary, for instance. When such evocations of stillness are placed in the context of a dance piece, where one expects motion, a disconcerting tension arises between movement and stasis, reality and representation. Vienne's exploration of these interstitial spaces—what one of her academic commentators calls zones of "indetermanence"—permits a questioning of the body's place in the contemporary world and, according to Vienne, also opens onto the space of poetry and the erotic.[9] She writes that her pieces "evoke the same sense of blending, which characterizes poetic experience as Georges Bataille described it: 'poetry leads us to the same place as all forms of eroticism: to the blending and fusion of separate objects. It leads us to eternity, it leads us to death, and through death to continuity . . .' It's likely that for these reasons the connection between image and movement, representation and reality has a fundamental place in my work."[10]

Given Vienne's focus on the body and the line between representation and reality, it's not surprising that she should have been curious about Cooper's work, which shares these concerns. When she heard he was visiting Lyon, Cooper recalls that "she wrote to me, said she liked my books, sent along DVDs of her work, and asked if I would consider staying a few extra days after the event and try to collaborate on a dance/theater piece. I liked what was on the DVD, so I said, Sure."[11] Vienne's use of life-size puppets and masks dovetailed with Cooper's employment of images of mannequins, dolls, and dummies across his oeuvre and aroused his long-standing interest in Bressonian "models" (those uncannily wooden nonprofessional actors, delivering their lines without emotion). Cooper and Vienne also had similar literary tastes, her experimental source texts and influences including the likes of Genet, Sacher-Masoch, and Bataille, as well as the Marquis de Sade and Nouveau Roman writers such as Alain Robbe-Grillet. All of this suggested that their meeting would be an exciting one, and in Lyon they duly hit it off. Cooper remembers that "we spent three or four days working together (also with [musician] Peter Rehberg and three performers), and by the end of that we had essentially made what ended up being *I Apologize*" (2017).[12] Thus began an immensely productive partnership between Cooper and Vienne that to date has yielded a startling array of critically acclaimed pieces, including theatrical performances, books, gallery installations, and, most recently, a TV show.

In the context of Cooper's previous work, the title of their first production, *I Apologize*, hints at some of its major themes. It refers to the novel *Try*—specifically the zine called *I Apologize: A Zine for the Sexually Abused* that the novel's protagonist Ziggy McCauley is found pasting together at the beginning of the book. Ziggy is a fan of the California punk/alt-rock group Hüsker Dü, and the title of his zine is taken from the song "I Apologize," a catchy punk-inflected track on the band's 1985 album *New Day Rising*, full of guilt and confusion about ambiguous events forgotten or misremembered for which an apology is deemed necessary (singer Bob Mould said it was about being an alcoholic). Regarding the content of Ziggy's fictional zine, Cooper states that it was based on a real zine called *Raised by Wolves*, edited by a New Mexico Queercore punk named Mr. Ed. Like the zine in *Try*, Mr. Ed's zine also included memories, stories, and poems about recovered memories of childhood sexual abuse. From the standpoint of Cooper's contribution, then, the title of his first collaboration with Vienne suggests that, like the Hüsker Dü song, it deals with memory and forgetting; like Mr. Ed's zine, it also deals with traumatic episodes and their reconstruction in and as art.

The piece opens on a set filled with twenty-seven pine boxes scattered around the stage, piled here and there in stacks. The boxes resemble rudimentary coffins, and each box in fact holds a five-foot mannequin dressed as a schoolgirl in a knee-length skirt, blouse, and tie. Over the course of the performance, all of the mannequins are unboxed, but to begin with they await exhumation, their coffin lids tightly shut. A teenager in a black hoodie (Jonathan Capdevielle) stomps back and forth over the set, eyeing the boxes warily. He exits stage left and returns carrying a mannequin with long dark hair and a blindfold over its eyes; sitting it upright on one of the boxes, he carefully positions its legs, bends its arms, and turns its head to face the audience. Exiting stage right, he returns with a chair on which he places another mannequin, also dressed as a schoolgirl, also wearing a blindfold.

The actions of Capdevielle's teenager are precise but hurried and almost brusque. They give the impression that he's done this before—so many times, in fact, that it's become quite routine to him. The stage darkens almost imperceptibly, and Cooper's sonorous monotone comes loud over the sound system, reading the first of seven pieces composed for the show.

"Great!" she yelled
when I reached inside her
to the elbow
and my hand tried
a slow dance with a lung,

when her back ripped
and sprayed us
under the lightning of my belt
as she crawled into
the quicksand of my bed,

when I choked her woozy
raised the toilet lid
and punched her face
until she saw the necklace
I'd given her.[13]

To one reviewer, Cooper's reading sounded like "a report delivered under hypnosis," which is not to say it is true or wholly intelligible.[14] The meaning of what he intones is as elusive as what the audience has just seen unfold on stage but, like the actions of the performer, it nonetheless conveys a mood. His imagery is violent and often sexualized—alluding, as in these lines, to the ecstasy ("Great!") experienced in BDSM practices like fisting ("when I reached inside her"), whipping ("under the lightning of my belt"), or asphyxiation ("when I choked her woozy"). Elsewhere in the same piece Cooper's text conjures scenes of jealousy ("You know who you fucked. If she's my wife so what . . . I'll tell you this. You're fucking evil if you did.") and death ("She's so dead. If I want / her ass again, I need to / love it."). Vague and fragmentary, none of his texts offer a narrative that might allow the audience to make sense of them or the piece as a whole (Julia Dobson calls them "oblique commentaries" on the action), but they create a powerful and pervasive feeling of desire, mistrust, and contempt.[15]

As the performance progresses, the teenager retrieves more mannequins from various wooden boxes and arranges them in a sequence of scenarios: some are positioned on chairs to one side of the stage in tiered seating that mirrors the audience's own; some are gathered together in a

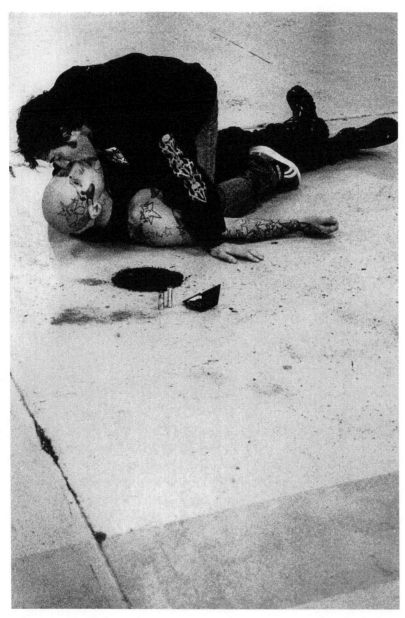

Jonathan Capdevielle and Jean-Luc Verna in *I Apologize* (2004). Courtesy of Gisèle
Vienne. Photo © Mathilde Darel.

semicircle at the back of the stage in a formation that recalls a classroom; a few are put into various awkward poses (prostrate, limbs akimbo) as the teenager prowls the stage in a deer mask, holding a revolver. Cooper's texts encircle the execution of these scenes, his lines filling the air with images of sex, exploitation, drug abuse, and desperation while the teenager rushes through his meticulous staging.

Before long we begin to suspect that the mise-en-scène has something compulsive about it and that each scene might be a warped rendition of another—a repetition with minor variations, as if the original has somehow been lost and can't be accurately remembered. These suspicions are confirmed when the teenager is joined on stage by another performer (Jean-Luc Verna), a tattooed colossus in jeans and combat boots, who lies down on the stage and assumes a position similar to a mannequin's from earlier in the performance, a pool of fake blood encircling his head. The sequence is repeated once more later on, as the performance nears its conclusion. When the third and final performer arrives on stage (Anja Röttgerkamp)—a dark-haired woman dressed in black who navigates the stage with ticking, spasmodic movements that are eerily mechanical—she too is implicated in the cycle of repeated stagings. Picked up by the teenager like one of his mannequins, she's arranged and directed by him in the same way.

The structured repetitions of the performance stood out to reviewers like Marie-Pierre Genecand, who wrote in the Swiss daily *Le Temps* that *I Apologize* read as the "compulsive organization" by a young man, of a "spectral dance where desire and death engage in an obsessive, recursive dialogue" and guessed that perhaps he was trying to reconstruct an accident where a number of young girls had been thrown from a school bus, "legs twisted under pleated skirts. Blood on their broken bones."[16] In France's *Libération*, Bruno Masi suggested that it was murder rather than an accident that was being compulsively restaged: "The murders are reconstructed in fragments, roles are reversed: who will play the master and who will play the slave?"[17] Julia Dobson's more scholarly appraisal found a number of echoes between *I Apologize* and its sequel *Une belle enfant blonde* (2005) (created using Cooper's *Violence, faits divers, littérature* text and featuring Catherine Robbe-Grillet, the writer, actress, and widow of Alain Robbe-Grillet); most notably, "both of these works stage attempts to reconstruct violent incidents in which the audience struggle to piece together parallel discourses (textual interventions, traumatic memories, or projected fantasies) of killing and being killed."[18]

In her critique, Dobson also points out that Vienne's productions are heavily influenced by Alain Robbe-Grillet but surprisingly doesn't comment on the form of *I Apologize*, where the Nouveau Romancier's influence is most evident.[19] According to Betty Rahv, Robbe-Grillet's novels are noteworthy for their iterative structure—the kind of repetition with variation that characterizes the stagings (and restagings) of Capdevielle's teenager—and she states that "each form, scene, or event in a novel by Robbe-Grillet repeats itself in various reflections that always vary so that ultimately each retains a constant core of sameness with slight variations."[20] This kind of iterative structure is broadly applicable to *I Apologize*, but Robbe-Grillet's formal experiments have other, more wide-ranging effects in the piece.

Cooper first came across the Nouveau Roman in the late 1980s when he was staying in Amsterdam, struggling with his health and the construction of what would become the George Miles Cycle. He found himself in an American used bookstore where, he says,

> someone had unloaded about thirty nouveau roman novels by Robbe-Grillet, Robert Pinget, Claude Simon, Nathalie Sarraute, Marguerite Duras, and Michel Butor, and I bought and read all of them. For some reason, in terms of literary influences, they were the kind of last piece of the puzzle, and *Closer* came together with their help. . . . Something about those writers' interest in an objective voice and the way their experiments with narrative were terse and kind of voluptuous at the same time excited me. (2006)[21]

Lesser-known authors like Pinget and Butor had what he calls a "really huge" influence on him, but it was Robbe-Grillet, the most famous of the Nouveau Roman group, who seems to have had the most profound impact. Cooper is quick to acknowledge the influence of Robbe-Grillet's novels, such as *The Voyeur* (1955) and *Topography of a Phantom City* (1976), as well as *For a New Novel* (1965), a collection of Robbe-Grillet's essays published in English.[22]

Refusing to accept what they considered to be the moribund state of the novel, in the 1950s and 1960s Robbe-Grillet and his fellow Nouveau Romanciers radically remade it, transforming its subjects, language, and narrative structures. The new forms this revivification took varied from writer to writer: the way Simon conducts the cadence of cinematic montage into his *Triptych* (1976), for instance, differs greatly from Butor's self-reflexive treatise on writing in *Degrees* (1960). For his part, Robbe-Grillet (in his early novels at least) focused most famously and prodigiously on the meticulous description of inert objects that, when placed in the midst of his deliberately vague and deceptive narratives, produced rather unsettling portraits of his narrators' mental state.

This style is most apparent in Robbe-Grillet's popular novel *The Voyeur*. A lacunary tale set on an unidentified island off the coast of Brittany, the novel follows the movements of Mathias, a watch salesman with an unreliable memory who may or may not have murdered a young island girl. The account opens as the protagonist's boat approaches the island jetty:

> The pier, which seemed longer than it actually was as an effect of perspective, extended from both sides of this base line in a cluster of parallels describing, with a precision accentuated even more sharply by the morning light, a series of elongated planes alternately horizontal and vertical: the crest of the massive parapet that protected the tidal basin from the open sea, the inner wall of the parapet, the jetty along the top of the pier and the vertical embankment that plunged straight into the water of the harbor.[23]

The jetty's geometric arrangement and the lapping of the sea against its walls could easily be a synecdoche for the structure of the novel as a whole, where formalism and fluidity are continually at odds. Time and again, geometric descriptions expressed with a marked evenness of tone protrude from a narrative whose structure is resonant with the rhythms of the sea breaking on the Breton shore—waves of repetition alternately revealing and quickly obscuring essential details of the plot and the sadistic murder, possibly committed by Mathias.

There are many correspondences between Vienne and Cooper's production and Robbe-Grillet's tale, not least in their employment of mannequins as a proxy for violence that otherwise remains largely implicit: in *The Voyeur* Robbe-Grillet's narrator describes a mannequin in a window display as "a young woman's body with the limbs cut off—the arms just below the shoulder and the legs twenty centimeters from the trunk."[24] But *I Apologize*'s principal debt to Robbe-Grillet lies in how it adopts the intermingling of formalism and fluidity exemplified by the structure of *The Voyeur*, how Vienne's piece manages to be both exacting and indeterminate at the same time, composed of precisely arranged set pieces that serve only to exacerbate the overall incoherence of a narrative that loops back on itself irregularly, fusing memory and projection. In Robbe-Grillet's book, the oscillation between formalism and fluidity conveys the impression of his narrator's disturbed mental state. Critics like Erwan Rault have read it more specifically as the author's attempt to portray the mind of a schizophrenic where, as Raylene Ramsay also noted, "there is no way of knowing, no way of differentiating between unconscious phantasy, daydream, and reality."[25] Likewise, *I Apologize*'s reworking of *The Voyeur*'s style produces a ubiquitous unease and intimates the presence of a pathological relationship to memory and the traumatic incidents of one's past—a pathology that may be attributable to Capdevielle's teenage character specifically or more diffusely to the piece as a whole.

VIENNE'S OEUVRE is remarkable for the subtle echoes that carry across from one piece to the next—the way a performance will pick up certain tropes or themes or images from a previous one and enlarge them or slightly contort them. She refers to this process as "quoting" and says that "all my different works are always quoting one another. It is a game of dark and uncanny associations for the audience."[26] Like the novels in Cooper's George Miles Cycle, her performances produce relations of reflection or refraction between one another, and a number of her subsequent productions have redeployed elements of her first collaboration with Cooper. *Jerk* (2007) in particular extends *I Apologize*'s exploration of disturbing, pathological states and psychologies by delving into the suffocating and sadistic world of a gay serial killer.

Based on Cooper's 1993 art book of the same name, which featured photographs of marionettes and hand puppets made by artist Nayland Blake alongside Cooper's text, *Jerk* is inspired by the infamous case of Dean Corll, a gay serial killer who tortured and murdered at least twenty-eight young men in Texas in the early seventies with the help of his teenage accomplices, David Brooks and Elmer Wayne Henley. In Blake and Cooper's book, Brooks has been asked by a professor to speak to a group of students from the University of Texas about his experiences; given that his preferred medium for depicting the atrocities he witnessed (and participated in) is puppetry, the story cried out for an adaptation by Vienne.

In her piece, Capdevielle assumes the role of Brooks, seated alone on stage as the audience files in and takes their seats. As in *I Apologize*, he's dressed in jeans and a hoodie, this time with the word "JERK" emblazoned on it. As Jordan Schildcrout observes, "Capdevielle's David is the killer as brooding hipster . . . a handsome but disheveled young man—with a neck tattoo, bed head, and a few days' worth of stubble," and Brooks duly greets his audience of undergraduates and pronounces the title of their course of study, "Freudian Psychology Refracted Through Postmodern Example," with a sneer.[27]

Following a brief introduction, he then acts out various scenes of molestation, torture, and murder using glove puppets similar to the ones made by Blake for the book. Capdevielle/Brooks switches between a variety of faintly absurd voices to distinguish each character—a menacing growl for the voice of Corll, a falsetto for Henley, an ethereal moan for the ghosts of the boys they've just killed. On a couple of occasions, he asks the audience to read from a zine given to them before the performance, which describes the background and lead-up to the violent scenes that are then performed for them. One text finds Corll in a reflective mood, expounding to Brooks and Henley on a typically Cooperian theme: the impossibility of truly knowing the beloved other.

> "Yeah," Dean says, and looks squarely at both of their cute, jaded faces. "That. 'Cos I've been kidding myself . . . thinking us killing those boys was . . . like . . . an accomplishment? Only I realized today that there's tons of shit going on inside those boys' heads while we've been killing them that we don't know about. That . . . all this time I've been thinking, 'They're cute,' you know, period. So killing them was like . . . the big finish. But I realized today that we haven't . . . known them at all. Not any of them. So it's like they're not ours anymore, not even dead. They got away from us."[28]

The act of reading Brooks's text implicates the audience into Vienne's piece: they assume their roles as University of Texas undergraduates by agreeing to read when they are asked and become part of the performance as a result. This is a more direct involvement than the implication by analogy in *I Apologize*, where the audience observes a mirror audience of

Jonathan Capdevielle
in *Jerk* (2008). Courtesy
of Gisèle Vienne.
Photo © Alain Monot.

mannequins erected on stage by Capdevielle's teenager. A safe separation
between the audience and the action maintained in the earlier piece is
here collapsed. This implication is intensified by the psychological effect
of what the audience reads: following Brooks's account on the page and
imagining scenes that provide a background for his puppet reconstruc-
tions, audience members are put into the position of his coconspirators.
(Cooper experimented with a similar effect in *Frisk*, written around the
same time as *Jerk*, which required his reader to read and imagine the
violent and wholly invented scenarios recounted in the narrator's pornographic letter from Amsterdam.)

This alternation between three modes (puppet play by Brooks, silent reading by the audience, narration by Brooks as director of the play) continues as the story becomes more frantic and macabre, following the death of puppet Corll at the hands of puppet Henley. The piece culminates in an extraordinary and disturbing finale where the characters in Brooks's play are no longer physically present in the form of puppets—but their voices are. Vienne explains:

> We were working on *Jerk*, and I wanted Jonathan to do this last scene, which is particularly intense. Over the course of the performance, his character is trying to distance himself from his story by writing it down, playing with these puppets, performing it for the audience, and by the end he is confused. It was here that I wanted his character to forget to use the puppets and do all the voices of his victims using the techniques of ventriloquy. So Jonathan learned ventriloquy for this final scene, and he became extremely good.[29]

During the final scene of *Jerk*, Brooks is seated almost motionless on stage. No puppets in his hands, his lips unmoving, voices emanate from him making declarations of devotion, horror, disgust; they vie with one another, murder one another painfully, and die with long, agonizing gurgles. There's something of the séance to what is unfolding and, like a medium channeling resentful spirits, Brooks seems to space out, drool trickling now and then from his lips. The effect of Capdevielle's performance is unexpected and unsettling (audience members have been known to faint or simply leave the theater during this sequence) and it astonished even Vienne when she first saw it: "We were totally amazed by what ventriloquy can achieve," she said. "Ventriloquy helped create this paranormal feeling. It is this mesmerizing auditory magical trick, and even if we are familiar with the trick, it doesn't lose anything of its power."[30] So startling was the impact of this scene that Vienne and Cooper frequently returned to ventriloquism in subsequent performances, notably in *Last Spring: A Prequel*, an installation at the 2012 Whitney Biennial that doubled the effect, featuring an animatronic teenager locked into a dialogue with his wicked ventriloquist's dummy. In *The Ventriloquists Convention* (2015), they built a whole production around the technique.

Vienne's pieces are often described in terms of their uncanniness, an idea most famously theorized by Freud in his essay "The Uncanny" (1919), where he explored the feelings of "dread and horror" attendant to things

like automata, doubles, and the sensation of involuntary repetition—all
of which Vienne's work with Cooper has in abundance.[31] As students in
the University of Texas Freudian psychology class would no doubt have
read, Freud posits that the uncanny "is in reality nothing new or alien, but
something that is familiar and old-established in the mind and that has
become alienated from it only through the process of repression," such
as the repression of "a primitive fear of the dead," which is "always ready
to come to the surface."[32] But the scenes of ventriloquism in *Jerk* and
other pieces by Vienne might be better described as "eerie," a term less
frequently attached to Vienne's work, which Robert Macfarlane calls "that
form of fear that is felt first as unease, then as dread, and that is incited
by glimpses and tremors rather than outright attack. . . . Its physical consequences tend to be gradual and compound: swarming in the stomach's
pit, the tell-tale prickle of the skin."[33]

According to Mark Fisher, the eerie comprises a specific realm of the
uncanny left unexamined by Freud, which is aroused by "a failure of absence or a failure of presence": "The eerie concerns the most fundamental
metaphysical questions one could pose, questions to do with existence
and non-existence: *Why is there something here when there should be
nothing? Why is there nothing here when there should be something?* The
unseeing eyes of the dead; the bewildered eyes of an amnesiac—these
provoke a sense of the eerie, just as surely as an abandoned village or a
stone circle do."[34] As it's used by Vienne, ventriloquism seems to engage
with these kinds of ideas: in the final scene of *Jerk*, Capdevielle's virtuosic
display *without the use of puppets* is eerie, not simply because a voice is
present where there should be none (given that his lips don't move), but
also, defying the norms of ventriloquism, puppets are not present when
we expect them to be. This style, which Vienne calls the "third voice," de-
noting "a voice performed in ventriloquy with no dolls or physical objects
personifying it," evokes what Fisher describes as "the intrinsically eerie
dimension to acousmatic sound—sound that is detached from a visible
source."[35]

For Macfarlane, Fisher, and other critics, contemporary art and culture
that seems eerie tends to have a kind of progressivism at its heart. Macfarlane claims that there is a "dissenting left politics" at work in eerie British art and culture of the landscape; such writing, music, and visual art
that "invokes the pastoral—that green dream of natural tranquility and

social order—only to traumatize it," he says, pushes back against jingoistic nostalgia and the pastoral as a key symbol of austerity politics under successive Conservative governments in the United Kingdom.[36] Fisher's essay goes deeper, trying to find out what it is about this particular form of uncanny experience that lends itself so easily to these leftist positions. He hypothesizes that eerie incidents or moments offer a "release from the mundane" and suggests that "the perspective of the eerie can give us access to the forces that govern mundane reality but which are ordinarily obscured, just as it can give us access to spaces beyond mundane reality altogether."[37] In other words, the eerie is a form of perception and critique that simultaneously allows us to recognize the forces (of history, for example, or of capital) that make up the world as we know it and also empowers us to visualize alternative ways of constructing the world. It is, therefore, an indispensable tool for those who wish to challenge the status quo and the homogenization of the social order, which Fisher elsewhere calls "capitalist realism."[38]

Fisher and Macfarlane are evidently keen to emphasize the positive effects of the eerie; it offers what Fisher calls "an escape from the confines of what is ordinarily taken for reality."[39] In Vienne and Cooper's pieces, however, the eerie conveys something different from—even antithetical to—this. Far from representing escape or release, moments of third-voice ventriloquism in their work suggest instead confinement, insularity, and imprisonment. As a consequence of his crimes, David Brooks is obviously physically imprisoned (the real Brooks was sentenced to life and is currently an inmate of the Ramsey Unit prison in Texas), but as the eerie finale of *Jerk* chillingly reveals, he is also psychologically imprisoned, a captive of the violent, traumatic incidents he was party to as a teenager, which he forever repeats and tries quixotically to distance himself from. In *Last Spring: A Prequel*, the teenage character portrayed by the animatronic doll claims to be the prisoner of the ventriloquist dummy that hangs limp by his side, locked in a labyrinthine castle whose blueprints adorn the walls of the cell where he recounts his story. His feeling of imprisonment, which is psychological as much as physical (the demon dummy may simply be himself, after all), is also palpable in the eeriness that envelops the scene—quarreling voices emerging from an unknown source. In short, Vienne and Cooper's eerie pieces disturb and unsettle in

The animatronic protagonist
of *Last Spring: A Prequel* (2011).
Courtesy of Gisèle Vienne.
Photo © Gisèle Vienne.

large part because they arouse the sense of psychological enclosure—the sensation of an interminable, inescapable confinement in the prison of a traumatized mind.

In their ever-evolving partnership, Cooper and Vienne, along with their frequent collaborators, including Capdevielle, Verna, Röttgerkamp, Rehberg, and Stephen O'Malley of the doom metal group Sunn O))), have explored ideas as diverse as the place of ritual in the contemporary world (*Kindertotenlieder*, 2007), the relationship between parent and child (*The Pyre*, 2013), and, most recently, the euphoria of teen raves (*Crowd*, 2017). However, as Betty Rahv detected a "constant core of sameness" in the iterations of Robbe-Grillet, the numerous varied pieces by Cooper and Vienne (who wear Robbe-Grillet's influence on their sleeve) share the interior life of the adolescent as a constant, recurring theme. Their work is distinguished by its sympathetic, gently probing investigations into the minds of troubled teenagers—and the adults they become. If Cooper's early poetry, characterized by individual isolation and a pained yearning for intersubjective communion, could be said to evoke a poetics of adolescence, his collaborations with Vienne describe something like a *choreography* of adolescence where such attributes are still very much present—even if Cooper's own isolation is somewhat displaced by his participation in the artistic collective.

Dennis Cooper's Blog

"You're the Mysterious Ones"

11 IF THE PUBLICATION of *Period* in 2000 drew the George Miles Cycle to a close, the release of *God Jr.* in July 2005 showed that, where Miles was concerned, closure was still a ways off for Cooper. Revolving around a father's attempts to build a monument in his backyard to the memory of his dead teenage son, the novel is about grief, guilt, and the work of mourning; remarkable in Cooper's oeuvre for its omission of sexual themes, the book's preoccupation with memorialization nonetheless intimately connects it to the concerns of the Cycle. Cooper told Danny Kennedy, "At the heart of it, it's true, it doesn't have a lot of things the other books had in it, but in terms of like its internal structure . . . it's another book about George Miles and about my own process" (2007).[1] The book's protagonist, Jim, builds an enormous edifice in his backyard to the memory of his son, Tommy, based on surreal sketches Tommy made that look like a puzzle from his favorite video game: "Look, here's the deal," Jim says. "Tommy was my son. He liked that puzzle. I don't know why. He did a lot of drugs. So do I. Maybe that's the only reason. Now Tommy's dead. I loved Tommy. I think that's safe to assume. But he's gone, and that puzzle's still there."[2] As a result, much of the novel takes place inside the video game, a stoned Jim desperately trying to connect with his dead son by meandering through a 64-bit universe in the guise of a talking bear.

God Jr.'s partial incorporation of the video-game format extended the stylistic innovations of *Period*, which had also incorporated the layout of computing technology in its instant message (IM) séances. However, *God Jr.* was swiftly eclipsed by *The Sluts*, a much more graphic and sensational work, which was published to much acclaim in October 2005 by Carroll and Graf (Void Books had put out a small run of the book the previous year). One of Cooper's most critically and commercially successful novels, *The Sluts* took on the appearance of web-based communication technologies like review websites, message boards, email, and IM. Its curious mix of lowbrow detective fiction and Nouveau Roman experimentalism was celebrated everywhere, and it was awarded two major prizes, the Lambda Literary Award, for fictional works that explore LGBT issues, and the Prix Sade, for writers who go "beyond all forms of censure and who [defy] the moral or political order against all forms of intellectual terrorism."[3]

Despite its unconventional design, the plot is relatively sequential and takes place between June 2001 and May 2002, opening with reviews of a teenage hustler named Brad, on a website for regular customers of gay male escorts. User bigman60 contributes a long physical description of Brad using the appropriate fields (age, height, weight, prices, dick size, etc.) before going on to describe a night during which "unbelievable" sex ended with Brad having a severe psychological episode that was "very spooky."[4] This is followed by a similarly comprehensive review by user llbean that challenges certain details of Brad's physical appearance in the previous report (here, for example, he is two inches shorter) but depicts a sex scene and conclusion analogous to the one before: "I did have to order him to leave, and he was very out of it and acting pretty strange. But let me tell you, he's worth it," he says.[5] In another review, self-proclaimed "caretaker" JoseR72 posts a description of Brad (eye color blue, not hazel or green as in the previous reviews) and outlines his failed attempt to rehabilitate him.[6]

Fifteen more lengthy reviews are posted by a variety of other users, which contest previous submissions and revise aspects of Brad's physique or behavior. The object of these reviews cycles through various weights (from 115 to 165 pounds) and hair colors (blond, dyed blond, dishwater blond, brown) and alternates between being circumcised and uncircumcised, chatty and laconic: "Despite what has been said about him, he was quite talkative, too talkative if anything," user bizeeb7 writes.[7] With each new report, Brad acquires more and more minutely dissimilar attributes; his portrait warps and becomes incrementally more sprawling and mysterious, eliciting phenomenal interest and, we are told, drawing huge traffic to the website. Who is Brad? Is he a burned-out porn star called Stevie Sexed? Was he murdered in August 2001? As user thetimmonster observes, "We're all caught up in this Brad thing because we're obsessed with him and want to fuck him."[8] User sammyd says, "I'm addicted to this saga because it's like a great mystery novel with a lot of sex scenes in it. . . . It's like cutting-edge escapism."[9]

In subsequent sections of the novel—"Ad," "Board," and "Email/Fax"— the Brad mystery is amplified and distorted, with users and commenters finding themselves entangled in it, drawn inexorably to the thread in order to engage with other Brad fans and have their fantasies affirmed and augmented by one another. Like Faulknerian voices circling the corpse of Addie Bundren in *As I Lay Dying* (1930), members of the "escort-loving community" depicted in *The Sluts* all orbit the text's Brad-shaped lacuna.[10] Yet as they interact, their online personae become subject to the same modifications and revisions as the expansive but gradually receding nucleus of their discussions. User egarrison, who claims to be Brad's pregnant girlfriend, movingly begs the users of the message board for donations, only to have her appeals undermined by user builtlikeatruck44, who alleges that she is a "well known Portland skeezebag who takes in street hustlers, addicts them to heroin, and pimps them to support her and their drug habits."[11] The mix of suspense and confusion that envelops participants in the Brad thread at times surpasses that which surrounds Brad himself: Was user jimmytaylor murdered by Brian? Is builtlikeatruck44 a guardian angel or a violent pedophile? Is Zack Young behind it all?

Although the story concludes in a bathetic fashion typical of Cooper's works, revealing the loneliness that underlies the collective fantasy in which user and reader alike have been implicated, this depiction of Brad and the community that surrounds him remains the most startling accomplishment of Cooper's novel. With the character or fictional space of Brad, Cooper convincingly limns the periphery of a void by focusing on the individual voices who seem to gravitate toward it. Timothy Baker writes, "As a protagonist and sometime narrator, Brad is revealed to be completely unknowable: he is a blank identity that can be filled both by himself and by others, whether those be direct imitators such as Thad [a Brad clone] or by the board commenters who vicariously live through him."[12]

This structure recalls a work like *Closer*, which tries to pinpoint George Miles by peering through the eyes of his admirers; given that *The Sluts* was originally conceived as the fourth book in the Cycle, it's tempting to see the same strategy replicated here. Yet in *Closer* and in the George Miles Cycle as a whole, Cooper's thought is turned inward: as we saw in the case of *Frisk*, he writes with an obsessive, navel-gazing attentiveness to the center. With *The Sluts*, on the other hand, he seems determined to identify the impulses that attract his protagonists to Brad and the forces that bind them loosely together as an "escort loving community." His focus shifts from the shimmering presence in the middle to the voices that encircle it, from the singular to the plural. The structure of the work may well be similar to works in the Cycle, but here the author seems more interested in the periphery than the hub.

During his time at Beyond Baroque, Cooper was in the middle of a radical, avant-garde society of like-minded poets including Amy Gerstler, Jack Skelley, and Bob Flanagan. While their veneration of the individual voice and contempt for its dissolution in "the common" could be read as anarchistic, the very centrality of Cooper to the community indicated the persistence of a social hierarchy inimical to anarchist thought. Cooper brought the punk poets together as the Beyond Baroque reading-series coordinator and helped to cultivate a vibrant literary scene in Los Angeles; once he departed for New York in 1983, the community stopped growing and eventually broke apart. If, as poet Lynne Bronstein defensively remarked at the time, the young poets of Beyond Baroque were a "poetry mafia," then Cooper was their unwilling don.

Looking back on his time in Los Angeles, he confesses to a discomfort with this status: "I was in a rut, *really* in a rut. I was seeing only poets, particularly a group of poets who sort of looked up to me, as a person who could give advice as well as be a friend. I was, like, a big fish in a small pond out there. I was pretty famous, but it was so *easy*. I didn't deserve the attention I was getting. It was ridiculous" (1983).[13] For a writer who, by his own admission, "like[s] situations where I can't possibly be the center of attention, or where I can believe that such a thing is possible," being so famous and indispensable to the punk poet scene was unbearable and was one of the factors that led him to abscond to the anonymity of Down-town New York (2000).[14]

Yet this experience of fame—and its capacity to bring a group of people together in their shared desire for intimacy with a celebrated figure—seems to have stayed with Cooper and emerges as a prominent theme in *The Sluts*. Woven from the stuff of his previous novels, sexual desire and morbid fantasy are of course ubiquitous in the book and, as Leora Lev points out, "collusion, complicity, love, hate, victimization, caretaking, and salvation all appear hopelessly intertwined."[15] In addition to these familiar features, fandom, celebrity, and idolization—with the exception of *Try*, ideas largely passed over by Cooper since *Idols*—are equally insis-tent leitmotifs. The final reviews of the escort named Brad, for instance, illustrate the lengths some obsessed "Brad fans" will go to in order to orchestrate a rendezvous with their favorite celebrity: in his review, Sand-man808 exclaims, "Watching his cute face go through its range of emo-tions was very hot and knowing he was the legendary Brad made it even more special."[16]

Returning to the idea of community in the wake of widespread digiti-zation, *The Sluts* finds Cooper at work sketching a fictional blueprint for an online community, drawn together by intrigue and held together by the promise of sex or fame or an elusive brush with celebrity. Somewhat like the one at Beyond Baroque, this community bonds through a shared attraction to a celebrated center (there Cooper, here Brad), but the society in *The Sluts* is markedly more horizontal, and, the center having absented itself, the text is made up solely of lateral conversations between partici-pants. Speaking with Danny Kennedy in July 2007, Cooper commented that the book "has no center at all. All the other books have an emotional center to them and this one has no emotional center to it at all, it's purely abstract. Brad is not an emotionally riveting character, he's just an ex-ample and he's just a whatever, he doesn't even exist."[17]

In *The Sluts*, Cooper explores the ways that one might effect the devel-opment of a network—a social formation where relationships between members are nonhierarchical. Can the internet admit kinds of commu-nity that are more open, flexible, and robust than previous examples? What is the most effective way to build such a community? Can it be sustained? If *The Sluts* introduces Cooper's response to these questions, his blog—a "major project" for more than a decade—is the main event.[18] Investigating the forms and concepts necessary to bring about the emergence of an anarchistic community online, the blog capitalized on some of the ideas discussed here, namely the capacity of desire and celebrity to join various individuals together in a supple, noncoercive social structure. Philosophically and politically, the phenomenon of the network is indispensable to Cooper's efforts: as an archetypal network and a sprawling, "live" version of *The Sluts*' cyberfictional simulation, Cooper's blog allowed him to experiment in miniature with the makings of an anarchist community.

A RUDIMENTARY DEFINITION of a network might start with what it is not: namely, a hierarchical, centralized, and hermetic system comprising homogeneous elements, rigidly arranged. The bureaucracy of the state in its traditional form might epitomize such a system, in its compartmentalization and hierarchization of parts, cascading down from the upper echelons of central government (e.g., ministries of the state, the criminal justice system, civil servants). Formations such as these tend toward stasis, conveying information relatively slowly and changing only gradually and with much effort. Kafka is perhaps their scribe, drawn to the maddeningly illogical excrescences produced by their inflexible logic and documenting the glacial pace with which information passes through their layers. In the vocabulary of Gilles Deleuze and Félix Guattari, these centralized, homogeneous systems are "arborescent" and are the anachronistic vestiges of feudal or sovereign societies: "Arborescent systems are hierarchical systems with centers of significance and subjectification, central automata like organized memories. In the corresponding models an element only receives information from a higher unit and only receives a subjective affection along pre-established paths."[19] According to Deleuze and Guattari, such arborescent structures not only shape the ruling-class system but also overcode the psychosexual landscape of the modern subject. As a result, opposition to the status quo usually advances "along pre-established paths" too: in their congregation around the issue of homosexual orientation, for instance, gay advocacy groups could be said to replicate and inadvertently validate the systems to which they are opposed.

In place of the arborescent, Deleuze and Guattari offer the rhizomatic: "finite networks of automata in which communication runs from any neighbor to any other, the stems or channels do not pre-exist and all individuals are interchangeable, defined only by their *state* at a given moment such that the local operations are coordinated and the final, global result synchronized without a central agency."[20] The rhizome or network, then, may be distinguished primarily by its horizontal and spontaneous distribution of different parts, which provisionally connect with one another through currents of information, energy, or, particularly for Deleuze and Guattari, desire. In place of centralizing forces and slow, incremental adaptation, the network is instead made up of an ever-expanding number of nodes and change is rapid, extensive, and continual. Networks are heterogeneous, mutating multiplicities. As Alexander Galloway and Eugene Thacker explain:

> Networks are multiplicities, not because they are constructed of numerous parts but because they are organized around the principle of perpetual inclusion. It is a question of a formal arrangement, not a finite count. This not only means that networks can and must grow (adding nodes or edges) but, more important, means that networks are reconfigurable in new ways and at all scales. Perhaps this is what it means to be a network, to be capable of radically heterogeneous transformation and reconfiguration.[21]

The necessity for continual transformation and reconfiguration in networks should be emphasized here. Whereas the potency of a top-down, arborescent structure comes from the perpetuation of its rigidity, that of the network lies in its dynamism: "Networks are only networks when they are live: when they are enacted, embodied or rendered operational."[22]

As a nonhierarchical, decentralized assemblage of independent nodes, the network is an anarchistic structure par excellence, and it surfaces repeatedly in anarchist culture. If gay rights groups could be associated with a conventionally centralized arrangement around a shared concept of gay identity, then we might consider Queercore activism of the '80s and '90s as an example of an anarchistic network formation. Proliferating via an abundance of zines that were dear to Cooper, these acephalous (or headless) groups thrived without an organizing principle or a core belief. "Xeroxed and/or cheaply offset-printed publications . . . constituting a network of sub-desktop alternatives to established, large circulation periodicals," they were oriented instead toward the peripheral and perverse.[23] The Queercore movement, which had such a formative influence on Cooper's anarchism, and other grassroots movements of the '90s such as Riot Grrrl, which combined radical feminism with punk rock, generated their networks during these years through the dissemination of DIY print culture, including zines and newsletters. But the elemental tendency of networks toward expansion was impeded by the pace of distribution: acquiring the latest issue of a zine meant posting cash or a check to the address of its publisher and then waiting for it to be delivered, which could take weeks, depending on its popularity. In *Girls to the Front: The True Story of the Riot Grrrl Revolution* (2010), Riot Grrrl historian Sara Marcus attests to a massive backlog of unanswered mail requests at the headquarters of the Riot Grrrl chapter in Washington, DC.[24] While the US postal system cannot be held wholly accountable for the demise of these movements, the slow calcifying of their communication channels may have contributed to their inevitable disintegration—as Galloway and Thacker remind us, "networks are only networks when they are live."

With the arrival of affordable dial-up internet in the late 1990s, however, communication technologies began to develop the speeds necessary to sustain a network's requisite rate of growth and change. As a "network of networks," or a "hypernetwork," the internet has always been especially adept at cultivating horizontal networks, and from its inception it was envisaged as a tool with which to build distributed systems.[25] Ironically enough, it was the US military that came up with the idea: as its creation myth now famously holds, the internet was the result of attempts by the Defense Advanced Research Projects Agency (DARPA) to set up a decentralized system of computers that could survive in the event of an enemy attack. Should an air strike incapacitate a hub in the Middle East, for instance, interaction between other hubs in the network would be unaffected, and commands communicated via that hub would be would be sheltered within the structure.

While the number and scale of networks undoubtedly increased with the advent of open architecture (where hermetic computerized systems under the control of a single entity gave way to interoperable TCP/IP systems) and continued to grow at an unprecedented rate, particularly during the dot-com boom of the 1990s, limited technological know-how also restricted the advance of networks. Becoming an active participant or node of a cyber network required more than an email account—it required an in-depth understanding of computer programming. Consequently, while the first weblogs that arose in the late 1990s catalyzed the proliferation of small, discrete networks, as Rebecca Blood confirms, some knowledge of basic coding language like HTML (hypertext markup language) was needed in order to participate: "When I started mine in 1999 no tools had yet been designed specifically for creating weblogs. Some programmers created or adapted their own software. The rest of us hand-coded our sites."[26]

In the 2000s, "everything changed": the arrival of next-generation web technologies unlocked the opportunity for apparently unlimited interaction and connectivity between even the uneducated and uninitiated would-be nodes of the internet's emergent networks.[27] Offering free software that was easy to operate and needed no real training, the primary function of these technologies, grouped under the name "Web 2.0," was to enable user-generated content and communication.[28] Media theorist Lev Manovich credits Web 2.0 with a fundamental shift in the orientation of the internet from professional to amateur and from a broadcast to an engagement model, exemplified by the popularity of social media hubs such as Wikipedia, Facebook, and YouTube. "Two commonly held ideas about Web 2.0 are most relevant," he wrote in 2009. "First, in the 2000s, we are supposedly seeing a gradual shift from the majority of internet users accessing content produced by a much smaller number of professional producers to users increasingly accessing content produced by other nonprofessional users. Second, if in the 1990s the web was mostly a publishing medium, in the 2000s it has increasingly become a communication medium."[29]

Most importantly for our consideration of Cooper's blog, the implementation of Web 2.0 technology also changed how weblogs were used and who used them: by providing a precoded interface, companies like Blogger and WordPress arguably democratized blogging and made participation in the blog network possible for millions of people. Neither the time for coding nor an education in the finer points of CSS or JavaScript was a prerequisite—everyone could now have their own blog and manage their own node. Geert Lovink argues that "whereas the dot.com suits dreamt of mobbed customers flooding their e-commerce portals, blogs were the actual catalysts that realized democratization worldwide, of the internet."[30] It's against this theoretical and technological background that the conception and development of Dennis Cooper's blog must be understood.

IN MAY 2005, extending his research into communication technologies conducted for *The Sluts* and responding to a fan survey on his website, Cooper began blogging at http://denniscooper.blogspot.co.uk. The blog has been forced to relocate on a couple of occasions and has been known as *The Weaklings* and *DC's*: for simplicity's sake, in what follows I call it *Dennis Cooper's*, which was its first name. Cooper's debut post, "I Think I'm Ill-Suited to Blogging," made plain his initial unease with the project; he wrote, "I'm shy, not particularly talkative, and I don't really like talking about myself."[31] He seems nonetheless to have rapidly acclimatized to the form, posting entries onto the site daily and engaging with a growing number of fans and friends who stumbled across his site or found their way there thanks to word of mouth.

Blogs like his were wildly popular at the time: widespread public adoption of free blogging software and web hosting services provided by Blogger, WordPress, LiveJournal, and others resulted in a massive increase in the number of online blogs from three million in May 2004 to more than ten million by the time Cooper wrote his first post (the following year growth was even greater, jumping to thirty-five million).[32] He and a legion of other bloggers could easily create content made up of text, picture files, or video and quickly upload it to the internet without knowledge of even basic computer coding. Permalinks gave each individual post a URL (i.e., uniform resource locator, a stable identity and location on the web) that could be emailed to friends and linked to on other blogs, while a comments facility beneath each post allowed bloggers to interact with other members of the so-called blogosphere.

Cooper has blogged continually since the beginning, creating large posts full of content six days a week—a routine that has been interrupted only by incidents that were out of his control, like when his blog was deleted by Google in 2016 (more on that later). It would be unrealistic to try to describe such a huge, amorphous project, so in what follows I use a small, representative selection of posts taken mostly from the blog's inception to its one-year anniversary to chart its history from its inauspicious beginnings to its evolution into a sprawling participatory artwork and queer subcultural hub.

Many of the posts published on the blog were made up of in-depth, eye-catching explorations of modern and contemporary writers, artists, filmmakers, and musicians. They typically included a short introductory text followed by curated examples of the subject's work, including text, JPEGs, YouTube clips, and so on. Cooper also provided an extensive list of links from around the web that explored the topic in greater depth (articles, interviews, more YouTube clips, etc.). The expansive range of material ensured both established and relatively unknown subjects received equal exposure; a post considering the work of austere British writer Ivy Compton-Burnett, for example, was sandwiched rather incongruously between posts devoted to the American rock band Butthole Surfers and the German visual artist Susanne Hay. As one of Cooper's heroes, Robert Pollard of the indie rock outfit Guided by Voices was a recurring presence, but Cooper also considered little-known or recently discovered subjects such as French writer Tony Duvert, visual artist Ryan Trecartin, and Australian photographer Bill Henson.[33]

Along with these posts dedicated to particular subjects and artists, the blog also provided insight into how Cooper's own works were conceived and created, usually in response to questions posed in the blog comments section. In early 2006, Cooper compiled a series of posts that painstakingly outlined the architecture of the George Miles Cycle. Before unveiling a sequence of equations and graphs used to construct the five novels, his opening post made clear why they were important to him.

> When I was developing the cycle, I realized that what I wanted to do wouldn't work if I wrote in a straightforward narrative style. I realized I would have to figure out and design a particular kind of container suitable for the content and subjects I wanted to explore—a container that would organize, display, house comfortably, and allow a productive interaction [*sic*] between subjects that would otherwise either deflect or destroy one another. One thing I did was devise a large number of charts and graphs in order to predetermine the cycle's form, which I wanted to be rather simple in appearance and yet very complex when examined, sort of like the things I wanted to write about.[34]

In addition to publicly dissecting his previous novels, Cooper also provided excerpts from smaller pieces and progress reports on new work. While writing *The Marbled Swarm: A Novel* (2011), he gradually revealed key facts about its influences, spoke at length about its structure and themes, and posted photos of people who inspired its characters.

While these kinds of posts might be found on other writers' personal websites and blogs, it's obvious that Cooper's blog was different from the majority of blogs in circulation. The difference was not merely one of longevity (unofficial statistics estimate that 60–80 percent of new blogs are abandoned after a month; Cooper blogged regularly from the start in 2005). Though similarly focused on the life and work of its author, Cooper's blog seemed to reach for something broader, more plural than most blogs' subjective takes on mainstream media or reflections on the blogger's personal interests.[35] Underneath or adjacent to Cooper's front page pulsed something multiple and cooperative: a cursory scroll through the site found the names and voices of numerous others swarming at the margins of Cooper's own. A click through to the comments section unearthed a hive of bloggers chatting, arguing, boasting, devising collaborative projects, and sharing links—relays issuing back and forth, out of the comments section, and beyond the blog itself.

Guided by the thoughts and activities of the writer, most blogs display an attentiveness to the self that verges on the egotistical—yet this egocentric facet of blogging culture is in fact antithetical to its technological basis. One of the fundamental qualities of a blog is its ability to establish and maintain instant, easy interaction between bloggers and their peers: blogs were designed to promote participation. The comments section that follows each blog post, in particular, offers the opportunity for bloggers to support one another, disagree, or discuss issues raised in the post. Yochai Benkler sees these comments as a principal feature of blogs, symptomatic of a changeover from a read-only web to a writeable web: "The result [of blogging's commenting facility] is therefore not only that many more people write finished statements and disseminate them widely, but also that the end product is a weighted conversation, rather than a finished good. It is a conversation because of the common practice of allowing and posting comments, as well as comments to these comments."[36]

For technopositivists like Benkler, commenting can make the relationship between reader and writer/publisher more horizontal, turning a monologue into a dialogue and the act of publishing into an interactive conversation between writer and reader. However, a glance at the comments sections of many blogs reveals that although this facility certainly exists, its use is not as widespread or radical as Benkler would have us believe. Innumerable blog posts are in fact followed by no comments at all; if any comments have been left, the blogger hasn't responded to them. This suggests that although blogging is an inherently networked form, the threat of the arborescent or pyramidal is never far away: all too easily an engagement model lapses into a broadcast model and openness gives way to solipsism. The capacity of a blog to be what it *is*, therefore, depends wholly on its author's commitment to generating networks and ability to draw enough users to the site to ensure the network's growth. Cooper industriously and ingenuously addressed himself to both of these conditions.

In the first instance, comments were key: on his blog, in contrast to innumerable other examples, feedback was vital to supporting and maintaining the network. He warmly encouraged readers to react to the day's post, offer their opinions on his work, or talk about themselves in the comments section, and his responses to these comments formed a subsection of the next post. Cooper's commitment to replying to each commenter every day—even when the number of comments ballooned from about twenty per post in 2005 to over a hundred per post in 2007—illustrates how important this interaction was to him. "I go through them one by one and answer them," Cooper said of the comments left on his blog. "It really does take about three to five hours every morning to do" (2011).[37] This ongoing conversation between Cooper and his readers, known as "distinguished locals," or DLs, perforated the stratification of front page and comments section, setting up a circuit that rendered their interactions less hierarchical.

But what of the comments section itself? Composed of what artist and Irish DL Jonathan Mayhew calls "a mixed bunch of writers, artists and other ne'er-do-wells of the interwebs," the comments section of Cooper's blog saw DLs chatting with one another about their work and offering one another advice or support; they also debated aesthetic interests, offered recommendations for further reading, and sometimes argued passionately with each other.[38] Tokyo-based writer and DL Paul Curran recalls that "my first comments were directed at Dennis and were related to my own writing and getting-to-know-you kind of things, or joining questions he asked to everyone, but then I started interacting with other DLs as we commented on each other's comments." The comments section, he claims, "became an extraordinarily vibrant and occasionally volatile virtual conversation or interactive text."[39]

In spring 2003, Cooper had launched Little House on the Bowery, a series with Akashic Books that was envisaged as "a line of fiction books in the tradition of the young New Directions and Grove Press."[40] Drawing on his experience as editor of Little Caesar Press, Cooper focused on challenging new work by young American writers (and some more established voices), publishing books by the likes of Trinie Dalton, Richard Hell, Martha Kinney, Derek McCormack, and Matthew Stokoe. In 2007, as part of the Little House on the Bowery series, he published an edited anthology of fiction by his blog's DLs called *Userlands: New Fiction Writers from the Blogging Underground.* His introduction to the volume acknowledges the importance of the conversations that circulated in the comments section, and he writes, "The comments section had become something of a virtual workshop full of supportive yet sharp discussions about writing by the people posting there. While I still used the blog as a creative outlet and playground for my own ideas, it seemed to me that my creations were less the point than the lure that brought newcomers into the growing artistic community that had formed backstage of the blog's main page."[41] These sentiments are echoed by other DLs, who attest to the importance of the community built in the comments section and its effects away from the blog. DL Mark Gluth says, "I love how the community that formed on his blog, in the comments section, has spilled over into social media (most of us are active in some way on Facebook) and the real world." Indicating an inherent understanding of the networked form of this particular community, he adds, "I think it presents this idyllic model for what the internet can be, at its best."[42]

In addition to forming the "backstage" part of *Dennis Cooper's*, the blog's relatively small but enthusiastic community also frequently dictated the content of the front page and the trajectory of the blog itself. If Cooper were asked a question in the comments section, the next day that question might be relayed to the group on the front page, and the day after it might form the subject of a subsequent post (e.g., "The Ideal Music Festival," June 28, 2005). Recurring "Self-Portrait Days" allowed DLs to scrapbook their memories by posting pictures of themselves as kids (July 15, 2006) or on Halloween (October 20, 2006); for Paul Curran, days like these "helped to gel the blog."[43] DLs were also encouraged to research their own posts on any topic; put together text, JPEGs, and video links; and then submit them to Cooper for publication. Guest posts were frequently as detailed and encyclopedic as Cooper's own, on subjects as varied as free jazz (curated by DL Jeff Jackson, October 9, 2006), British comedian Chris Morris (curated by DL Joe Mills, November 10, 2006), and American crooner Lorenz Hart (curated by DL David Ehrenstein, November 17, 2006).

As Gluth observes, the community generated by the comments section of Cooper's blog had a tendency to "spill over" into other areas of the internet and into the "real world," affecting the personal lives and careers of those who socialized in the comments section. A case in point, Gluth's first novella, *The Late Work of Margaret Kroftis* (2010), was published by Cooper in the Little House on the Bowery series, and two of his other books were put out by small presses run by friends he met on Cooper's blog—his novel, *No Other*, came out in 2014 with DL Ken Baumann's Sator Press, and his collection of short stories, *The Goners*, was released in February 2015 by DL Michael Salerno's Kiddiepunk Press. "My career would exist in some radically different form were it not for Dennis's blog," Gluth says.[44] Salerno, an Australian photographer and filmmaker whose Kiddiepunk Press website hosts Cooper's GIF novels, including *Zac's Haunted House* (2015), has also published poetry collections by DL Thomas Moore, adding his scarred photographic images of bare-chested young men to Moore's unsettling poems about sadomasochism and neglect. Although DLs tend to be mostly male-identified, Salerno also met the female illustrator and performance artist O. B. De Alessi in the comments section of Cooper's blog, and the two were married in 2011. The comments section at *Dennis Cooper's* was the site of innumerable other meetings, collaborations, encounters, intrigues, and even altercations; its development was nurtured and sustained by Cooper's feedback and the enthusiasm of the commenters themselves.

"A Place to Experiment"

Cooper's blog began as a type of informal personal website and a supplement to his official site. Launching the blog on May 15, 2005, he wrote, "The guys who run my official website (www.denniscooper.net) asked vistors [*sic*] what they'd most want to be added to the site, and they chose a blog by me. (Note to voters: I wish you'd picked a message board. You're the mysterious ones, not me.)"[45] Despite this initial reluctance, his blog quickly filled with the kind of information Dennis Cooper fans would love. He wrote, for instance, that some of his favorite films are Robert Bresson's *The Devil, Probably*; Orson Welles's *The Magnificent Ambersons*; and Andy Warhol's *Chelsea Girls*.[46] In June we found out he disliked Smashing Pumpkins singer Billy Corgan.[47] In July he revealed that his favorite *Simpsons* character was Barney.[48] From May to August 2005, dramatic details emerged about Cooper's repeated attempts to secure an American visa for his Russian boyfriend, the failure of these attempts, and his ultimate relocation from Los Angeles to Paris where, to his relief, his boyfriend acquired a visa from the French government. Other posts consisted of numerous Polaroid pictures taken during the 1970s and 1980s, where Cooper appeared alongside celebrities of the New York and LA literary scenes; John Ashbery, Donald Britton, Kenward Elmslie, Robert Glück, and Brad Gooch all made regular appearances.[49]

By revealing this kind of material about his life and offering readers the opportunity to chat with him, Cooper drew many fans to the site, a number of whom became part of the blog's community of commenters. DL Thomas Moore recalls being "very excited" when he found the blog: "I was a huge fan of Dennis Cooper's books. I can't remember when I first read the blog but I think I was looking for interviews with Cooper online, and reading bits and pieces about him and I saw the blog linked or listed somewhere."[50] Similarly, DL George Wines claims that "what drew me to the blog was an interest in Dennis's work. When I saw what was going on at the blog and that he actually responded to commenters there, I commented. I've been commenting almost daily ever since."[51] For DL Mark Gluth it was a short step from his own Dennis Cooper fan website to the blog and conversing with fans who were also drawn there in the hope of finding out new facts about their cult idol.

These DLs were not alone in their interest, and traffic to the blog was immense—at one point racking up more than eighty thousand hits per day.[52] Suddenly, a relatively little-known cult writer found himself with a huge audience turning up every day to read his opinions on, say, the latest indie film or Guided by Voices album, check out his work in progress, or just send him a message to say hi. Given the massive increase in Cooper's renown, it could be argued that a major reason for the blog's existence was to market him and his work. The popularity of the blog undoubtedly contributed to HarperCollins offering Cooper a three-book deal with the Harper Perennial imprint in 2008. But if the popularity of the blog resulted in increased visibility, even a cursory scan of Cooper's earlier work undermines any suggestion that selling books was the blog's principal goal. The phenomenon of fandom is far too interesting and important to Cooper to be used in a grasping and utilitarian way; he frequently identifies as a fan (of Rimbaud, for instance) and writes about fans, hero-worship, and idolization in thoughtful and compassionate ways.

His liner notes for the 1994 reissue of Sonic Youth's album *Sister* are dedicated to exploring the relationship between fans and their heroes. "Phoner," a fictional telephone interview between teenage Cubby and Thurston Moore of Sonic Youth, is written from the perspective of a teenage fan trying to make sense of the desire that underpins his relationship to Moore and to Sonic Youth's music. "What do you think of . . . fans like me?" Cubby asks Moore. "You're glad we worship you? Cos we *do*."[53] Later Cubby's "worshipping question" becomes more explicitly about the erotics of fandom, when he confesses:

> Shit. . . . Don't, like, hate me, but . . . your music gives me a boner, ha ha ha. Always. It's weird. Especially the, uh, *Sister* album and . . . *especially* when *you're* singing. And *especially especially* on. . . . You know in "Schizophrenia" when you sing that line about, uh, "Her brother says she's just a bitch with a golden chain"? Well, when you sing that, I'm thinking, "Yeah I *am* a bitch, Thurston," you know?[54]

The character of Cubby is tenderly drawn, allowing Sonic Youth fans (including Cooper himself) to identify with the teenager's hesitation, excitement, awkwardness, and hyperbolic appreciation of Moore: "He has *such a beautiful fucking surferish way of talking*. Wow! There *is* a God."[55] This encounter between Cubby and Moore is just one instance of Cooper taking fandom seriously and demonstrates his sensitivity to the vulnerability of the fan, offering an empathetic portrait of his powerlessness before his idol.

Moreover, the sheer volume of largely inconsequential, sometimes sensational biographical detail pasted daily onto the blog's front page was too insistent and prolific to be driven by a mere opportunistic exploitation of his fan base. Something was going on that was qualitatively different from a desire to make money from these disclosures, and Cooper seemed to be playing with his readers' expectations of what a blog is supposed to do—with surprising results. This tallied with his stated intention to use the blog as an opportunity for formal improvisation; early posts, for instance, described it as "a place to experiment," specifically "having to do with structure and form."[56] "I'm trying to do something really different with the blog," he said:

> But the blog is interesting because the blog really can be almost anything. It's a very limited form. Because I feel like in a way it's like going back to the beginning again, because I can do anything inside these rules and these strict things about what size the pictures can be and where they can be placed and what links you can do and what you can't do and all that stuff. . . . It's me using the blog and not having any kind of respect for what a blog is. (2007)[57]

As we saw in the case of *Frisk*, Cooper's writing often takes certain forms that would seem to bind his creative expression and bends them to his will (the Möbius strip that would seem to put limits on subjective expression ultimately comes to amplify its effect). Similarly, Cooper manipulated blogging's "totally degraded form," turning its traditional use as a site of autobiographical revelation into something altogether weirder and more compelling.[58]

One of the unusual effects of Cooper's blogging experiment was that the patient, meticulous collection and display of Dennis Cooper–related paraphernalia seemed to transcribe Cooper's biography with the compulsive care of a Dennis Cooper fan. His blog began to resemble a fan's scrapbook of a literary idol. Dennis Cooper's "Rules of Writing" were pasted into the entry of June 27, 2005 ("Characters are not real people. They are designs with human names"). July filled with photos of Dennis Cooper's LA pad, French friends, and Russian boyfriend. August 11 brought another "Dennis Cooper Writing Exercise" where readers could learn to write like Dennis. The intimate association between these blog postings and a fan's scrapbook looks intentional on Cooper's part when we consider his repeated use of scrapbooks in the early stages of his work, a technique he first encountered while working with William S. Burroughs's archive in the 1970s.

> I was able to really study the scrapbooks that Burroughs had made while writing his early novels, and I was very inspired and influenced by the way Burroughs had combined texts, both original and found, with magazine images and photographs in a collage-like way, and I thought that trying to work out my ideas and sense of style and structure through that kind of multi-media approach without the pressure of having to start writing novels might help me, and it really did. (2014)[59]

In the 1970s and 1980s, Cooper used scrapbooks to assist his exploration of contemporary celebrity culture and idolization—efforts that fed into the writing of *Idols* and other works from that period. His extensive JFK Jr. scrapbook, for instance (now held at NYU's Fales Library), forms the basis of *Idols'* "Some Adventures of John F. Kennedy Jr." series. Made up of 112 pages of clippings, including photos, news items, and gossip columns taken from celebrity magazines and newspapers like the *National Enquirer* and *Movie Life*, the scrapbook documents John Fitzgerald Kennedy Jr.'s adolescence, from the death of his father to his entrance to Brown University. JFK Jr. stares out from every page of this obsessively compiled folder. In grainy black and white, "John-John" stands solemnly by his father's grave; in a full two-page spread, he plays in the snow with his mother; three pages depict John on the beach, older now and naked from the waist up.

Cooper's scrapbooks are meditations on the phenomenon of celebrity in American post-1950s culture. Reminiscent of Andy Warhol's serial paintings of Marilyn Monroe and Jackie Kennedy (John-John's mother), they explore an American obsession with the rich and famous, a symptom of a "spectaclist" American society of Debordian proportions that "announces itself as an immense accumulation of spectacles," where "everything that was directly lived has moved away into a representation."[60] Specifically, Cooper's scrapbooks investigate the dislocation of subjectivity induced by the media's repeated representation of celebrity: how a bombardment of images of the same person may result in the

disappearance of their subject such that representation comes to supersede reality. Cooper stresses this in a recent interview about his scrapbooks: "I was very interested in 'the teen idol' at the time," he recalls. "I
was very interested by the way those boys were emptied out of meaning
by the media and by their image-makers" (2014).[61] Cooper's scrapbooks
trace the becoming-idol of teenage celebrities like John F. Kennedy Jr. and
offer a glimpse of the process he would later undertake on his blog.

The blog format, which encourages and even expects persistent self-
presentation, constantly offers writers the opportunity (or responsibility) to promote themselves and their work and construct hasty autobi-
ographies that structure their discussions. Cooper's blog executed its
form of self-presentation as a kind of scrapbook, akin those that might
be compiled by a teen heartthrob's young admirer or those assembled by
Cooper himself in previous decades. However, taking scrapbooks as one
of the conceptual supports of Cooper's much later blog-as-scrapbook introduces an estranging effect into this archetypally autobiographical text.
In short, the blog bore witness to the becoming-idol of Dennis Cooper,
and though his name hovered over every post, *Dennis Cooper's* ironically
failed to ever capture its subject.

THE POINT OF Cooper's self-scrapbooking was to maintain an alluring,
almost holographic presence in the middle of the blog that stoked the interest of Dennis Cooper fans, drew them to the site, and kept them there
as a loosely bound community while simultaneously removing himself
from the center. In effect, Cooper tried to create a network that avoided
the errors of the Beyond Baroque scene, creating a community that had a
magnetic, affective charge but that was also acephalous. Cooper usually
undertook this process slowly and subtly; its effect was necessarily cumu-
lative, so it was normally only perceptible on a macro level. Nonetheless,
there were particular instances where Cooper tipped his hand and his
project appeared in microcosm. On August 13, 2005, he published the
following post.

Saturday
—Wake up feeling burnt out. Our hotel room window faces an
apartment building where very late last night some young gay

guy and his mother had a screaming, hysterical, hours-long, sleep destroying fight. (Sample dialogue: Mom: "Louie! Louie! Louie! I'm your fucking mother! I don't want you to do that!" Louie: "Fuck you, mother! This is my life! This is my fucking life! Get out of my fucking life! I'm nothing, mother! Nothing! Nothing!")
—Drink lots of coffee, smoke a few cigarettes. (Remember to try to find a store, any store in Paris that sells Camel Wide Lights as I'm scarily down to three packs.)
—Walk to Columbus Café to buy a caramel-apple muffin.
(Observation: when French guys are beautiful, they're knee-buckling beautiful; when they're ugly, they're interesting ugly like character actors.)
—Fiddle with the order, contents of my poetry collection. Work on this one longish, fucked up prose poem I've been trying and failing to salvage for about a year now.
—Read the International Herald Tribune. (The Dodgers lost again?! No impeachment proceedings against Bush yet?! Courtney Love isn't really clean and sober?! "Stealth" is a box office flop?!)
—Sex. (n.o.y.b., m.f.)[62]

This apparently throwaway piece is important because it reveals the continual oscillation between self-assertion and self-abnegation that was underway in Cooper's blog. The conspicuous absence of a subject is the most explicit indication of this: the post recounts events, makes plans, registers observations, and notes reminders, all without the presence of an "I." Ostensibly itemizing a day in the life of Dennis Cooper, the erasure of a subject immediately puts the notion of an agent behind these activities into question.

The key to understanding the post lies in its opening section, which finds Cooper awake in a hotel, exhausted after a sleepless night. The setting is crucial as the hotel itself signifies the theme of selfhood and its abolition. Hotel rooms offer a few square feet of personal space in the vast, often foreign, urban sprawl. Individual cells to which visitors may retreat to recompose themselves after a day in the crowded city, they can also be blank spaces hospitable to the expression of desires that might otherwise be impeded by one's moral or ethical attachments. Wayne Koestenbaum remarks that "hotel uncanniness wakes us from lostness in the

'They'—peer pressure, social norms, the noise of crowd-think."[63] Yet, he continues, "the hallmarks of hotel experience are not-being-there, emptiness, automation, mechanical transmission," and if hotel rooms grant their occupants a certain liberty from "lostness," the iterability of the space also induces anonymity.[64] Tourists, traveling business types, drifters, runaways . . . for this procession of unknown characters, home is briefly a bed with starchy sheets, a Formica table, single-serving coffee, and a glass wrapped in plastic. To inhabit a hotel room is to partially identify oneself with its identikit accommodations; to become lost in that endless, faceless procession of guests; and to concede one's anonymity within it.

For the subject, therefore, hotel rooms are paradoxical zones where one's identity is continually menaced by the vacancy of being-identical. Cooper is predisposed to ideas of symmetry (and vacancy), so it is not surprising that Louie's hysterical declarations in the apartment opposite reflect this aspect of hotel rooms. "Fuck you, mother! This is my life! This is my fucking life! Get out of my fucking life! I'm nothing, mother! Nothing! Nothing!" Poised between a vehement affirmation of selfhood ("This is my life!") and an almost simultaneous withdrawal of that self ("Nothing! Nothing!"), Louie's dialogue mirrors the status of Cooper in his hotel room, which itself stands for his blog's attempt to scrapbook himself into obscurity.

This amplification of autobiography to the paradoxical point of opaqueness extended into the twenty-first century a mode of poetic composition undertaken by Cooper's friend Joe Brainard in the 1970s. Brainard's famous poem "I Remember" (1970–75), for instance, bears a striking resemblance to the blog's almost compulsive self-presentation and manipulation through extension of authorial identity. In Brainard's work, a lengthy series of aphoristic (and apparently honest) memories are announced by a ubiquitous "I remember."

> I remember the first time I got a letter that said "After Five Days
>   Return To" on the envelope, and I thought that after I had kept
>   the letter for five days I was supposed to return it to the sender.
> I remember the kick I used to get going through my parents' drawers
>   looking for rubbers. (Peacock.)
> I remember when polio was the worst thing in the world.
> I remember pink dress shirts. And bola ties.[65]

This sequence continues in the original 1970 edition for 32 pages and in subsequent editions for up to 138 pages and has lately become the focus of critical interest for the way it engages with contemporary Pop Art to produce a serial self. The thinking goes that while lines such as these evoke the lyric subject ("I"), their collection of biographical detail arranged in a series and stamped with a recurring brand speaks more to Pop Art works like Andy Warhol's famous *Campbell's Soup Cans* (1962) than the postwar Confessionalism of Robert Lowell and Anne Sexton. For critic Andy Fitch especially, Brainard's incessant "serial realist" display of what looks like a transparent self produces a queer effect: "Brainard's project at first appears to provide a fixed focal-point of projective identification, but finally presents an amorphous, polytemporal subject beyond the range of even the most empathic reader."[66] *I Remember*'s poetic voice is therefore discrete but indistinct, everywhere but elusive. Fitch continues, "Anticipating poststructuralist calls to deauthor poetic production, Brainard elects not to explode or erase the 'I,' but (all the more devastatingly, as Warhol and Lichtenstein prove through their departures from previous abstract painting) to repeat it—confounding rather than parodying the lyric subject's authentic coordinates at a particular time and place."[67] The cyber scrapbook of Dennis Cooper's blog updated Brainard's strategy of serial repetition that curves toward anonymity while retaining an affective, lyrical charge.

In adopting this mode of composition, Cooper affirmed his continued interest in a tradition of Pop-inflected, post–New York School poetry influenced by Brainard, which includes Cooper's friends like Eileen Myles and David Trinidad. According to Fitch, such work constructs "a pixelated, post-Romantic lyric 'I,' an 'eye' that enables post-War poetics to assimilate the affect-heavy, perspectively fluid simulacra of pop-cultural narrative."[68] Myles's work is especially close to Cooper's in this regard, and Myles's famous "An American Poem" in particular riffs on a confessional register, expanding its voluminous lyric subject so as to accommodate the entirety of the poem's imagined audience.

The poem starts, "I was born in Boston in / 1949," and right away this reads like a Confessional piece: Myles *was* born in Boston in 1949. Other details revealed—the speaker is a poet, a fixture of the 1970s New York scene, and an out lesbian—are also part of Myles's personal history. Yet the apparently autobiographical voice Myles sets up soon reveals that the "famous / Boston family" the speaker has supposedly run away from is in fact the Kennedys. "Yes / I am a Kennedy," the speaker declares, "And I await / your orders."[69] Coming out of a specific, factually anchored, quasi-autobiographical "I" into the rather more indefinite "a Kennedy," this confession also causes a shift in the poem from a confessional tone toward an oratorical one as the poet assumes the status of the people's candidate and rails against homelessness, AIDS, lack of basic medical care, and rising rents. As a Kennedy, the speaker has been sheltered from these problems, but "shouldn't we all be Kennedys?" they ask. The poem's closing lines then insist with expansive, Whitmanesque inclusivity upon the Kennedy name as a point of collective identification that runs contrary to "the message of Western / Civilisation": "I am alone."

> It is not normal for
> me to be a Kennedy.
> But I am no longer
> ashamed, no longer
> alone. I am not
> alone tonight because
> we are all Kennedys.
> And I am your President.[70]

In a way that recalls Cooper's retreat behind the scrapbooked idol of Dennis Cooper, in Myles's poem a queer slumming heir that passes for Eileen Myles sheds the poet's rags and is cast as a member of the Kennedy clan. For Myles, being a Kennedy means being a somebody, cloaking oneself in the mantle of privilege and celebrity, yet as Maggie Nelson succinctly observes, the poem "cannily performs being 'somebody' and 'nobody' at the same time."[71] Fame is crucial to Myles's improvisation. Here the famous image can conceal the self, an operation that is characteristic of the self-scrapbooking Cooper performed with his blog.

For both Cooper and Myles, this image may be used as a focal point from which to challenge the loneliness and isolation of modern society. It's something "we" may all gather around. "An American Poem" attests to Myles's commitment to retooling the lyric subject in order to implicate the reader in a communal experience comparable to the one Cooper tried to bring about on his blog. Myles's poem expands the self and the all-American family such that it can include all of the poem's implied

(American) audience, yet developing an online network out of a multitude of independent voices is a more involved affair and requires more than inclusion by fiat. For this network to come into being, Cooper had to both attract fans to his site *and* keep them there. By engaging with them every day, provoking and facilitating interactions between them, and regularly handing over the front page to them, Cooper turned his blog into a participatory artwork that was coauthored by a network of collaborators.

Deleted

On June 27, 2016, Cooper tried to log in to his blog as he had almost every day for the previous decade, only to find that his account had been shut down and his blog removed. An automated message informed him that Google had revoked his access because he had violated Blogger's terms of service. He and his lawyer repeatedly asked Google for more information, but for over a month no response was forthcoming. The incident quickly caught the attention of the international media, with articles appearing in venues such as the *New Yorker*, the *Guardian*, *Le Figaro*, and the *New York Times*. An online petition was also launched, demanding that Google reinstate the blog, and was signed by over four and a half thousand people.

In the absence of any official word from Google, speculation was rife about the cause of the blog's removal. One guess that gained traction as the weeks went on was that Cooper posted "risqué material" deemed inappropriate by the tech behemoth, which has owned Blogger since 2003.[72] The suggestion carried some weight; Cooper is evidently no stranger to controversy and over the years has found himself pilloried both by the conservative right (we recall James Gardner's assertion that *Try* represented "literature of self-defined immorality, anguish, and degradation") and an uninformed fringe of the queer left—in 1991 a Queer Nation affiliate group calling themselves Hookers Undivided Liberation Army (HULA) took umbrage at his depiction of at-risk gay teens and issued him a death threat.[73] Why Google would suddenly become offended by his blog content after ten years and about three thousand posts was anyone's guess, however.

Regardless, most media pieces decried Google's apparent act of censorship, tapping into widespread fears about the increasing proportion of the internet controlled by a tiny number of big tech firms with obscure links to three-letter government agencies. Yet few of the many articles that followed in the wake of the Google incident peered past the front page of the blog, and none reflected in any depth on its community, which, as I've argued, made Cooper's blog what it was. Content to portray Cooper as a wronged legislator of the world whose work had been shamefully desecrated, journalists mostly overlooked or marginalized the fact that for over ten years his blog was home to a dynamic and rapidly expanding network of queer subcultural producers and consumers.

On August 26, after two months of stonewalling him in defiance of mounting public pressure, Google finally returned *Dennis Cooper's* data to Cooper, and the blog relocated to a new web address. It was deleted, they said, when someone flagged an image from one of the blog's old "Self-Portrait Days" as child pornography. Cooper explains:

> According to Google, around the time my account was disabled, some unknown person came across this ten-year-old page, thought one of the images on it constituted child pornography, and reported it to Google who immediately disabled my account. Now let me just say that I know there are people who don't know me or my work well and think I'm some kind of ultra-transgressive shock-creating monster, but I completely assure you that if someone had sent me an image that I thought was child pornography, I would never have uploaded it, period.[74]

The blog reappeared, however, shorn of its archives. Although the data are now available, each post and its accompanying comments must be individually reinstated by Cooper by hand, an immense effort that will take years—if indeed it will ever be completed. All of the blog posts referenced in this chapter were deleted; all of their URLs redirect to a Blogger web page that states simply, "Blog has been removed" (the passive voice diminishing any real responsibility on Google's part, as if the removal were somehow an act of God). Given that they describe a place and a community that now no longer exists, the question of how to properly cite the sources named in these pages has flummoxed author and editor alike. It's one thing for an author to scrapbook himself into obscurity and engineer his withdrawal using "a pixelated, post-Romantic lyric 'I'"; it's quite another for him to be deleted along with ten years of work.

Sometime after the debacle I wrote a piece for a special issue of *GLQ:*

A Journal of Lesbian and Gay Studies that Gavin Butt and Nadja Millner-Larsen were putting together on the subject of the queer commons. I told them I wanted to write about how the structure of Cooper's blog engaged with the idea of the anarcho-queer commons. Inextricable from this was a compulsion to write down a history of the blog and have it recorded in the pages of what is, for some, the journal of record for queer studies. It was important to me that the enormity of Google's act be declared and its impact on the blog's community past, present, and future be known. I also wanted to counteract the deletion in some way—by testifying to the blog's existence and the existence of a once-thriving anarchistic network of distinguished locals that loitered in its comments section.

An important touchstone for my contribution was the work of queer theorist José Esteban Muñoz. In a 2013 article Muñoz set out to describe the LA punk scene of the 1970s and 1980s and theorize its affective and social relations, which he called "circuits of being-with, in difference and discord, that are laden with potentiality and that manifest the desire to want something else."[75] It wasn't so much the specifics of Muñoz's portrayal of LA punk that struck a chord. As I've pointed out, the LA punk scene had little or no tangible connection with Cooper's punk poetry scene at Beyond Baroque, which was more East Coast in character. Cooper's story didn't gel with Muñoz's historical reflections in that regard. But the ideas Muñoz spun out of those reflections were uncannily apropos when it came to framing the achievements of Cooper's blog and the networks it created.

Muñoz's conjugation of queerness and the commons was especially resonant, in particular his intention "to look to queerness as a mode of 'being-with' that defies social conventions and conformism and is innately heretical yet still desirous for the world, actively attempting to enact a commons that is not a pulverizing, hierarchical one bequeathed through logics and practices of exploitation."[76] In the article Muñoz also admits that he writes from the position of a punk-rock fan, where the word *fan* is, he says, a "degraded term" connoting familiarity instead of professionalism and subjective attachment rather than critical objectivity. He adds, "*Fan* is also meant to mark that I was not 'there' in the time and place of the Masque club where the Germs performed or in Los Angeles in the late 1970s and early 1980s."[77] This read like an open invitation to consider Cooper's blog along similar lines: I *was* a fan and I *was* there.

Considering the deletion of Cooper's blog according to the logic of the commons, I suggested, would allow us to queerly intervene into contemporary debates about the status of the commons and illustrate how, in the words of Michael Hardt and Antonio Negri, "the common exists on a different plane from the private and the public, and is fundamentally autonomous to both."[78] A commons denotes a set of resources shared by all the members of a community, resources that are generally considered in material terms: land, water, air, and so forth. Yet theorists like Hardt have also argued for an immaterial twenty-first-century commons, made up of "ideas, information, images, knowledges, code, languages, social relationships, affects and the like."[79] Where *Dennis Cooper's* was concerned, this constituted the entire body of discourse that made up the comments section and Cooper's posts: the knowledge, gossip, hints, tips, *information* shared through conversation and a history of interactions freely available to view online by past, present, and future members of the blog community. By suppressing and withholding the blog data, Google effected the enclosure of a commons, where enclosure designates the illegitimate withdrawal of common resources from circulation and the dispossession of the communities bound to them and, in this case, composed by them. George Caffentzis and Silvia Federici insist that "history itself is a common": with total indifference, Google cut off access both to the community's refuge and to its *archive*—the discursive history that permitted it to develop, that sustained it, and that secured its continuity into the future.[80]

Hardt and Negri maintain that of late, "the common, which previously was cast as external, is becoming completely internalized"; rather than exist outside it, the (immaterial) commons is increasingly a process that occurs from within capital itself.[81] This addresses the apparently paradoxical idea that a commons such as that of *Dennis Cooper's* could be made manifest on corporate servers via privately owned tech. Yet queer subcultures have a long history of founding precarious commons within enclosures controlled by both private and public interests that would ordinarily subdue them, which, *pace* Hardt and Negri, predates our era of biopolitical production. Bars on the bad side of town rented from unscrupulous landlords, bathhouses run by the Mob, the intimate spaces of public restrooms—commons like these and their histories constitute a transtemporal network of queer subcultural commons in which the anarcho-queer commons of *Dennis Cooper's* participates. If the fate of these examples is a cause for sorrow (shut down, stamped out, scattered to the winds, and, most recently, deleted), the *persistence* of such queer commons even online, even under the constant threat of erasure, remains a source of joy. Their histories—including the one written down in this book—are an archive of hope and an invaluable resource for queer communities to come.

Reading for Queer Subculture
in *The Marbled Swarm*

12 IN *DISCIPLINE AND PUNISH* (1975), Michel Foucault famously charted the evolution of the disciplinary regime, outlining the principal features of a transition from a sovereign society, where discipline was enforced through confinement and seclusion, to a modern disciplinary society, remarkable for the primacy of visibility and observation, moving "from a schema of exceptional discipline to one of a generalized surveillance."[1] A disciplinary society, according to Foucault, is predicated on the permanent visibility of the social subject, who must be legible at all times to an all-seeing or "panoptic" gaze. To be seen is to be subject to a disciplinary apparatus.

Under these conditions, the constant exposure of the subject to real—and imagined—surveillance results in an internalization and proliferation of the machinery of discipline. "He who is subjected to a field of visibility, and who knows it, assumes responsibility for the constraints of power," Foucault writes. "He makes them play spontaneously upon himself; he inscribes in himself the power relation in which he simultaneously plays both roles; he becomes the principle of his own subjection."[2] Constant visibility effectively induces individuals to forever unveil themselves and become the means of their own oppression. Foucault states that, "on the whole, therefore, one can speak of the formation of a disciplinary society in this movement that stretches from the enclosed disciplines, a sort of social 'quarantine' to an indefinitely generalizable mechanism of 'panopticism.'"[3]

In the twenty-first century, where the primacy of the visible seems absolute, Foucault's diagnosis is now more pertinent than ever. Individuals eagerly reveal a profusion of private information before the data bank of social media. Governments demand absolute transparency of the biopolitical subject in order to demonstrate their innocence until proven otherwise. Even dissent, in order to be considered as such, must present itself in terms that are immediately visible to the status quo and legible according to its definitions: criticisms of quasi-anarchist collectives such as Occupy Wall Street, for instance, spoke of the need for it to outline its "positive objectives"—"to be for something specific and not just against something."[4] Within this panoptic landscape, a subject's commitment to secrecy and concealment—effective negations of the sine qua non of such a social context—is imbued with a radical significance.

Foucault offers an especially useful lens through which to read *The Marbled Swarm: A Novel*, one of Cooper's most experimental and complex books. The strategies of encryption that structure the work indicate the importance of obscurity to its author: in its very form the novel explores alternatives to the ceaseless exposure (and concomitant subjugation) that marks the modern disciplinary society and how it regulates resistance. A counterpoint to the blog, whose autobiographical revelations allowed Cooper to conjure up an online community, sociability is also suggested in *The Marbled Swarm*, but it's the kind that works through ciphers rather than public confessions. As we'll see, Cooper's employment of these techniques, and indeed the way the novel brings into being a reader who can understand and enjoy them, resonates with queer subcultural traditions that run through the twentieth century in the decades before Gay Liberation.

The Marbled Swarm is a perplexing text made up of the testimony of an arrogant, rich, French twenty-year-old; the unnamed narrator describes, in baroque prose, a circuitous journey from a labyrinthine chateau in the French countryside to his flat in the Marais area of Paris. Along the way, he alludes to the fact that he's part of a small group of affluent Parisian cannibals, with whose help he murders his brother, a depressive teenager and manga fanatic, by fucking him violently then repeatedly rolling a heavy barrel over him. Hidden passageways behind false walls of French chateaus and mansions abound, and voyeurism is a recurring theme. Cooper has said that the book is "an homage to Robbe-Grillet—although not in the way you might expect" (2012).[5]

But the work is much more layered and multiplicitous than this outline might suggest, and its ostensible plot is something of a literary MacGuffin—a device that stokes readers' initial interest only to fade into irrelevance once they've been hooked. Far more interesting is the surface of the writing itself—the eponymous marbled swarm that denotes the narrator's manner of speaking, which we're told he inherited from his stepfather. Intricately brocaded, the father's authoritative version of the marbled swarm is made up of number of interlocking systems of speech taken from a variety of European languages and registers. According to the narrator, these are

> spoken at a taxing pace in trains of sticky sentences that round up thoughts as broadly as a vacuum. Ideally its tedium is counteracted by linguistic decorations with which the speaker can design the spiel to his requirements. The result, according to this mode's inventor, is that one's speech becomes an entity as open-ended as the air it fills and yet as dangerous to travel as a cluttered, unlit room in which someone has hidden, say, a billion euros.[6]

According to the narrator's riddling descriptions of it, the father's marbled swarm may have magical or manipulative effects; he suggests, for instance, that it may have helped him accumulate a vast fortune. However, the son's version—the one we're reading—is a flawed imitation, involving different systems amateurishly combined, that fails to come up with the same manipulative effect. The narrator laments that it's a bad cover version of an original classic: "My marbled swarm is more of an atonal, fussy bleat—somewhat marbled yet far too frozen tight and thinned by my loquaciousness to do the swarming it implies."[7] His version is nonetheless sufficiently marbled to produce the novel's disconcerting effect, which gradually turns the reader's curiosity away from the goal-driven pursuit of a Sadean murder-mystery plot toward a more expansive attentiveness to the simultaneous narrative threads swarming on the surface of the text.

Cooper describes how, "with *The Marbled Swarm*, I was trying to write a novel the way a sound technician mixes a song or piece of music into its final form." He continues:

I thought about each element of the novel, whether it was a narrative thread or character or reference point or an on-going motif or tone or rhythm. The idea was that they would always be there, but they would be emphasized or de-emphasized at different points, mixed into the foreground, middle ground, or background, being moved around constantly so the reader's attention would be directed all over the place. My idea was that it would give the writing a three-dimensional quality, as the reader is carried along by the musical surface of the novel, but he or she would also be chasing different story lines and recurring ideas as they waver and scamper about and hide inside the prose. (2011)[8]

A brief look at one of the more densely plotted sequences of *The Marbled Swarm* shows how this works. The fifth part of the novel opens with the revelation that, unbeknownst to all including his lawyer, the narrator's recently deceased stepfather was in possession of a chateau in northern France. Trying to find out more about the property and ascertain its value, the lawyer tells the narrator that he has found scant reference to it despite his extensive searches. However, he was informed by the mayor of a nearby village that in the chateau's gardens there exists a mysterious playhouse designed to resemble something from a comic book. The account then segues into a description of the narrator's final meal with his father, who reveals his discovery, years earlier, of a network of hidden rooms and passages in their previous home that were installed by a contemporary of Sade. The father then confides that his attraction to magic, rather than voyeurism, motivated the construction of secret rooms and passageways in their *new* home, which is an old shoe factory in Paris.

The rest of the section continues in this way, shifting from one narrative track to another, splicing sequences together, taking up themes discarded in previous sections. Fraying ideas are replaced by others, and storylines intersect at unexpected moments or escape in surprising directions. Embedded within these prominent threads (the spooky chateau, magic, the culinary arts, and so on) are hints at still more minor or "de-emphasized" ones. Passages in this section evoke fairy tales (we are told that "the playhouse would huff and puff"), Disney motifs (a child is said to be "goofy"), and comic books (the narrator refers to himself as "a kind of Robin who wasn't wedded to uncley Batman").[9]

Cooper by turns reveals and conceals constitutive storylines, tones, and ideas in the throng of the marbled swarm. This teasing kind of encryption is the overriding feature of *The Marbled Swarm*. The narrator repeatedly draws attention to it; reflecting on his story's construction, he confides, "Everything you've read thus far was more mischievous than you imagined . . . you're advised that what you see around you—walls, if you're hallucinating, or certain facts, if you're my readers—are potentially encrypted—with passageways if you're chateau guests, or subtexts if you're with me."[10] Speaking with Joshua Chaplinsky in November 2011, Cooper was similarly candid about the way the text plays with various codes to create its effect, remarking that "it is a puzzle and it can be solved. There's many, many, many clues—everything there is kind of a clue. You can believe the narrator when he says, 'I have an emotional problem and I've been lying to you,' if you want. But it is solvable."[11]

To someone committed to reading in a linear, teleological kind of way—that is, someone who comes to a text looking for story arcs and character development and all the predictable features of a strictly narrative reading—the book is likely to be dissatisfying. (Some readers even found it infuriating; one Amazon reviewer called it "Dennis Cooper's most maddening book so far," despite giving it four out of five stars.)[12] It's not hard to see why readers might be frustrated by it: *The Marbled Swarm* subverts conventional modes of reading such that the ultimate fate of a particular character or plotline is often beside the point. What *is* important is the kind of reading that takes the place of a teleological one—how Cooper initiates receptive readers into a new experience of reading where their attention is "directed all over the place." I'm tempted to borrow Samuel Delany's assessment of Ursule Molinaro's work here and suggest that "we must virtually learn *how* to read" the "all-over" construction of *The Marbled Swarm*.[13] Once initiated, however, the reader becomes attuned to the multiple, simultaneously functioning plots and themes, without privileging one over the other. The reader consequently becomes more attentive than assumptive—*presuming* less and *perceiving* more.

THINKING ABOUT Cooper's novel in this way—how its form encourages or creates conditions for the emergence of a nonteleological, nonhierarchical reading experience—brings to mind Eve Kosofsky Sedgwick's discussion of paranoid and reparative reading. In a well-known 2003 essay, Sedgwick reevaluated the kinds of reading practices cultivated by critical theory and queer theory, a field of study that she herself pioneered with works like *Between Men: English Literature and Male Homosocial Desire* (1985). Theory-based methods like New Historicism, deconstruction, and queer theory, she argued, were characterized by what Paul Ricœur called a "hermeneutics of suspicion."[14] Critical theory was built on the findings of Marx, Nietzsche, and Freud, whose work shared a conviction that the true nature of politics, society, or the mind was hidden and needed to be exposed in order to be understood and transformed; theory was thus wedded from the outset to a suspicious disposition. Over the years, however, this hardened into something less responsive and more pathological: "Not surprisingly," says Sedgwick, "the methodological centrality of suspicion to current critical practice has involved a concomitant privileging of the concept of paranoia" such that at the time she was writing, "to theorize out of anything *but* a paranoid critical stance has come to seem naïve, pious, or complaisant."[15]

In Sedgwick's formulation, paranoid reading has a number of attributes. It's programmatic, for one thing. Paranoid readers approach an individual text (or movement, or social phenomenon, etc.) intent on making a generalization about it based on predetermined ideas. The text is legible to them only insofar as it fulfills their expectations about what it *should* do; the specifics of this or that are irrelevant beyond their capacity to support an ideological position. In this way, paranoid reading is also hierarchical. Such is their zeal for the program, paranoid readers are fully prepared to ignore a text's specifics to demonstrate catchall theories.

In terms of Sedgwick's connection with Cooper, most significant is her characterization of paranoid reading as a "strong theory" that "places its faith in exposure."[16] In general, a paranoid reading produces a selective and rigorous interpretation designed to support a preconceived way of thinking. It is, Sedgwick writes, a "powerfully ranging and reductive" operation that presses a partial view into the service of theories that have been repeated so often and imitated so widely they've taken on the appearance of fact.[17] In addition, as we might expect given critical theory's basis in Marxist, Freudian, and Nietzschean thought, paranoid readings are all about exposure. "Paranoia for all its vaunted suspicion acts as though its work would be accomplished if only it could finally, this time, somehow get its story truly known," says Sedgwick, and her improvisation on Ricœur's phrase sees her recast it as a "hermeneutics of suspicion *and exposure*."[18]

While she stops short of condemning paranoid reading, which includes much of her earlier work and which she has a grudging admiration for, Sedgwick does seriously question its usefulness and suggests that its strong theoretical suppositions have meant that it's become unresponsive to changes in culture and society.[19] "The force of any interpretive project of *unveiling hidden violence* would seem to depend on a cultural context," she writes. "What does a hermeneutics of suspicion and exposure have to say to social formations in which visibility itself constitutes much of the violence?"[20] Indeed, given Foucault's remarks on "an indefinitely generalizable mechanism of 'panopticism,'" we might extend her question and wonder about the political efficacy of any contemporary work of exposure that, in making the invisible visible, would also seem to make it available for surveillance and capture by a disciplinary society.

In previous decades, exposure had enormous purchase for an emergent queer politics. Publicly exposing queer lives and making them visible before the law was a central feature of Gay Liberation and its efforts to secure for queers the same civil rights as straights. Outing and coming out of the closet were thus of a piece with the slogan often heard at Gay Liberation rallies, "We're Here, We're Queer, Get Used to It," which Laurie Marhoefer contends was "an answer-back to the debate about *discretion* that had marked the long history of gay and trans activism."[21] In the 1980s and 1990s, groups like ACT UP and later Queer Nation doubled down on the Gay Liberation project of exposure, combining spectacular public demonstrations such as die-ins with media-savvy tactics to draw maximum attention to the AIDS crisis and the plight of people living with AIDS. For six long years of the epidemic, Ronald Reagan, the president of the United States, refused even to pronounce the word "AIDS" publicly; under these conditions, queer pleas for homosexual visibility under the law necessarily morphed into angry, righteous demands to be seen and heard. As ACT UP's famous slogan "Silence = Death" attests, their lives depended on it.

But by the time Sedgwick drafted her essay in the mid-'90s, change was already underway. Indeed, she wrote it from a desire to reassess the legacy of HIV/AIDS and how it influenced her thought. During the AIDS crisis, she suggests, the primacy of the visible in activist circles for the most part went unquestioned. In hindsight, however, Sedgwick questions the necessity of proceeding directly from suspicion to exposure. It's not that exposure wasn't an effective strategy for contesting the negligence of the state and the ignorance of the general public vis-à-vis AIDS, but she's curious about the legacy of that knotting together of suspicion and exposure and the impact it had on her work. That impact, she concludes, manifests as paranoid reading.

Sedgwick's essay thus interrogates a mode of reading that was in the ascendancy at the time, which was determined to pursue a single inves-tigative or explanatory track and approached the task of reading with certain preconceptions in mind, most notably the value of exposure. This paranoid mode is comparable to the kind of reading elicited (and quickly withdrawn) by *The Marbled Swarm*—that teleological, strictly narrative reading that is aroused by the Sadean murder-mystery plot as a MacGuf-fin. It might seem counterintuitive to link Cooper and Sedgwick in this way, given that paranoid reading strategies are generally critical of teleo-logical accounts and often try to show the complicity of goal-oriented narratives with oppressive, capitalist ideologies. (See, for instance, the Language poets' criticisms of narrative, which we looked at in chapter 6, where they argued it was inherently conservative and bourgeois.) But the reading *position* in both cases is comparable: the paranoid reader and the narrative reader both approach a text in similar ways, reading with "strong" preconceptions in mind and looking to have their expectations (narrative or theoretical) confirmed rather than challenged—which is precisely why the MacGuffin works and why, as Sedgwick writes, "para-noia is nothing if not teachable."[22]

The mode of reading that takes the place of a teleological one, fur-thermore, resonates closely with the alternative kind of reading practice favored by Sedgwick, which she names "reparative." The "reparatively positioned reader," she says, is driven by pleasure. Such readers display an impulse that is "additive and accretive," which favors plenitude over reduction and a weak and contingent approach over a strong theoretical devotion to "regularity and repetitiveness."[23] In Heather Love's helpful gloss, reparative reading "stays local, gives up on hypervigilance for atten-tiveness; instead of powerful reductions it prefers acts of noticing, being affected, taking joy and making whole."[24] Crucially, a reparative reading position is open to the possibility of surprise, which could equally describe the reading position demanded of Cooper's book; as we have seen, it requires its reader be receptive and alert, open to the appearance of new clues or encrypted tones and themes.

SEDGWICK'S AND COOPER'S encouragement of analogous reading positions, which prefer "acts of noticing" over the determined pursuit of a single narrative (or theoretical) thread, can be better understood when viewed against the backdrop of queer subcultural communication in the decades before Gay Liberation. Looking at examples of textual and linguistic artifacts that came out of oppressed and clandestine queer communities in the early twentieth century, we can make out a continuity between reparative or all-over readings and the kinds of readings these previous artifacts required and solicited. As we'll see, Sapphic romans à clef, Polari or gayspeak, and other forms of encrypted subcultural expression often passed as straight discourse but offered much more to the engaged queer reader. In the years before secrecy became synonymous with the closet and invisibility with political quietism, these subcultural forms circulated as open secrets within mainstream culture, speaking to and in a sense creating the kind of reader later interpellated by Cooper and Sedgwick.

The roman à clef is a novel in which biographical detail is concealed beneath anodyne prose. While its origin dates from seventeenth-century France, its function as a satirical or parodic mode of address that speaks uncomfortable truths to power from behind a fictional screen has assured its continued use to the present day; Joe Klein's *Primary Colors* (1996), Roberto Bolaño's *2666* (2005), and Robert Harris's *The Ghost* (2007) are all popular works that use roman à clef techniques. For modernist women writers who wanted to distribute stories featuring same-sex desire, the roman à clef also offered a unique opportunity to get their work published and circulating in the straight mainstream. American (and some English) writers of so-called Sapphic romans à clef used the form to express personal attachments and describe private trysts in ways that circumvented the panoptic gaze of anti-obscenity legislation. Sashi Nair writes, "In the period between the world wars, a number of female modernist authors mobilized a particular version of the roman à clef genre in order to represent a desire that was seemingly unspeakable, strategically deploying references to personal experience as a means to simultaneously reveal and encrypt same-sex emotional and physical attachments."[25]

Djuna Barnes was one notable writer of the Sapphic roman à clef, and her work, as Thomas Heise points out, is marked by a preoccupation with secrecy and writing's capacity for encryption. Her early journalism depicting the space and community of New York's Greenwich Village, for example, shows that "for Barnes, authentic queer life was contingent upon being submerged, unknowable and away from the prying eyes of New York. . . . Ultimately the [queer] underworld—hidden below the basements of a depraved neighborhood—remained concealed within her prose as a means of staving off the erosion of local detail in the community she seeks to shield."[26] Her novel *Nightwood* (1936) extends this project, conducting an interest in obscurity and concealment though the form of the roman à clef.

An oneiric ramble through the streets of interwar Paris, the novel is full of eccentric characters, most notably Dr. Matthew-Mighty-grain-of-salt-Dante-O'Connor, melancholic Nora Flood, and her promiscuous, alcoholic lover, Robin Vote. T. S. Eliot was a friend of Barnes's and wrote a preface to the text when it was republished 1937; in it he diverts the reader's attention away from lurid fascination with the oddballs who populate the text and encourages us to appreciate instead its lyricism and the universality of its humanist achievement. To mistake its representation of "the human misery and bondage which is universal" for a "horrid sideshow of freaks," he says, is "to miss the point."[27]

However, in addition to these two interpretations or readings—one Eliot anticipates and scorns, one he construes and endorses—there exists yet another, the point of which is unsurprisingly missed by him. Couched within the form of the roman à clef, *Nightwood* also describes, in detail but at a safe remove, the disintegration of Barnes's relationship with her lover Thelma Wood. Nora Flood thus stands in for Barnes and Robin Vote stands in for Wood, and the novel as a whole is an attempt by Barnes to share how she felt with a coterie of friends, which scholarship has taken to be the group that moved through Natalie Barney's salon in Paris between the wars (including the likes of Colette, Gertrude Stein, and Isadora Duncan, among others). Thus when Nora sadly reflects on her fraught liaison with Robin, Barnes's prose broadcasts on at least two different frequencies, embedding within a fictional register an autobiographical account that she, Wood, and the members of their circle would understand: "Looking at every couple as they passed, into every carriage and car, up to the lighted windows of the houses, trying to discover not Robin any longer, but traces of Robin, influences in her life (and those who were yet to be betrayed), Nora watched every moving figure for some gesture that might turn up in the movements made by Robin."[28] *Nightwood*'s "layered, simultaneous address to public, counterpublic and coterie audiences" thus scrambles the salient features of Barnes's relationship with Wood and makes them decipherable to a small clique of readers.[29]

Barnes's encoding of her relationship into a roman à clef foreshadows the later use of Polari, or gayspeak, by queer British subculture in the years that followed the Second World War. Immortalized in British singer Morrissey's 1990 single "Piccadilly Palare," parlyaree, parlare, or Polari, despite its heterogeneous origins in the murky depths of Britain's urban spaces, is now synonymous with the gay scene of postwar London and Manchester; "put simply, [it was] a secret language mainly used by gay men and lesbians in London and other UK cities with an established gay subculture, in the first 70 or so years of the twentieth century."[30] Similar to other types of midcentury slang in its use of metonymy ("handbag," for example, denotes money) and anagrams ("ecaf," often shortened to "eek," is a face), Polari is less a discrete language than a composite lingo made up of a special mix of linguistic elements and registers. In terms that are uncannily redolent of those used by the narrator of *The Marbled Swarm* to describe his father's speech, cultural historian Matt Houlbrook says of Polari, "Derived from a mixture of lingua franca, Italian, Romany, and backslang originally associated with eighteenth-century theatrical troupes, by the twentieth-century Polari was part of that amorphous 'underworld' slang current amongst dockside labourers, seamen, prostitutes and tramps. By the 1920s it had clearly entered common usage within queer urban life."[31]

The most significant feature of Polari, and one of the primary reasons for its emergence within certain urban gay communities in Britain, was its facilitation of secrecy. Faced with the threat of arrest and prosecution until the decriminalization of homosexuality in 1967, anti-languages and asignifying systems such as Polari enabled the gay subcultures of cities like London to continue to circulate within, around, and beneath the prevailing language of society at large.[32] Identifying gay men with other ostracized, often criminalized groups at the time, Leslie Cox and Richard Fay affirm the importance of this aspect of Polari's genesis and employment, arguing that "just as some marginalized groups developed secret codes, such as criminals' cant or tinkers' shelta, so gay men developed Polari. These codes developed from the need to express common identity, for self-protection, and for secrecy."[33] Houlbrook similarly asserts that, if "Polari was a linguistic practice through which men enacted their difference, it was simultaneously a tactic of concealment, evasion and invisibility. . . . Whatever their degree of fluency, these 'special words' allowed men to hide their character and conversation from all but those in the know."[34]

In the following passage, evocative of the vocabulary and cadence of the Polari that was used in London, discernible English terms and phrasing give way to code-encrusted arabesques designed to foil the intrusion of a mainstream audience and evade its penetrating glare while remaining open to the initiates of the queer underworld.

> As feely homies [young men], when we launched ourselves on the gay scene, Polari was all the rage. We would zhoosh [fix] our riahs [hair], powder our eeks [faces], climb into our bona [nice] new drag [clothes], don our batts [shoes] and troll off [cruise] to some bona bijou [nice, small] bar. In the bar, we would stand around parlyaring [chatting] with our sisters [gay acquaintances], varda [look at] the bona cartes [nice genitals] on the butch homie [masculine male] ajax [nearby] who, if we fluttered our ogleriahs [eyelashes], might just troll over [wander over] to offer a light.[35]

The distribution of Polari textures in the conversations of some gay men at this time—the surfacing of encoded terms (riah, ajax, bona drag, etc.) within their speech—evokes the alternately visible and invisible circulation of gay subcultures within the heteronormative terrain of British urban spaces in the 1940s and 1950s.

The Marbled Swarm resembles earlier forms of queer subcultural communication in its wariness about exposure and its abundant use of codes. The narrator's language is full of elisions, looping and folding in an apparent attempt to avoid being pinned down. Lines typically corkscrew through repeated future unreal conditional formulations that conceal their ultimate destination; he elusively states, for instance, "If vampire movies hadn't been the franchise of that year, and were wastrel fashion models and feeble-looking bands not so incredibly in vogue, and if a wary-eyed pallor were not, as a consequence, the diamond in the rough of facial options, my sad state might have turned the single-minded nerds and fops moseying around me into Good Samaritans."[36] The narrator is particularly evasive when he talks about his sexuality and repeatedly declines to be outed: "Were I gay and not the creep to whom you'll turn the other cheek soon enough"; "were I even half as gay as you imagine"; "were I gay or, if you insist, entirely gay I would have . . . well you tell me. I'm not gay enough to know."[37] Like the Polari-peppered speech of queer Londoners, the novel's prose, as we have seen, is also littered with key words and phrases that signal the surfacing of a particular narrative strand that the attentive reader will recognize. The phrase "One day . . ." or the suggestion of a "trail of breadcrumbs" indicate the proximity of a fairy-tale thread, for instance, while the sudden appearance of a carousel or a roller coaster denotes the arcing of the story toward a Disneyland thread.[38]

The form of *The Marbled Swarm* is thus reminiscent of the form of certain queer subcultural artifacts that were similarly evasive and cryptic in their expression; as a consequence, the kind of reading it demands also resembles the reading practices demanded by those earlier forms. Sapphic romans à clef, Polari or gayspeak, and other examples of encrypted queer language required particular reading publics to decode them; emerging out of incipient queer communities, they also fed back into them in a recursive feedback loop that reinforced a sense of queer belonging. But they also required their readers to be alert enough to notice queer codes as they floated by on the tide of a dominant culture—a word in Polari overheard amid idle chatter on a London bus or a poem found in a literary magazine that seemed just a little *too* paratactical to be straight. With few obvious places to go to find overt queer representation (and fewer legal places), it's possible that one could find covert queer representation *anywhere*; one needed to be attentive and alert to its possible appearance should it, perchance, come. In other words, although encoded queer communication evolved as a reaction to homophobic violence and the threat of surveillance, it also cultivated and catered to a public that had the necessary skills in reading against the grain, that was observant and receptive to the sudden appearance of a familiar clue that hinted at a disguised queer alliance—a community, even. It's this kind of all-over reading position that Cooper calls upon in his work and, with reparative reading, Sedgwick also evokes: their work recuperates and revives a queer reading position that prevailed in queer subcultures in the pre-Stonewall days. In doing so, their works address themselves to a cultural rift that came about during the gay civil rights era and was more apparent in its aftermath.

GAY LIBERATION brought about a sea change in queer culture. In keeping with a project of exposure, queer desire could now be theoretically expressed in public, openly, in forms previously reserved for a straight majority (theoretically—needless to say, public expression of homosexual desire was and continues to be restricted both by institutional homophobia and the threat of violence). The embrace of such cultural forms came at a cost, however, and the successes of Gay Liberation in terms of queer visibility and gay rights entailed a renunciation of previous modes of expression that, to the out, proud, post-Stonewall queer, were a painful reminder of a secretive and shameful past. As David M. Halperin recalls in *How to Be Gay* (2012):

> Gay men my age prided themselves on their generational difference. We were dimly aware that for a lot of gay men ten or twenty years older than us, being gay had something to do with liking Broadway musicals, or listening to show tunes or torch songs or Judy Garland, or playing the piano, wearing fluffy sweaters, drinking cocktails, smoking cigarettes, and calling each other "girlfriend". . . . From my youthful perspective, which aspired fervently to qualify as "liberated," those old queens were sad remnants from a bygone era of sexual repression—victims of self-hatred, internalized homophobia, social isolation, and state terror.[39]

In his essay on the Broadway musical, D. A. Miller similarly sees the forsaking of earlier forms of queer culture as an attempted negation by younger queers of the imagined secrecy and shame of their predecessors. Broadway, he argues, is bound up with the realities of the gay experience, including "the solitude, shame, secretiveness by which the impossibility of social integration was first internalized." "Precisely against such realities," he writes, "is post-Stonewall gay identity defined: a declarable, dignified thing, rooted in a community, and taking manifestly sexual pleasures on this affirmative basis." Consequently, the pleasures of Broadway had to be renounced and, Miller wryly adds, "No gay man could possibly regret the trade, could be anything but grateful for it."[40]

We might put the forms of queer subcultural expression explored in this chapter—those varieties of verbal and written communication that not only *connoted* the secrecy of pre-Stonewall life but actually *facilitated* it—in the same category as the likes of Miller's Broadway musical and the artifacts Halperin explores in his study of traditional gay male culture, including the films of Joan Crawford. These cultural modes didn't so much fall out of fashion after Stonewall as they were pushed, disowned by an out gay public bent on visibility and representation beyond the implied, the encrypted, and the encoded; beyond shame and beyond secrecy. This before/after discontinuity was compounded by the AIDS crisis; activist groups like ACT UP and Queer Nation were committed to the project of exposure and cast the nonexplicit as not merely shameful or outmoded but actually dangerous and potentially in league with a repressive, homicidal state. Moreover, the AIDS death toll in the 1980s and 1990s ruptured a line of cultural inheritance between members of successive generations of gay men. Pre-Stonewall cultural forms and reading practices might have endured longer and circulated less shamefully had the dialogue between older and younger generations of gay men not been interrupted in such a devastating way.

The rejection of previous subcultural forms contributed to a less obvious but no less momentous shift in the ways queer publics read. As the implicit gave way to the explicit, skills like decoding were no longer all that relevant to an emergent queer community whose motto was We're Here, We're Queer. You also didn't need to be all that alert and receptive if what you were looking for was *right there*. In their different ways, Cooper's *The Marbled Swarm* and Sedgwick's disquisition on paranoid/reparative reading draw our attention to what was lost in that shift: a healthy skepticism about the primacy of the visible, for instance; a receptivity to possibility and surprise, the skill of reading against the grain, or an antinomian (or even anarchistic) cynicism about dominant ideas and "strong" theories.

By eliciting a reading position akin to that of a queer, pre-Stonewall subject who is attentive, perceptive, and prefers "acts of noticing" over grand reductions, their work also offers the opportunity to reverse this shift. Something different from nostalgia is at work here ("I really, really hate nostalgia," Cooper has said. "I think it's a bad, distorting thing, so I never romanticize things from the past." [2014]); we might instead consider their recovery of a discarded queer subcultural reading position as *itself* a reparative gesture.[41] This gesture seeks to overcome the rupture or discontinuity in queer cultural life before and after Gay Liberation, drawing on a pre-Stonewall past in an attempt to learn, once more, *how* to read.

Asignifying Desire |
HTML Novels and Feature Films

13 SOON AFTER THE appearance of *The Marbled Swarm*, Cooper set to work on another novel, which would more closely resemble a memoir than any of his other books. "I would like it to be a very emotional novel," he told Ira Silverberg in the fall of 2011.[1] Building on ideas of memory and representation explored in his Villa Gillet lecture and his work with Vienne, in this new book Cooper planned to focus exclusively on his relationship with George Miles. He also planned to make the novel his last, closing the circle that began twenty-three years earlier with the publication of *Closer*. Ever drawn to concepts of symmetry and balance, completing ten novels—five Cycle novels and five post-Cycle novels—greatly appealed to him.

Things did not go well from the start. Trying to write about Miles in a direct way deeply saddened and disturbed him, and his efforts to describe their relationship often left him tearful and dejected. By September 2012, the impact of writing the novel was apparent on his blog, where he admitted that he was "suffering"; he worried the book would not do justice to Miles or their friendship and was "just a cathartic explosion of love and pain that deserves no better than a diary." Miles was evidently on Cooper's mind all the time during this period and became a recurring preoccupation in his conversations on the blog. "I'm writing this book about George Miles right now," he wrote to DL Dom Lyne on September 10, 2012. "I loved him like I've never loved anyone else in my life, and I would still be with him if that had been possible, and the things his condition forced into our relationship were nothing compared to the complete privilege and joy that every minute with him gave me."[2]

At the end of his tether, in October Cooper made the uncharacteristic decision to have his tarot read, trying to make contact with Miles and find a direction for the project. He told blog regular James Champagne, "You know, I'm a big skeptic, although I'm as open to the idea as I have ever been. Someone is going to do a Tarot reading for me early next week to try to contact him. I decided to go for it out of a combo of desperation and thinking I can do something with it in the novel."[3] It's unclear exactly what the outcome of the reading was (Cooper intimated to me that in spite of his skepticism, he was troubled by what he was told); in any case, he gave up working on the novel shortly afterward. Years later he would refer to it only as "the novel I tried to write about my real relationship with George Miles. That crashed and burned badly" (2016).[4] When one door closes, however, another often opens—and in Cooper's case it would open wide onto vistas and adventures that would lead his work in exciting new directions. While his most recent attempts at a print novel had been preoccupied with the solemn work of completion and closure, these new projects would inaugurate a fresh, future-oriented phase of his career that would take its principal cues from collaboration and friendship, specifically his new friendship with the young Franco-American video artist Zac Farley, whom he met in December 2012.

Born in 1988, Farley grew up in France but moved to the United States when he was sixteen. He attended American high school and after graduation went to the California Institute of the Arts, where he was first introduced to Cooper's work by Matias Viegener, who had included *The Sluts* in his course on sex, writing, and pornography. Farley dropped out of CalArts after a couple of years and found his way to Northwestern University in Illinois, where he took a degree in art history and gender studies. Fascinated from an early age with video art and editing processes, he also attests to the influence of video artist Steve Reinke, with whom he studied at Northwestern. He returned to France in 2012 and first met Cooper in Paris a couple of months later. "We immediately felt a strong personal kinship, and our interests as artists were very similar," Cooper says (2018).[5] Farley remembers that "our collaborations started really organically, with friendship, and weren't strictly limited to the realm of film."[6] They quickly became close friends and began collaborating on a range of projects, including books, documentaries, music videos, and, as we shall see, feature films.

IN 2015 COOPER RELEASED *Zac's Haunted House*, the first of a number of "HTML books" dedicated to Farley, composed solely of large columns of GIFs, or graphics interchange format files, a ubiquitous image format normally used on blogs or social media to punctuate a reaction. Popular GIFs are most often short, looping snippets of film or TV, taken from the larger narrative and uploaded to the internet by users themselves. In terms of their aesthetic, they recall zoetropes or kinetoscopes, which similarly featured short, silent, looping sequences of images that conveyed the impression of movement.

Critics account for the renewed popularity of GIFs more than three decades after their first release in 1987 by pointing to the ease with which they can be made and circulated online. This free circulation of GIFs, coupled with their emergence out of an amateur or DIY milieu, has led scholars like Graig Uhlin to stress their opposition to the commodity form and a capitalist system of exchange; for him, GIFs are "illustrative examples of an alternative economy of exchange enabled by digital technologies, namely the sharing economy of the internet."[7] Other critics suggest that because it was originally published as an open format, the GIF has the ethos of the commons encoded into its history. Jason Eppink writes, "A successful gif is one that is shared, eclipsing its creator to become an essential part of a cultural conversation. The result is a digital slang, a visual vocabulary, unencumbered with authorship, where countless media artifacts are viewed, deployed, and elaborated upon as a language more than as a product. Even though individuals process the pixels, communities make the GIFs."[8] This notion of the GIF commons is crucial where Cooper's HTML books are concerned: all of the GIFs used in the books were sourced online using a simple keyword search; none were specifically created by him. All of the completed works were also made available to download for free, allowing them to circulate back into the alternative economy of exchange their constituent GIFs came from.

The idea for creating a novel in GIFs came to Cooper through his blog. "I was making these posts that were tall stacks of GIFs organized along a thematic," he says. "I started to realize that really interesting things were happening between the GIFs—rhythmic, poetic, narrative, associative things. So I started experimenting with organizing them in a deliberate way, and then dividing them into groupings."[9] Those groupings first started to look like sentences, then paragraphs, then chapters; soon he realized that he was writing fiction in much the same way as he'd written his previous novels and short stories, but instead of using words, he was using silent, low-quality looping clips retrieved online. "I take the GIF fiction as seriously as I do my written fiction," says Cooper, adding that he considers his HTML books to be among his finest works (2016).[10]

Reading a book like *Zac's Haunted House* is like looking at someone's blog or Tumblr (a visuals-heavy microblog). Clicking on the index.html file opens the book in an internet browser; to read it, you simply scroll through huge vertical towers of GIFs taken from innumerable sources (films, TV shows, cartoons, workout videos, etc.). But even on first impression, the arrangement looks much more deliberate than the mood board of most blogs: thematic or rhythmic echoes join together clusters of images, divided from the clusters above and below by a serrated pause line.

The novel's preface, consisting of two contrasting GIFs, indicates the best way for the reader to approach the work. A hand-drawn animation of a Vibroplex Morse code key tapping out an irregular pattern is followed by a clip taken from a horror movie, where flashes of lightning intermittently illuminate two demonic red eyes. Wildly different both in terms of how they look and what they represent, the attentive reader will nonetheless sense a kind of continuity between them—the spasmodic tapping of the Morse key, for instance, coincides on occasion with the fitful rhythm of the lightning flashes, and this rhythmic communication between the GIFs seems to supersede signification. Put differently, the GIFs don't share a *meaning* as such; instead, something like sensation joins them together. The preface announces that in the novel that follows, readers should expect surface resonance to supersede narrative. Even when sequences are less visually jarring than this one, the chains of signification created by them are perpetually undermined. In one early sequence, a flow of water gushes from a shower hose, arcing down into subsequent images of flowing particles, tumbling grain, and a cartoon waterfall, all

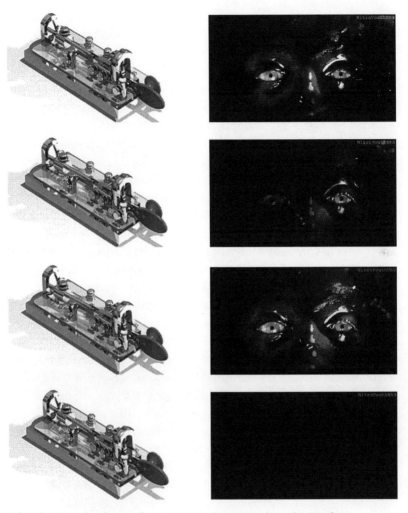

Vibroplex Morse key from preface
to *Zac's Haunted House* (2015).

Demonic red eyes from preface
to *Zac's Haunted House* (2015).

trickling down interminably and pooling in the last image, a non sequitur where a goth teenager in black and white convulses in despair while clutching a book to his chest.

Cooper is evidently still interested in bringing about an all-over reading experience where the reader's attention is drawn away from the pursuit of a narrative to what's happening on the surface of the text. The HTML novels seem highly successful in this regard. Readers of *Zac's Haunted House* and its sequel, *Zac's Freight Elevator* (2016), have described the "intense emotional response—fear, disgust, hope, anxiety, joy" provoked by the novels' arrangement of GIFs and have spoken of the works evoking "powerful and gnarled emotions."[11] Such readers are far more reluctant to discuss what the books are *about*, however, and there seems to be a tacit understanding that what the books *mean* in a traditional sense isn't really the point. This assault on normative reading practices irritated some; just as *The Marbled Swarm* had its frustrated detractors, *Zac's Haunted House* caused conservative readers to round on the idea that it was even a novel. "Can something be described as fiction if it has no narrative?" moaned the *Huffington Post*'s Claire Fallon, adding that "there's a pretty solid genre already suited to [Cooper's] GIF sequence: video art."[12]

For his part Cooper maintains that they are novels, even if they are "emotion and sensation"–based works whose sequences of GIFs try to convey "a doomed or dooming relentlessness" like the feeling of being in a free-falling elevator.[13] Elsewhere he says writing the books felt like sculpture or even landscaping: "When you combine gifs," he says, "you get this immediate intense energy, and then it's just modulating that through editing choices . . . it was very strangely so calculated but also like trying to landscape a rushing river" (2015).[14]

While Cooper's HTML books may not be typically novelistic, contrary to Fallon's suggestion they also differ greatly from video art—or even GIF art, which is itself now a legitimate genre, with GIF artists exhibiting at the Whitney Biennial. For one thing, video art and GIF art are produced as commodities, but Cooper's works are distributed for free online. While much GIF art can be slick or affected, Cooper's works are also markedly demotic. *Zac's Haunted House*, *Zac's Freight Elevator*, and the other HTML "Zac" books, *Zac's Control Panel* (2015) and *Zac's Coral Reef* (2018), revel in the clichéd iconography of internet chatter. Paul Soulellis calls Cooper's GIFs examples of "poor media"—that is, "compressed forms

that privilege accessibility, remixability, and circulation over quality"—
but what's true for the books' medium is also true for their message, which
is anything but highfalutin.[15] Emblematic of this is the final GIF of *Zac's
Haunted House*, a legendary 2.4-second loop of a kangaroo dropping a
yellow ball. With each repetition, the kangaroo appears alternately absurd, pathetic, or irritated, and the GIF's polysemy has led to it becoming
a fixture of the listicle, or list-based article. In concluding the novel with
this coup de grâce, Cooper attests to his appreciation for the vernacular
cultures of the internet.

COOPER'S HTML BOOKS may be aligned with the popular cultures
of the web, but they're also curiously reminiscent of the work of the
twentieth-century avant-garde. As assemblages of found GIFs, we might
consider them as digital counterparts to Robert Rauschenberg's combines
or Joseph Cornell's shadow boxes, which similarly juxtaposed salvaged
objects in unique and complex arrangements. Cooper insists that we
should think of his works not as visual art but as novels, however, which
puts them more in line with a literary tradition of appropriation and the
cut-up method.

With a cut-up, phrases, sentences, or whole sections of written works
are removed from their original context and relocated elsewhere, in a
different arrangement, producing a different effect. Appropriation was all
the rage among literary experimentalists in the last century: William S.
Burroughs and Brion Gysin might have been its most famous practitioners, but they certainly weren't the only ones to try it, and of the circle of
writers Cooper knew or was familiar with, John Ashbery, Ted Berrigan,
and Kathy Acker (to name just a few) all flirted with it. Acker seems to
have been its most sustained—and controversial—practitioner; cut-ups
were a constant in her writing and were a prime example of what Georgina Colby calls her "antiabsorptive experimental practices" that aimed
to undermine traditional structures of signification.[16] Although Cooper's
early scrapbooks (and his blog as an online scrapbook) demonstrate an
abiding interest in cut-up techniques, his HTML books are his first publicly available works composed entirely of appropriated material. They are
in fact a twofold appropriation: the GIFs in these novels and stories are
recontextualized from their usual setting of blogs and online chat, but

these GIFs are *themselves* the result of an appropriation, generally cut from a larger, mass-media product, looped, and redeployed online.

One overriding feature of the GIF's particular form of appropriation is its focus on movement and gesture. James Van Der Beek crying, Jean-Luc Picard covering his face with a hand, Keanu Reeves giving a thumbs-up—these well-known GIFs are created by extracting a gesture from the narrative flow of a film or TV show and isolating it from the source text. Looping the decontextualized gesture over and over, which excludes its target and infinitely defers its end point, liberates it from participating in a narrative or needing to refer to anything in particular. By bracketing narrative, the GIF hypostatizes the gesture (i.e., gives it a distinct material existence) such that it can be easily redeployed in another context.

The hypostatization of gesture by the GIF sets it apart from the source text narrative but also puts it in opposition to the narrative as a meaning-making apparatus. According to Hampus Hagman, the GIF is characterized by "the attempt to make movement strange again, to assert a power of movement all its own, liberated from the responsibility of making it mean and carry out narrative goals." In general, movement is important in a narrative-driven mass-media product like a film or a TV show only insofar as it helps the plot along or contributes to character development. GIFs retrieve these otherwise meaningless movements and gestures. For Hagman, "the animated gifs that are encountered all over the internet very seldom tell a story: on the contrary they seize hold of those purely excessive moments that carry little to no narrative purpose."[17] Félix Guattari would call such "excessive" moments *asignifying* elements, which play a crucial role in his consideration of how cinema intersects with revolutionary desire. Guattari's 1973 essay "Cinema of Desire" offers vital insight into the importance of these asignifying elements and indeed how to interpret their isolation in the animated GIF.

For Guattari, modern capitalist society is characterized by the monopoly of eros, a systematized form of attachment that channels libidinal energies toward particular objects. These attachments could be the binary relation of man/woman but equally mother/child or father/child—what matters is that the ensuing couplings uphold the status quo and maximize production. What Guattari calls "a dominant semiology" is essential to producing and disseminating these models of eros and eroticism: "Power can only be maintained insofar as it relies on the semiologies of signification," he writes.[18] A dominant culture thus maintains control over its subjects by proliferating sanctioned models of eros through its meaning-making systems; by participating in those systems and reproducing them, subjects affirm their reality and complete their own subjugation. The media play an essential role in the proliferation of dominant semiologies: "Cinema, television, and the press have become fundamental instruments of forming and imposing a dominant reality and dominant significations . . . they are instruments of power."[19]

According to Guattari, the media for the most part "function in the service of repression," but, he significantly adds, "they could become instruments of liberation of great importance."[20] His vision of this liberatory potential comes from his observation that the media are more than just vehicles of signification. Their expressions are multifaceted, made up of many components that do not signify correctly—if indeed they signify at all. Cinema especially is composed of multiple asignifying elements, including "linkages, internal movements, colors, sounds, rhythms, gestures, speech, etc."[21] Asignifying components participate in a counter-semiotics, or what Guattari calls an "asemiotics," and they are important for him because of their connection to "desire and desiring energy."[22] For Guattari, desire is the antithesis to eros and eroticism; it predates their imposition and challenges their appeals to nature.

> Desire is not, like eros, tied down with the body, the person, and the law; it is no more dependent on the shameful body—with its hidden organs and its incestuous taboo—than to a fascination with and to myths about the nude body, the all-powerful phallus, and sublimation. Desire is constituted *before* the crystallization of the body and the organs, *before* the division of the sexes, *before* the separation between the familiarized self and the social field.[23]

Desire, unlike eros, "is not centered on dominant significations and values: it participates in open, asignifying semiotics."[24] The asignifying elements of cinema—like the movement or gesture isolated by the GIF that plays no role in the propagation of meaning—are the locus of a liberated, uncodified desire that subverts the dominant semiologies of status quo; in Guattari's more ambitious moments, they are said to indicate a "revolutionary breakthrough."[25]

Cinema is therefore Janus-faced. It can be both "the machine of eros," which disseminates dominant social and relational models through sig-nification, and also "the machine of liberated desire," where the asignify-ing component is discharged into the social sphere subverting the status quo.[26] How might "a machine of liberated desire" be brought into being? Guattari is less forthcoming on this score: "No theory can furnish the keys to a correct orientation in this domain," he unhelpfully admits.[27] Nonetheless, he does refer to a future "miniaturization" of media that, he writes cryptically, "could become a determining factor" in the evolution of an alternative to established powers of signification.[28] Here he seems to be talking about the masses seizing the means to proliferate an asemiot-ics via nonmainstream channels—through Super 8 cameras, for instance. But what if we were to take "miniaturization" to mean the shrinking of mainstream media products to small, looping two-second clips? We have seen that a principal feature of GIF creation is its hypostatization of the asignifying component of gesture. Does this mean that animated GIFs approximate Guattari's desire?

Any contention that GIFs imply Guattari's notion of desire and as a re-sult run counter to the dominant semiology of a capitalist system should take into account the kind of temporality the GIF seems to fetishize and *its* apparent complicity with the "perpetual present" of late capital-ism.[29] In an essay on the avant-garde filmmaker Martin Arnold, David Bering-Porter argues that the looping temporality of the GIF and the cin-emagraph (a high-quality GIF that loops endlessly without an apparent "hard" reset point) are revealing of a particular experience of time under contemporary global capitalism that he calls, following Eric Cazdyn, "chronic time." Quoting Cazdyn, he states that the chronic constitutes "a looping of time in which the future is spelled out in advance, granting to the meantime an impossible location that is heading somewhere and nowhere at once."[30]

Chronic temporality is representative of a capitalist logic that doesn't deal with systemic crises but simply manages them in the "perpetual present" and eschews any kind of drastic change. The GIF is its symp-tom: "The looped and looping temporality of the gif and the cinemagraph reveals something important about the cultural logic of our age. This kind of temporality is without beginnings or endings but preserves and tends to the present moment—it is a system of time that is antithetical to real change."[31] Can this vision of the GIF as a mere by-product of the temporality of global capitalism be reconciled with a Guattarian reading, which would see it express instead a subversive desire and subvert a capitalist order?

Bering-Porter's reading of Arnold's films offers one possible resolution—and a way of thinking through how Cooper's HTML books fit into this schema. Arnold is most widely known for his appropriation of Hollywood films from the 1940s and 1950s: running 16mm film through an optical printer, he alters the progression of the scene, looping it backward and forward. Bering-Porter describes the effect as "like that of a DJ scratching a record: the motion of the film seems to seize, to convulse in repetitive patterns of time."[32] Arnold's editing of early Andy Hardy films starring Mickey Rooney in *Alone. Life Wastes Andy Hardy* (1998), for instance, includes an extended instant where, through deceleration and looping of the film, Andy innocently kissing his mother on the cheek comes across as altogether more lascivious—and funny—than it would have been at normal speed.

This sets up Bering-Porter's comparison of Arnold's work, the GIF, and the cinemagraph: "The kind of temporality evinced by the cinemagraph, the films of Martin Arnold, and the circulation of the gif within contemporary digital culture is markedly different from the increasing speed associated with modernity and the heterogenous and heterochronic temporality of the postmodern," he writes.[33] Ultimately, however, he finds that Arnold's films differ significantly from GIFs and cinemagraphs: the use of variable loops and "development across the work" actually evinces a *critique* of the chronic time of which loops are symptomatic.[34] According to Bering-Porter, Arnold's films "offer a model of a temporal loop that does not flatten and smooth time into the homogenous and empty form of late capital."[35]

Cooper's HTML books may be considered along similar lines. Like Arnold, Cooper's books play with a variety of loops: some, like the Morse key and the demonic eyes of the preface to *Zac's Haunted House*, have a rhythm that occasionally coincides; others have no discernible agreement—or at least one that alternates in curious and undecipherable patterns. Take the second chapter of *Zac's Haunted House*, which is made up mostly of falling GIFs: video-game footballers pratfall over and over; a cat repeatedly falls and lands on its feet in an animated chronograph by Étienne-Jules Marey; Harry Styles of boy band One Direction slips on stage to the recurrent surprise of his bandmates; animated coins drop and bounce. . . . With no obvious connection between subjects (aside from the theme of falling), the variety of speeds at which things are looped and their subjects fall emerges most forcefully as the chapter's theme. Cooper's GIF phrases set up peculiar, mesmerizing relays between GIFs, generating optical illusions where loop rates seem to slow down and speed up depending on what other GIFs are in the frame. If, as Bering-Porter suggests, "the loop underscores the temporality of our time," then Cooper's sequences defamiliarize the loop and draw attention to the multiple paces and rhythms a loop might have.[36] We might see these sequences as less a critique of life lived under the infernal loops of global capitalism than a demonstration of how the subjects of chronic time might make different kinds of loops that can loop at different rates.

Like Arnold's films, Cooper's HTML books also allow for development across the work—a development that is, significantly, not narrative but based on "emotion and sensation." This not only counteracts the closed and flattened temporality of its constituent GIFs but also augments the asignifying elements of their gestures, producing a plane of intensity that we might liken to a Guattarian asemiotics.

If there is a problem with animated GIFs like the ones employed in Cooper's HTML books, it's that even though their appropriation of mass-media products and hypostatization of gesture are remarkable, any subversive potential is rendered all but useless when the liberated gesture is routed back into the service of another, rather banal meaning-making system—that is, the online conversation. The reaction GIF in particular puts the gesture once more in the service of a dominant mode of signification: a GIF of James Van Der Beek crying tells you I'm sad (or perhaps I'm ironically sad), Jean-Luc Picard with a hand over his face tells you I'm disappointed, and so on. From a Deleuzoguattarian perspective, we might say that while the creation of the GIF deterritorializes the gesture through appropriation, the circulation of the GIF in online chatter reterritorializes it (Hagman says something similar when he suggests that in online conversations, "the empty signifier of the gif is completed with a signified with the consequence that pure gesture is reified into image").[37] The GIF's dissemination in this milieu popularizes the GIF-gesture, and its popularity makes it available for Bering-Porter's reading, where it assumes the nature of a symptom of chronic time.

But what if GIFs were taken from this milieu not with the intention of putting them back in the service of another regime of signification but with the idea of making them interact with *one another* in ways that could circumvent or supersede those kinds of regimes? Of reaction GIFs, Eppink writes, "The role of these GIFs is not primarily aesthetic; they are gestures, performed reactions that are not fully realized until they meet their catalysts."[38] The catalyst in this description refers to a statement or event to which the user reacts by means of a GIF; a statement or event is thus a complement to the reaction GIF, which permits the gesture it represents to become, in Eppink's words, "fully realized." Cooper's HTML books demonstrate what happens when the catalysts for these incomplete GIF-gestures aren't statements or events at all but other GIF-gestures—which catalyze further GIF-gestures, which in turn catalyze still more GIF-gestures, and so on. The ensuing "immediate intense energy" of Cooper's sensational stacks of GIFs—which Guattari might call "desiring energy"—arguably eludes capture by a dominant semiotics by refusing to allow its GIF-gestures to be reterritorialized according to recognizable meaning-making systems.[39] The fields of intensity generated by these books—the "intense emotional reactions" produced by them—carry readers away from sanctioned and privileged forms of communication toward a pleasurable engagement with the text that cannot be codified— or commodified.[40]

SOME OF THE IDEAS Cooper developed in his HTML books are brought forward in his first film collaboration with Farley, *Like Cattle Towards Glow* (2015). The film, which was written by Cooper and directed by Farley with Cooper's assistance, is made up of five very different vignettes. In the first section, a blond emo strips naked and plays dead for someone who wants to relive a relationship with his dead friend; next, an Asian vocalist in a noise band screams about his traumatic youth while being molested by two audience members; the third section depicts two young gay lovers in a pastoral scene; a stagey fourth section finds two young anarchists in Krampus costumes murdering a kid from a neighboring village; and in the final section a solitary male figure wanders around a beach, observed by cameras controlled by a woman hidden in a control booth.

The film is extremely disjointed in terms of its subjects, themes, and styles (Cooper and Farley obviously tried to experiment with as many ideas as their small $40,000 budget would allow), but there are nonetheless powerful resonances between individual sections. Cooper's GIF work seems to have fed into how he and Farley edited the sections together as a feature film, and in moving from one section to the next, the sequencing of tableaux and relationships between them evokes a comparable affective charge as the HTML books. The film connects with Cooper's other works too, notably his collaborations with Vienne, who appears in the film as the woman in the final section. Cooper is keen to acknowledge the impact of having worked with Vienne, stating that "the process of making the film was familiar to me because of my ongoing collaboration with the French theater director Gisèle Vienne."[41] Indeed, Cooper and Vienne's partnership manifests elsewhere in the film in a very material sense—their 2007 piece, *Kindertotenlieder*, provides the fourth section of the film with its wintry setting of artificial snow and the anarchists' Krampus costumes.

Despite its minuscule budget and lack of any real distribution, *Like Cattle Towards Glow* received lots of solid reviews, and Cooper's turn to filmmaking was well received. John Waters listed the film in his top ten best films of 2016 for *Artforum*: "Arty teenage death, Gallic rimming, and a maddening passion for punk penises make this Eric Rohmer–like porno a real French tickler for the fucked-up literary set," he wrote.[42] The film also appeared in *Paper* magazine's end of year top-ten list, and Dennis Dermody memorably called it "Bresson, but with boners."[43] The positive reaction to the film encouraged Cooper and Farley to continue working together on film projects and allowed them to secure a more reasonable budget of $160,000 for their second feature film, *Permanent Green Light*, which started filming in April 2017 and premiered at the International Film Festival Rotterdam in January 2018.

Permanent Green Light is about a boy who wants to explode. Played by Benjamin Sulpice, Roman is a disabled teenager who's fascinated by the idea of disappearing without a trace. As his friend Ollie (Julien Fayeulle) puts it, Roman wants an explosion to "turn him into nothing." He discusses this "project" with a small circle of friends who are dismayed but nonetheless fervent in their support of him. "It's not that I don't like having him around," says his friend Tim (Théo Cholbi), "but I'm mostly

Roman (Benjamin Sulpice, center) surrounded by his friends in *Permanent Green Light* (2018), directed by Zac Farley and Dennis Cooper.

worried he might not do it." Roman obsesses over others who have disappeared, namely an internet legend called Pentti Monkkonen, and devises ways to make his dream come true: he meets a girl who collects suicide bomber vests and gets in touch with someone who sells explosives. As he explains to the explosives trader, he wants there to be nothing left of him, "or barely anything . . . maybe a mist," and it's important that only he explodes. Killing is almost beside the point for Roman; he doesn't want to kill other people and seems to consider the explosion itself as disappearance rather than death. To this end, in the closing scene he invites his friends to join him in the countryside in a large open field where they watch from a safe distance as he blows himself up. Their four faces arrayed in the final shot are inscrutable, expressing a blankness that could be read as awe as much as surprise or even terror.

Comparisons with radical Islamic suicide bombers are perhaps inevitable given that the film is inspired by the true story of Jake Bilardi, an Australian teenager who joined ISIS in 2014 and later blew himself up in a failed terror attack. But *Permanent Green Light* is too elliptical to be read as a straightforward comment on Islamic extremism, and Cooper has said that "what interested me was not the ISIS thing at all, but the question: What if he had really wanted to disappear, so he chased this really loaded context that would erase him. That was really interesting to me and Zac" (2018).[44] Disappearing is, of course, a recurring concern in many of Cooper's post–George Miles Cycle projects, and his blog and *The Marbled Swarm* deal respectively with forms of vanishing and invisibility. In *Permanent Green Light* Cooper continues to explore the theme of disappearance, elaborating on his investigations in a cinematic vein, and this collaboration with Farley attests to his fascination with voiding and withdrawal in particular.

Roman's becoming-void, his desire to disappear—what the filmmakers call "his goal to erase his own humanity through a cloud of ingenuity and sensationalism"—is naturally the film's most striking example of withdrawal, but it's supported by a tissue of references to removal and extraction that expand the terms of Roman's "project."[45] Withdrawal is immediately implied in, for instance, *Permanent Green Light*'s mise-en-scène. The film was shot in Cherbourg, a dull grey metropolis in northern France remarkable for its port and its location on the Normandy coastline, but none of the city's distinguishing features appear on screen. Cooper and Farley remove the port, the sea, and all other particulars from their shots—a subtraction that results in a setting that feels abstract and unspecific. Visual examples like this combine with a comparable auditory emphasis on removal. Music is used sparingly in the film, but "PSA," a track by German minimal-techno producer Thomas Brinkmann played in a nightclub scene, seems to insist on silence as the *subtraction of sound*: with tears streaming down his face, Roman's friend Guillaume (Sylvain Decloitre) dances to a beat that's arrhythmic, pitted with holes through which seeps an abyssal silence.

As one might expect of a work whose creators adore Robert Bresson, there's a lot going on in *Permanent Green Light* that belies the subdued performances of its (mostly nonprofessional) actors. Its theme is deceptively simple; its characters are elusive; the dialogue is dense and beguiling. But in one sense what Cooper and Farley are trying to achieve here isn't so different from what other writers or filmmakers have attempted to do in their work: have their artistic subjects transcend their material and conceptual constraints via the formal properties of the medium itself. In a statement distributed at the UK premiere of the film in September 2018, they state that, "although [Roman's] goal to erase his own humanity through a cloud of ingenuity and sensationalism is doomed, our film gives him a chance to succeed"—in other words, Roman's "project" finds its completion in the film itself. Collapsing diegetic and extra-diegetic space (i.e., the space inside the film and outside the film), Cooper and Farley's film guarantees that Roman gets his wish. "I would like the explosion and what it leaves behind to be so incredible that people will go 'thank you so much, whoever did this,'" Roman says to the explosives dealer. The filmmakers ensure that in the final scene, Roman's explosion leaves nothing behind, save the impressions—fascinated, startled, and confused—inscribed on the faces of his on-screen audience *and* those in the auditorium.

A useful comparison might be made here with the work of Gaspar Noé, the notorious French-Argentinian director whom Cooper and Farley are friendly with. Noé first came to the attention of international audiences in the early 2000s as a leading auteur of what James Quandt derisively called "New French Extremity." This grouping included other creators of similarly transgressive films like Catherine Breillat, Philippe Grandrieux, and Christophe Honoré—the associate producer of *Like Cattle Towards Glow* and director of *Homme au bain* (2010), in which Cooper played a small role. Cinema of the New French Extremity was, Quandt wrote, "determined to break every taboo, to wade in rivers of viscera and spumes of sperm, to fill each frame with flesh, nubile or gnarled, and subject it to all manner of penetration, mutilation, and defilement."[46] His description was particularly apposite where Noé's 2002 film *Irréversible* was concerned: it infamously featured a nine-minute rape scene and an excruciatingly extended shot of someone having his head smashed in with a fire extinguisher.

In the years since Quandt made his reductive assessment, New French Extremity has turned out to be about as useful a coinage as Michael Silverblatt's "transgressive writing" (i.e., not very). As his oeuvre has grown, it's evident that Noé's stylistically experimental films have more in common than "extremity"; they also conjoin style and scenario in radical, unprecedented ways. In all of Noé's works characters repeatedly vie with the situations in which the director has placed them, and they attempt in an almost Rimbaldian way to loosen the strictures of their subjectivities through a derangement of the senses. This is represented on screen through their experiments with violence, sex, and drugs, but, most strikingly, their efforts are also aided and abetted by the *form* of the film itself.

In *Enter the Void* (2009), Oscar (Nathaniel Brown) is an American living in Tokyo with his sister. Their parents died when they were children and, in a flashback, he promises never to leave her; when a drug bust goes wrong, he gets shot and his spirit returns to haunt his sister. Noé called the film a "psychedelic melodrama," and on one level the banality of its melodramatic story is matched only by the formulaic dialogue pronounced by its characters.[47] Viewed in another way, however, the characters seem to be cognizant of the tedium, and Oscar for one is constantly trying to escape the identity he's been assigned by getting high and tripping out. Noé's camera both evokes and facilitates these color-saturated drug binges. In death, Oscar's spirit communes with the camera, and his drifting through the past, present, and future is expressed in some of the most astounding visual effects ever committed to film—the camera/Oscar zooms high above the city, passes through walls, and, most remarkably, enters his sister's body while she has sex to observe an interior cum shot.

The protagonist of *Love* (2015) also appears aware of his incarceration in the film's predictable plot (this time involving a breakup and pining for a lost love). Murphy (Karl Glusman) compulsively has sex or immerses himself in the memory of sexual encounters, which offer fleeting moments that liberate him from the banality of the scenario he is compelled to move through. Like *Enter the Void*, the film itself acknowledges this pervasive monotony and stylistically attempts to alleviate Murphy's predicament. Shot in sensational 3-D that pushes the format to its limits, Murphy literally walks off the screen and into the movie theater, tethered only tenuously to a flatlining narrative going on behind him. Critic Mark Kermode inadvertently stumbled onto the crux of Noé's vision when he wrote in his dismissive review of *Love* that "Gaspar Noé's bid to shock us into submission with 3-D sex is let down by two-dimensional performances"—in Noé's work "two-dimensional" subjects are always implicated in cinematic techniques that echo and participate in their (quixotic) attempts to go beyond the limits of their character.[48]

In its Bressonian austerity, Cooper and Farley's style in *Permanent Green Light* couldn't be more different from Noé's, which often feels like an extended riff on the *giallo* aesthetic of Italian horror maestro Dario Argento. Nonetheless, by participating in Roman's "project" and giving him "a chance to succeed" in his attempts to spectacularly disappear, the filmmakers render the boundary between what is told and how it's told porous, encouraging a kind of complicity between characters and their representation in ways that echo Noé's work. This enfolding of form and content in support of Roman's endeavors effectively aligns the film itself with Roman's teenage friends, whose love and support for him is similarly resolute and unquestioning. Declaring its sympathy for and devotion to its teenage protagonist and his inexplicable project via its form and structure, *Permanent Green Light* is, among many other things, a moving testament to the importance of friendship.

Afterword | Starting with Friendship

IN MAURICE BLANCHOT'S *The Space of Literature* (1955)—a work that Cooper lists among his biggest influences, along with Bresson's *Notes on Cinematography* (1975), Robert Pollard's 1999 album *Kid Marine*, and the Disneyland attraction Mr. Toad's Wild Ride—Blanchot extends his reflections on the idea of solitude, which had underwritten his earlier treatment of egoism in the Marquis de Sade.[1] For Blanchot, solitude is the precondition of presence. In saying "I am," the individual's assertion of presence also negates what it is not, namely that undifferentiated existence called "being." "'I am' (in the world) tends to signify that I am only if I can separate myself from being," Blanchot says. "In this negation which is action and which is time, beings are brought to fruition, and men stand forth erect in the liberty of the 'I am.'"[2] Philosophically speaking, then, the discrete individual exists only by virtue of its separation from generic being. This is what Blanchot calls "the essential solitude" of the subject.[3]

An important outcome of Blanchot's meditation on solitude is his denaturalization of relation. If individual presence is founded on an essential solitude, then a connection with others cannot be assumed and must, in fact, be created. Friendship, what he calls "this relation without dependence, without episode, yet into which all the simplicity of life enters," is for him a privileged form of relation that bears witness to relation's supplementary character. (Thus do we say we *make* friends.) The relation of friendship therefore "passes by way of the recognition of the common strangeness" that makes friends who they are as individuals; of the friend, Blanchot says, "speaking to us they reserve, even on the most familiar terms, an infinite distance, the fundamental separation on the basis of which what separates becomes relation."[4]

The qualities of friendship affirmed by Blanchot resonate closely with what I have called Cooper's ethics of distance—how works like *Safe* invite us to think about the fundamental estrangement of his characters as individuals. But Blanchot's comments also echo Cooper's own remarks on friendship. Asked recently about his thoughts on love, Cooper responded, "I sometimes think friendship love is the best, more than romantic love." Highlighting the advantages of friendship over romantic love, he continued, "You get more freedom? It's more trust and respect and you have to give other people room, and you have to have confidence and trust. I like that you would not attach yourself to someone, and become dependent on them" (2018).[5]

Looking back at Cooper's oeuvre, friendship is an ever-present if sometimes implicit theme. In the early poems of *Idols*, young male friends explore each other's bodies ("Early Riser"), wrestle and share secrets ("Two Friends"), or pledge to love each other forever ("Jeff and Steve Turn to Each Other"). In the George Miles Cycle, friends console, support, and inspire one another; *Try*'s central dynamic is Ziggy and Calhoun's intensely complicated friendship, and *Guide*'s group of friends make up "an offbeat family vibe" at the novel's core.[6] In *My Loose Thread*, meanwhile, the narrator's friendship with Will seems to be the only relation that remains untouched by the novel's homicidal climax; in the closing pages, Jim sits next to Will on the grass outside their high school, and a rare tranquility alights upon the scene.

> Then we just sit there and watch how the world works against us like always.
>
> "You want to know something?"
>
> "Not really," Will says.
>
> I don't care if he does. Maybe most friends don't. Maybe it's not that important. So I suddenly have a nice second or two of realizing we're friends, and actually look at him. I know I always do. "Wow."
>
> "What?" he says, and looks back at me.
>
> "I'm sorry about stealing Jude from you."
>
> "Okay," he says.

"You're a really good friend."
"Yeah, well, you suck," he says, and smiles.[7]

Friendship has been a vital feature of Cooper's writing career, too. Over the years, as we have seen, he has tirelessly created and maintained friendships with artists and writers whose talent he has believed in. From making a space for his friends to read at Beyond Baroque, to putting out his friends' work with *Little Caesar* and Little House on the Bowery and editing their work in anthologies like *Coming Attractions, Discontents: New Queer Writers* (1992) and *Userlands*, Cooper has used whatever status he has to support his friends and give them the chance to develop their careers. Cooper's friendship and trust were shamelessly exploited by Laura Albert and her JT LeRoy ruse, but as evidenced by his generation of international friendship networks through his blog—what José Muñoz might have likened to "circuits of being-with, in difference and discord, that are laden with potentiality and that manifest the desire to want something else"—his belief in the virtues of friendship remains.[8]

If a tension between individual and communal concerns has sometimes marked Cooper's life and work, his comments on "friendship love"—prompted no doubt by his burgeoning friendship with Zac Farley and the flourishing of their creative partnership—seem to indicate a solution or at least a kind of equanimity in the face of this tension. Cooper's reflections on friendship—as a relational mode that emerges out of and is maintained by mutual trust and respect, that is characterized by reciprocal support and not dependency, where the freedom of the individual is paramount—indicate a continued commitment to a way of working, living, *loving* that comes closest to an outlook he claims as anarchistic. In friendship, the persistent, push–pull demands of independence and togetherness are in equilibrium; as both a creative practice and a subject of that practice, friendship is the provisional resolution to what Cooper has called "this kind of weird detachment and longing for attachment and all that stuff."[9]

Notes

Chapter One

1. Cooper, "Dennis Cooper: On Avant-Garde Today."
2. Cooper, "Wrong."
3. Solomon-Godeau, "Rightness of Wrong," 30.
4. Edelman, *No Future*, 2.
5. Solomon-Godeau, "Rightness of Wrong," 32.
6. Cooper, "Charismatic Voice."
7. Stogdill, "Mrs. Thompson."
8. "Dennis Cooper: On Avant-Garde Today."
9. Cooper, *Violence, faits divers, littérature*, 11.
10. Cooper, interview by Dan Epstein.
11. Cooper, *Violence, faits divers, littérature*, 17.
12. Ibid., 18.
13. Ibid., 20.
14. Ibid., 13.
15. Cooper, "Dennis Cooper (Interview)," interview by Robert Glück, 244.
16. Ibid., 243–44.
17. Ibid., 243.
18. Ibid., 243.
19. Cooper, "Art of Fiction," 187–88.
20. Cooper, interview by Hester, August 31, 2018.
21. Ibid.
22. Ibid.
23. Ibid.
24. Ibid.
25. Ibid.

26. Ibid.
27. Ibid.
28. Ibid.
29. Cooper, "Art of Fiction," 189.
30. Ibid., 189.
31. Ibid., 189–91.
32. Ibid., 191.
33. Ibid., 191.
34. Cooper, "Charismatic Voice."
35. Cooper, "Dennis Cooper (Interview)," interview by Robert Glück, 244.
36. Cooper, "Charismatic Voice," 243.
37. Dennis Cooper, "I'm Sorry I Bent Your Feathers So Long," 1968, Dennis Cooper papers, box 10, folder 719, Fales Library and Special Collections, New York University Libraries.
38. Cooper, interview by Dan Epstein.
39. Ron Koertge, email to author, August 10, 2018.
40. Cooper, "Art of Fiction," 176.
41. Cooper and Myles, "Afterword," 464.
42. Cooper, "The Plague and Boredom," 30.
43. Ibid., 30.
44. O'Hara, "Personism," 498.
45. Burt, "Okay I'll Call You."
46. Cooper, "#19," 15.
47. Kane, *Do You Have a Band?,* 202.
48. Amy Gerstler, email to author, August 10, 2018.
49. Ibid.
50. Dennis Cooper, email to author, August 13, 2018.
51. Cooper, "Art of Fiction," 187.
52. Brian Tucker, email to author, August 23, 2018.
53. Cooper, "Boy Talk."
54. Cooper, "David Cassidy."
55. *Tiger Beat* promotional flyer, 1978, Dennis Cooper papers, box 1, folder 4, Fales Library and Special Collections, New York University Libraries.

Chapter Two

1. Cooper, "High School Basketball," 26.
2. Ibid., 26.
3. Cooper, "Greg Tomeoni," 11.
4. Cooper, "Bill McCall," 18.
5. Peters, "Youth-an-Agia," 22.

6. Hall, *Adolescence*, Vol. 1, 1:xiii.

7. Strobel, "Middle-Aged Adolescence," 76.

8. Cooper, "Some Adventures of John," 71.

9. Cooper, "Art of Fiction," 175.

10. Burt, *Forms of Youth*, 13.

11. Ibid., 14.

12. Bersani, *A Future for Astyanax*, 244.

13. Rimbaud, "Childhood," 11.

14. Cooper, "Early Riser," 23.

15. Cooper, "Art of Fiction," 183.

16. Ross, *Emergence of Social Space*, 3.

17. Ibid., 5; Bakunin, "Paris Commune," 268; 263.

18. Ross, *Emergence of Social Space*, 42.

19. Bey, "Part 3—TAZ."

20. Ross, *Emergence of Social Space*, 25.

21. Ibid., 48.

22. Ibid., 49.

23. Elkind, "Egocentrism in Adolescence," 1030.

24. Cooper, "Interview with Dennis Cooper from *Honcho Magazine*."

25. Viegener, "Philosophy in the Bedroom," 133.

26. Cooper, "Art of Fiction," 176.

27. Sade, *120 Days of Sodom*, 199.

28. Ibid., 198.

29. Ibid., 198.

30. Blanchot, "Sade," 40.

31. Sade, *120 Days of Sodom*, 252.

32. Blanchot, "Sade," 55.

33. Beauvoir, "Must We Burn Sade?," 50.

34. Ibid., 50.

35. Ibid., 58.

36. Cooper, "Scott Van Der Karr," 12.

37. Ibid., 12.

38. Ibid., 12.

39. Cooper, "First Sex," 20.

40. Ibid., 21.

41. Ibid., 21.

42. Cooper, "If I Were Peter Frampton," 30.

43. Cooper, "My Type," 29.

44. Beauvoir, "Must We Burn Sade?," 37.

45. Cooper, "Craig Tedesco," 10.

46. Cooper, "Scott Van Der Karr," 12.

47. Cooper, "Craig Tedesco," 10.
48. Cooper, "Jeff, After a Long Time," 86.
49. Ibid., 86.
50. Dennis Cooper, "Interview with Dennis Cooper by Steve Lafreniere," 1988, Dennis Cooper papers, box 10, folder 714, Fales Library and Special Collections, New York University Libraries.

Chapter Three

1. Cooper, "Dennis Cooper on Zine Days."
2. Cooper, "LC#1 Introduction," 1.
3. Mohr, *Hold-Outs*, 114–15.
4. Ashbery and Ford, *John Ashbery in Conversation with Mark Ford*, 45.
5. Herd, *John Ashbery and American Poetry*, 52.
6. Quoted in Padgett, *Ted*, 69.
7. Thorne, "New York School Is a Joke," 74–75.
8. Ibid., 81.
9. Kane, *All Poets Welcome*, 107.
10. Boyd, "Venice Recalled," 160.
11. Ellingham and Killian, *Poet Be like God*, 150.
12. Mohr, *Hold-Outs*, 90.
13. Quoted in Kikel, "Dennis Cooper," 57.
14. Cooper, "Charismatic Voice."
15. Stefans, "Lost Poets," 134.
16. Cooper, "Dennis Cooper on Zine Days."
17. Ibid.
18. Quoted in Cooper, "80s Then," 344, 349–50.
19. Lee, "Little Caesar."
20. Quoted in Mohr, *Hold-Outs*, 93.
21. Stefans, "Lost Poets," 134.
22. Trinidad, interview by D. A. Powell.
23. Equi, "The Switchboard"
24. Quoted in Moffet, "Poetic Licence."
25. Weissman, interview by Raul Deznermio.
26. Delp, "A Small Circle."
27. Cooper, *Coming Attractions*, n.p.
28. Trinidad, "The Party," 143; Skelley, "Juvenile Loitering," 127.
29. Flanagan, "Houses," 66.
30. Ibid., 67.
31. Ibid., 67.
32. Ibid., 67.

33. Ibid., 66.
34. Donne, "The Good-Morrow," 293.
35. Mohr, *Hold-Outs*, 118.
36. Cooper, "Dennis Cooper on Zine Days."
37. Cooper, "Charismatic Voice."
38. Lee, "Little Caesar."
39. Kane, *All Poets Welcome*, 113.
40. Kane, "Angel Hair," 95–96.
41. "Patti Smith," 108.
42. Ibid., 108–9.
43. Ibid., 110.
44. Noland, "Rimbaud and Patti Smith," 583–84.
45. Kane, "Nor Did I Socialise," 114.
46. Cooper, "Charismatic Voice."

Chapter Four

1. Goldman, "Tragedy of Woman's Emancipation," 213.
2. Proudhon, "System of Economical Contradictions."
3. Lehman, *The Last Avant-Garde*, 9.
4. O'Hara, "Today," 15.
5. Shaw, *Frank O'Hara*, 2.
6. Quoted in Gooch, *City Poet*, 187.
7. Goodman, "Advance-Guard Writing," 205.
8. Ibid., 211.
9. Epstein, *Beautiful Enemies*, 30.
10. Goodman, "Utopian Thinking," 5.
11. Ibid., 6 (original emphasis).
12. Goodman, "Post-Christian Man," 86.
13. Goodman, "Utopian Thinking," 13.
14. Goodman and Goodman, "Banning Cars from Manhattan," 145–46.
15. Goodman, Preface to *Utopian Essays*, xvi.
16. O'Hara, "Poem Read at Joan Mitchell's," 113.
17. Ibid., 113.
18. Epstein, *Beautiful Enemies*, 109.
19. LeSueur, *Digressions on Some Poems*, 5–6.
20. Honeywell, "Paul Goodman," 3.
21. See Lehman, *The Last Avant-Garde*, 287.
22. Sontag, "On Paul Goodman," 7–8.
23. LeSueur, *Digressions on Some Poems*, 117.
24. Cooper, "Dinner," 37–38.

25. Ibid., 38.

26. Ibid., 38.

27. Cooper, interview by Martin Bladh, n.p.

28. Cooper, "Grip," 44.

29. Cooper, "Darkens," 45.

30. Cooper, "Late Friends," 47.

31. Dennis Cooper, "Interview with Dennis Cooper by Steve Lafreniere," 1988, Dennis Cooper papers, box 10, folder 714, Fales Library and Special Collections, New York University Libraries.

32. Cooper, "A Herd," 73.

33. Ibid., 73.

34. Ibid., 73.

35. Ibid., 73.

36. Ibid., 73.

37. Ibid., 57.

38. Ibid., 60, 51, 51, 68.

39. Ibid., 51, 68.

40. Ibid., 51.

41. Ibid., 52.

42. Ibid., 56.

43. Sade, *120 Days of Sodom*, 252.

44. Cooper, "A Herd," 59.

Chapter Five

1. Dorn and Clark, "AIDS Awards."

2. Weinberger, "AIDS Hysteria," 40.

3. Abbott, *View Askew*, 169.

4. Killian, "Open Letter," 424–25.

5. Dorn, *Edward Dorn: Collected Poems*, 697.

6. CAConrad and Smith, "Dorn, AIDS, and Community."

7. *Edward Dorn: Collected Poems*, 749.

8. CAConrad and Smith, "Dorn, AIDS, and Community."

9. Dennis Cooper, email to author, February 22, 2018.

10. Cooper, "Dennis Cooper on Zine Days."

11. Dennis Cooper, email to author, February 22, 2018.

12. Ibid.

13. Tom Clark to Dennis Cooper, January 31, 1983, Dennis Cooper papers, box 6, folder 267, Fales Library and Special Collections, New York University Libraries.

14. Tom Clark to Dennis Cooper, November 27, 1982, Dennis Cooper papers,

box 6, folder 267, Fales Library and Special Collections, New York University Libraries.

15. Koestenbaum, "John Ashbery's Lazy Susan," 85.
16. Tom Clark to Dennis Cooper, September 14, 1983, Dennis Cooper papers, box 6, folder 267, Fales Library and Special Collections, New York University Libraries.
17. Dennis Cooper to Tom Clark, January 24, 1984, Dennis Cooper papers, box 6, folder 267, Fales Library and Special Collections, New York University Libraries.
18. Ibid.
19. Weinberger, "AIDS Hysteria," 40.
20. Felice Picano to Dennis Cooper, July 23, 1983, Dennis Cooper papers, box 1, folder 28, Fales Library and Special Collections, New York University Libraries.
21. Cooper, "Safe," 103–4.
22. Ibid., 131.
23. Ibid., 139.
24. Cooper, "DC on Mark Lewis."
25. Cooper, "Safe," 157.
26. Bellamy, "Digression as Power," 98.
27. Ibid., 99.
28. Ibid., 102.
29. Cooper, "Dennis Cooper (Interview)," interview by Robert Glück, 244.
30. Cooper, "Art of Fiction," 176–77.
31. Dennis Cooper, *Antoine Monnier* manuscript, 1978, Dennis Cooper papers, box 1, folder 5, Fales Library and Special Collections, New York University Libraries.
32. Cooper, "Art of Fiction," 177; Dennis Cooper, "Prose by a Punk Poet," unknown publication, undated, Dennis Cooper papers, box 1, folder 5, Fales Library and Special Collections, New York University Libraries.
33. Dennis Cooper, *Antoine Monnier* manuscript, n.p., 1978, Dennis Cooper papers, box 1, folder 5, Fales Library and Special Collections, New York University Libraries.
34. Kathy Acker to Dennis Cooper, 1981, Dennis Cooper papers, box 1, folder 19, Fales Library and Special Collections, New York University Libraries.
35. Ibid.
36. Dennis Cooper to Kathy Acker, September 8, 1981. Dennis Cooper papers, box 1, folder 19, Fales Library and Special Collections, New York University Libraries.
37. Ibid.
38. Cooper, "Safe," 105.

39. Ibid., 100.
40. Ibid., 100, 103.
41. Ibid., 100.
42. Ibid., 107.
43. Ibid., 115.
44. Ibid., 116.
45. Ibid., 146.
46. Scemama, "Robert Bresson," 101.
47. Ibid., 117.

Chapter Six

1. Schjeldahl, "Dennis Cooper's Molten Miracle."
2. Prager, "An Author Who Explores."
3. Abbott, "Gay Lit's Bad Boy."
4. Ibid.
5. Quoted in Jackson, "Bruce Boone," 26.
6. Glück, "Sanchez and Day," 1.
7. Abbott, "*SOUP* Intro," 1.
8. Boone, *Century of Clouds*, 62.
9. Ibid., 67–68.
10. Ibid., 4.
11. Ibid., 4.
12. Ibid., 15.
13. Glück, "Caricature," 94.
14. Harris, "New Narrative," 806.
15. Glück, *Jack the Modernist*, 171.
16. Ibid., 9.
17. Ibid., 33.
18. Ibid., 121.
19. Ibid., 177, 9.
20. Ibid., 56 (original emphasis).
21. McGann, "Contemporary Poetry, Alternate Routes," 638.
22. Harris, "New Narrative," 808.
23. Bernstein, "Narrating Narration," 308.
24. Silliman, *TJANTING*, 15.
25. Boone, "Language Writing," 7–8.
26. Halpern, "Realism and Utopia," 83.
27. Ibid., 90.
28. Glück, "Long Note," 24.

29. Abbott, "Notes on Boundaries," 211.

30. Ibid., 214.

31. Ibid., 211, 213.

32. Dennis Cooper, "Outwrite," 1991, Dennis Cooper papers, box 10, folder 724, Fales Library and Special Collections, New York University Libraries.

33. Bellamy and Killian, "Notes," 482.

34. Cooper quoted in Glück, *Jack the Modernist*, cover; Boone, "Stoned," 222.

35. Bellamy and Killian, *Writers Who Love Too Much*, 477.

36. Bellamy and Killian, "Introduction," iv.

37. Ibid., vii.

38. Ibid., iv.

39. Ibid., vi.

40. Bellamy and Killian, *Writers Who Love Too Much*, 479.

41. Bedoya, "Outside Is the Side."

42. Abbott, "*SOUP* Intro," 1.

43. Monte, "Political as Personal."

44. Killian, "Xerox Coup."

45. Michael Amnasan, email to author, October 26, 2017.

46. Amnasan, *I Can't Distinguish Opposites*, 11.

47. Tremblay-McGaw, "A Review of *LIAR*."

48. Killian, *Bedrooms Have Windows*, 1.

49. Ibid., 7–8.

50. Ibid., 26.

51. Ibid., 88.

52. Ibid., 106.

53. Bellamy, *Letters of Mina Harker*, 13 (original emphasis).

54. Ibid., 173 (original emphasis).

55. Ibid., 19.

56. Ibid., 29–30 (original emphasis).

Chapter Seven

1. Griffith, "Michael Lally," 3.

2. Welt, interview by Troy Elliott, 10.

3. Bernard Welt to Dennis Cooper, June 18, 1983, Dennis Cooper papers, box 2, folder 94, Fales Library and Special Collections, New York University Libraries.

4. Welt, "Silent Radio," 1.

5. Ibid., 2 (original emphasis).

6. Ibid., 6.

7. Kissack, *Free Comrades*, 4.
8. Cooper, "Homocore Rules," 1.
9. Quoted in Steiner, "Queercore U Kno."
10. Quoted in *She Said Boom*.
11. Quoted in Rathe, "Queer to the Core."
12. LaBruce and Jones, "Don't Be Gay," 27–28.
13. Ibid., 29.
14. Cooper, "Homocore Rules," 6–7.
15. LaBruce and Jones, "Don't Be Gay," 30.
16. Nault, *Queercore*, 107.
17. Quoted in Rathe, "Queer to the Core."
18. Cooper, "Homocore Rules," 2.
19. Jennings, "What the Fuck Is HOMOCORE?," 1.
20. Block, "Scanning the 'Zine Scene," 54.
21. Davis, interview by Abbe Schriber.
22. Cooper, "Homocore Rules," 2, 7.
23. Quoted in Rathe, "Queer to the Core."
24. Cooper, "Queercore," 292.
25. Ibid., 294.
26. Cooper, "Introducing Horror Hospital," 43.
27. Ibid., 44.
28. Ibid., 46.
29. Ibid., 47.
30. Ibid., 49.
31. Ibid., 51.
32. LaBruce, "Hard Driving Fiction," 11.
33. Dreher, "Homosexuals Are Enemies," 42.
34. Nault, *Queercore*, 133.
35. Dreher, "Homosexuals Are Enemies," 42.
36. Cooper, "Introducing Horror Hospital," 58.
37. Cooper, "Homocore Rules," 7.
38. Rich, "New Queer Cinema," 15.
39. Cooper, "Queercore," 294.
40. Quoted in *She Said Boom*.
41. See Nault, *Queercore*, 7.
42. Cooper, "Dennis Cooper (Interview)," 253.
43. Bakunin, "The Reaction in Germany."
44. Dennis Cooper to Jessica Pegis, fax, undated, Dennis Cooper papers, box 6, folder 274, Fales Library and Special Collections, New York University Libraries.

Chapter Eight

1. Cooper, "Wrong," 63.
2. Ibid., 64.
3. Ibid., 65.
4. Ibid., 65.
5. Ibid., 65.
6. Ibid., 66 (original emphasis).
7. Ibid., 67.
8. Quoted in Kikel, "Dennis Cooper," 57.
9. Acker, "Blood and Guts," 56.
10. Cooper and Myles, "Afterword," 463.
11. Quoted in Kikel, "Dennis Cooper," 57.
12. Cooper and Myles, "Afterword," 466.
13. Dennis Cooper, diary 1978–81, Dennis Cooper papers, box 10, folder 715, Fales Library and Special Collections, New York University Libraries.
14. Supree, "Men with Men," n.p.
15. Cooper, "East Village," 28.
16. Cooper and Myles, "Afterword," 478.
17. Ibid., 475–76.
18. Kikel, "Dennis Cooper," 57.
19. Cooper and Myles, "Afterword," 473.
20. Ibid., 469.
21. Cooper, interview by Dan Epstein.
22. Dennis Cooper to Lynne Tillman, April 1, 1987, Lynne Tillman papers, box 1, folder 14, Fales Library and Special Collections, New York University Libraries.
23. Cooper, "Art of Fiction," 189.
24. Cooper, *Closer*, 105.
25. Ibid., 44.
26. Cooper, interview by Tim Guest.
27. Dennis Cooper to Joel Rose and Catherine Texier, July 8, 1987, *Between C & D* papers, box 1, folder 18, Fales Library and Special Collections, New York University Libraries; Cooper to Joel Rose and Catherine Texier, April 22, 1987, *Between C & D* papers, box 1, folder 18, Fales Library and Special Collections, New York University Libraries.
28. Cooper to Rose and Texier, April 22, 1987.
29. Mark Polizzotti to Dennis Cooper, January 22, 1987, Denis Cooper papers, box 1, folder 35, Fales Library and Special Collections, New York University Libraries.

30. Jonathan Galassi to Dennis Cooper, December 18, 1986, Dennis Cooper papers, box 1, folder 35, Fales Library and Special Collections, New York University Libraries.

31. Dennis Cooper to Joel Rose and Catherine Texier, January 30, 1987, *Between C & D* papers, box 1, folder 18, Fales Library and Special Collections, New York University Libraries.

32. Cooper, interview by Alexander Laurence.

33. Cooper, *Frisk*, 67.

34. Dennis Cooper to Marcus Hu, undated, Dennis Cooper papers, box 3, folder 68, Fales Library and Special Collections, New York University Libraries.

35. Ibid.

36. Kevin Killian to Dennis Cooper, July 18, 1995, Dennis Cooper papers, box 8, folder 423, Fales Library and Special Collections, New York University Libraries.

37. White, "Out of the Closet."

38. Wickliffe, Ron, "Letter to the Editor: Flush Frisk," unknown publication, June 29, 1995, Dennis Cooper papers, box 3, folder 68, Fales Library and Special Collections, New York University Libraries.

39. Cooper, "Dennis Cooper Interviewed," interview by Larry-bob Roberts.

40. Texier, "Love."

41. Cooper, *Try*, 93.

42. Ibid., 93.

43. Grattan, *Hope Isn't Stupid*, 134.

44. Dennis Cooper to Ira Silverberg, May 6, 1992, Dennis Cooper papers, box 3, folder 85, Fales Library and Special Collections, New York University Libraries.

45. Ibid.

46. Dennis Cooper to Elizabeth Young, July 17, 1992, Dennis Cooper papers, box 3, folder 85, Fales Library and Special Collections, New York University Libraries.

47. Cooper, "Not Evil."

48. Morrison, "First Black President."

49. Quoted in France, *How to Survive a Plague*, 456–57.

50. Reynolds, *Energy Flash*, xxvi.

51. Ibid., xxvi.

52. Cooper and Westendorf, "A Raver Runs," 200.

53. Cooper, *Guide*, 131.

54. Ibid., 4.

55. Ibid., 155.

56. Ibid., 155, 170.

57. Ibid., 59.
58. Cooper and Westendorf, "A Raver Runs," 201.
59. Cooper, *Period*, 70.
60. Ronell, "Philosophical Code," 194.
61. Cooper, *Try*, 149.
62. Cooper, *Period*, 37.
63. Silverblatt, "Shock Appeal."
64. Ibid.
65. Chun, "Naked Breakfast," 49.
66. Quoted in Chun, "Naked Breakfast."
67. Gardner, "Transgressive Fiction," 55.
68. Ibid., 54.
69. Clarke, "Over Their Dead Bodies," 16.
70. Walsh, John Walsh Column, 5.
71. Young and Caveney, "Introduction," viii.
72. Young, "Death in Disneyland," 248.
73. Jackson, "Death Drives Across Pornotopia," 167.
74. Foster, "Obscene"; Bredbeck, "New Queer Narrative"; Aaron, "(Fill-in-the) Blank Fiction."
75. Taylor, "Geometries of Desire."
76. Taylor, "Dorian Gray," 197.
77. Ibid., 178.
78. Taylor, "Geometries of Desire."
79. Ibid.
80. Ibid.
81. Ibid.
82. Cooper, "Art of Fiction," 193–94.
83. Cooper, *Closer*, 21.
84. Ibid., 21.
85. Ibid., 26.
86. Cooper, *Period*, 8.
87. Ibid., 10.
88. Ibid., 11.
89. Cooper, *Try*, 45.
90. Rubin, "Thinking Sex," 149.
91. Ibid., 149.
92. Cooper, "DC on the Cycle."
93. Cooper, "Dennis Cooper (Interview)," interview by Robert Glück, 258.
94. Cooper, *Closer*, 5.
95. Goldman, preface to *Anarchism and Other Essays*, 41, 42.
96. Ibid., 42.

er2 Notes to Pages 159–173

97. Quoted in Hayles, "Chance Operations," 226.
98. Ibid., 238.
99. Weaver, "Divining the Derivers."
100. Mac Low, interview by Nicholas Zurbrugg, 400.
101. McHale, "Poetry as Prosthesis," 20.
102. Cooper, "Dennis Cooper (Interview)," interview by Robert Glück, 253–54.
103. Cooper, *Frisk*, 3, 127–28; 4, 128.
104. Ibid., 24, 27, 31.
105. Ibid., 70.
106. Ibid., 86–87.
107. Ibid., 40.
108. Ibid., 107.
109. Ibid., 107.
110. Ibid., 122.
111. Hegarty, *Frisk*, 181.
112. Cooper, "I Really, Really Hate Nostalgia."

Chapter Nine

1. Quoted in *The Cult of JT LeRoy*.
2. Quoted in Hester, *Beyond Explicit*, 164.
3. Cooper, interview by Dan Epstein.
4. Quoted in *The Cult of JT LeRoy*.
5. Benderson, interview by Alexander Laurence.
6. Benderson, "New Degenerate Narrative."
7. Benderson, "Terminator."
8. Quoted in *The Cult of JT LeRoy*.
9. Terminator, "Baby Doll," 42.
10. Ibid., 22.
11. Stone, "Introduction," xxi; Benderson, "Terminator."
12. Cooper, interview by Alexander Laurence.
13. Cooper, "Combustible Romanticism," 19.
14. Ibid., 19.
15. Cooper, *My Loose Thread*, 121.
16. Cooper, "High School Basketball," 26.
17. Cooper, *My Loose Thread*, 18–19.
18. Ibid., 23.
19. Ibid., 113.
20. Ibid., 45, 51 (emphasis added).
21. Ibid., 40.
22. Ibid., 47–48.

23. Lev, "Center Cannot Hold," 231; Cooper, *My Loose Thread*, 13.
24. Kinkel, "Kip's Writings & Statements."
25. Kinkel and Warthen, "Kip Kinkel's Confession."
26. Cooper, "*My Loose Thread* Interview."
27. Cooper, "Art of Fiction," 183.
28. Cooper, "*My Loose Thread* Interview."
29. Cooper, "Combustible Romanticism," 19.
30. Ibid., 19.
31. Quoted in *The Cult of JT LeRoy*.
32. Clarke, "The Tuesday Book," 38.
33. Quoted in Sturm, "Dennis Cooper."
34. Press, "Cult of J.T. LeRoy."
35. Quoted in Dennis Cooper, email to author, May 25, 2018.
36. Shields, *Reality Hunger*, 32.
37. Olbermann, "Heartbreaking Hoax."
38. HIV Epidemology and Field Services Program, "AIDS Diagnoses."
39. Schulman, *Gentrification of the Mind*, 45.
40. Quoted in St. John, "Unmasking of JT LeRoy."
41. Dennis Cooper, email to author, May 25, 2018.
42. Feuerzeig, "Jeff Feuerzeig Talks."
43. Beachy, "Who Is the Real JT LeRoy."

Chapter Ten

1. Cooper, *Violence, faits divers, littérature*, 11.
2. Ibid., 11.
3. Ibid., 15.
4. Cooper, "Gisèle Vienne Day."
5. Dobson, "Troubling Matters," 24.
6. Vienne, "*Showroomdummies*."
7. Vienne, "Érotisme," 91. All translations from the French are the author's own.
8. Vienne, "Entretien avec Gisèle Vienne," 86.
9. Barbéris, "*Jerk*, de Gisèle Vienne," 160.
10. Vienne, "Érotisme," 91–92.
11. Cooper, "Meet Hucow."
12. Ibid.
13. Cooper, "*I Apologize*: Extracts," 1.
14. Masi, "Giséle Vienne."
15. Dobson, "Troubling Matters," 24.
16. Genecand, "Critique."

17. Masi, "Giséle Vienne."
18. Dobson, "Troubling Matters," 24.
19. Ibid., 28.
20. Rahv, *New Novel*, 103.
21. Cooper, "Dennis Cooper (Interview)," 250.
22. Quoted in Hirsch, *Dennis Cooper*.
23. Robbe-Grillet, *The Voyeur*, 11.
24. Ibid., 49.
25. Rault, *Robbe-Grillet*; Ramsay, *Robbe-Grillet and Modernity*, 10.
26. Vienne, "Uncanny Landscapes," 41.
27. Schildcrout, *Murder Most Queer*, 171.
28. Blake and Cooper, *Jerk*, 15–16.
29. Vienne, "Uncanny Landscapes," 36.
30. Ibid., 36.
31. See, for example, Vienne, "Uncanny Landscapes," 34; Freud, "The Uncanny," 219.
32. Freud, "The Uncanny," 241; 242.
33. Macfarlane, "Eeriness."
34. Fisher, *The Weird and the Eerie*, 61, 12.
35. Vienne, "Uncanny Landscapes," 38; Fisher, *The Weird and the Eerie*, 81.
36. Macfarlane, "Eeriness."
37. Fisher, *The Weird and the Eerie*, 13.
38. See Fisher, *Capitalist Realism*.
39. Fisher, *The Weird and the Eerie*, 13.

Chapter Eleven

1. Cooper, "It's the Shift That Creates," 193.
2. Cooper, *God Jr.*, 159.
3. Prix Sade, "Lauréat 2007—Prix Sade."
4. Cooper, *The Sluts*, 4.
5. Ibid., 6.
6. Ibid., 8.
7. Ibid., 10.
8. Ibid., 110.
9. Ibid., 112.
10. Ibid., 110.
11. Ibid., 119.
12. T. C. Baker, "The Whole Is Untrue," 57.
13. Quoted in Kikel, "Dennis Cooper," 57.
14. Cooper, interview by Matthew Byloos, 9.

15. Lev, "Next," 99.
16. Cooper, *The Sluts*, 189.
17. Cooper, "It's the Shift That Creates," 196.
18. Ibid., 201.
19. Deleuze and Guattari, *A Thousand Plateaus*, 16.
20. Ibid., 17.
21. Galloway and Thacker, *The Exploit*, 70–71.
22. Ibid., 62.
23. Cooper, "Homocore," 2.
24. See Marcus, *Girls to the Front*, 8.
25. Terranova, *Network Culture*, 41.
26. Blood, "Blogging Software," 53.
27. Ibid., 55.
28. O'Reilly, "What Is Web 2.0."
29. Manovich, "Practice of Everyday (Media) Life," 319–20.
30. Lovink, *Zero Comments*, 4.
31. Cooper, "I Think I'm Ill-Suited."
32. Sifry, "Blog Usage."
33. Cooper, "Hero."
34. Cooper, "Some of You Asked."
35. Calson Analytics, "Blog Statistics and Demographics."
36. Benkler, *The Wealth of Networks*, 217.
37. Cooper, "My Dark Places."
38. Dennis Cooper, email to author, February 5, 2015.
39. Dennis Cooper, email to author, February 13, 2015.
40. Cooper, "Introducing Little House on the Bowery."
41. Cooper, "This Is Not an Isolated Incident," 12.
42. Dennis Cooper, email to author, February 2, 2015.
43. Dennis Cooper, email to author, February 13, 2015.
44. Mark Gluth, email to author, February 2, 2015.
45. Cooper, "I Think I'm Ill-Suited."
46. Cooper, "Some Stuff."
47. Cooper, "I'm Still Reeling."
48. Cooper, "Winners and Whatever Else."
49. See, for example, Cooper, "I Used to Throw These Literary Parties."
50. Dennis Cooper, email to author, February 9, 2015.
51. Dennis Cooper, email to author, February 13, 2015.
52. See Cooper, "It's the Shift That Creates," 202.
53. Cooper, "Phoner," 102 (original emphasis).
54. Ibid., 103 (original emphasis).
55. Ibid., 104 (original emphasis).

56. Cooper, "PS"; Cooper, "I Think I'm Ill-Suited."
57. Cooper, "It's the Shift That Creates," 198–99.
58. Ibid., 201.
59. Cooper, interview by Martin Bladh, n.p.
60. Debord, *Society of the Spectacle*, secs. 11; 1.
61. Cooper, interview by Martin Bladh, n.p.
62. Cooper, "Saturday."
63. Koestenbaum, *Hotel Theory*, 38.
64. Ibid., 48.
65. Brainard, *Collected Writings*, 5.
66. Fitch, *Pop Poetics*, 161; 179.
67. Ibid., 178–79.
68. Ibid., 48.
69. Myles, "An American Poem," 15.
70. Ibid., 16–17.
71. Nelson, *Women*, 182.
72. Cavalli, "Google Deletes Dennis Cooper's Blog."
73. Gardner, "Transgressive Fiction," 54.
74. Cooper, "I Am Very, Very Happy."
75. Muñoz, "Gimme Gimme This," 96.
76. Ibid., 96.
77. Ibid., 98.
78. Hardt and Negri, *Commonwealth*, 282.
79. Hardt, "The Common in Communism," 348–349.
80. Caffentzis and Federici, "Commons against and beyond Capitalism," 93.
81. Hardt and Negri, *Commonwealth*, 283.

Chapter Twelve

1. Foucault, *Discipline and Punish*, 207.
2. Ibid., 202–3.
3. Ibid., 216.
4. Bill Clinton, quoted in Weinger, "Bill Clinton."
5. Cooper, "My Fear Arouses Me."
6. Cooper, *The Marbled Swarm*, 49.
7. Ibid., 49.
8. Cooper, "Art of Fiction," 197.
9. Cooper, *The Marbled Swarm*, 129, 131, 132.
10. Ibid., 60.
11. Cooper, "Solving the Puzzle."
12. Heil, "It's Impossible to Figure."

13. Delany, *About Writing*, 234.
14. Sedgwick, "Paranoid Reading," 124.
15. Ibid., 125–26.
16. Ibid., 130.
17. Ibid., 136.
18. Ibid., 138, 140.
19. Ibid., 149.
20. Ibid., 140.
21. Marhoefer, "From Gay Nazis" (emphasis added).
22. Sedgwick, "Paranoid Reading," 136.
23. Ibid., 149, 147.
24. Love, "Truth and Consequences," 237–38.
25. Nair, *Sapphic Modernism*, 4.
26. Heise, *Urban Underworlds*, 100.
27. Eliot, Preface to *Nightwood*, xxi.
28. Barnes, *Nightwood*, 55.
29. Nair, *Sapphic Modernism*, 4.
30. P. Baker, *Polari*, 1.
31. Houlbrook, *Queer London*, 152.
32. P. Baker, *Polari*, 15.
33. Cox and Fay, "Gayspeak," 107.
34. Houlbrook, *Queer London*, 152.
35. Burton, "Gentle Art of Confounding Naffs," 23.
36. Cooper, *The Marbled Swarm*, 79.
37. Ibid., 5, 7, 46.
38. Ibid., 84, 91, 124.
39. Halperin, *How to Be Gay*, 39.
40. Miller, *Place for Us*, 26.
41. Cooper, "I Really, Really Hate Nostalgia."

Chapter Thirteen

1. Cooper, "Art of Fiction," 197.
2. Cooper, "Halloween Countdown."
3. Cooper, "DC's Writers Workshop."
4. Cooper, "DeAundra Peek."
5. Cooper and Farley, "Language, and How It's Used."
6. Ibid.
7. Uhlin, "Playing in the Gif(t) Economy," 518.
8. Eppink, "Brief History," 301.
9. Cooper, "Dennis Cooper on Writing."

10. Ibid.

11. McIntyre, quoted in Cooper, "Weirdest Work Yet"; Bradley, "Dennis Cooper's Haunted HTML."

12. Fallon, "Is It Still A Novel?"

13. Quoted in Henry, "GIFs Into Fiction"; Cooper, "In a State of Confusion."

14. Cooper, "In a State of Confusion."

15. Soulellis, "The Download."

16. Colby, *Kathy Acker*, 54.

17. Hagman, "Digital Gesture."

18. Guattari, "Cinema of Desire," 236.

19. Ibid., 238.

20. Ibid., 238.

21. Ibid., 242.

22. Ibid., 241, 245.

23. Ibid., 245.

24. Ibid., 245.

25. Ibid., 246.

26. Ibid., 245.

27. Ibid., 246.

28. Ibid., 244.

29. Bering-Porter, "Automaton," 185.

30. Quoted in Bering-Porter, "Automaton," 185.

31. Ibid., 190.

32. Ibid., 179.

33. Ibid., 185.

34. Ibid., 189.

35. Ibid., 190.

36. Ibid., 185.

37. Hagman, "Digital Gesture."

38. Eppink, "Brief History," 303.

39. Cooper, "In a State of Confusion"; Guattari, "Cinema of Desire," 245.

40. McIntyre, quoted in Cooper, "Weirdest Work Yet."

41. Cooper, "In a State of Confusion."

42. Waters, "Best Films of 2016."

43. Dermody, "Films of 2016."

44. Cooper, interview by Jennifer Krasinsky.

45. Cooper and Farley, document distributed at UK premiere, n.p.

46. Quandt, "Flesh and Blood," 18.

47. Noé, *Enter the Void* press kit, 10.

48. Kermode, "*Love* Review."

Afterword

1. See Cooper, "Dennis Cooper on Writing."
2. Blanchot, *Space of Literature*, 251.
3. Ibid., 19.
4. Blanchot, "Friendship," 291.
5. Cooper, "Novelist Dennis Cooper."
6. Cooper, *Guide*, 156.
7. Cooper, *My Loose Thread*, 120.
8. Muñoz, "Gimme Gimme This," 96.
9. Dennis Cooper, "Interview with Dennis Cooper by Steve Lafreniere," 1988, Dennis Cooper papers, box 10, folder 714, Fales Library and Special Collections, New York University Libraries.

Bibliography

Aaron, Michele. "(Fill-in-the) Blank Fiction: Dennis Cooper's Cinematics and the Complicitous Reader." *Journal of Modern Literature* 27, no. 3 (January 1, 2004): 115–27.

Abbott, Steve. "Gay Lit's Bad Boy." *San Francisco Sentinel*, December 19, 1986.

———. "Notes on Boundaries/New Narrative." In *Writers Who Love Too Much*, edited by Dodie Bellamy and Kevin Killian, 211–21. New York: Nightboat, 2017.

———. "*SOUP* Intro." *SOUP*, no. 2 (1981): 1.

———. *View Askew: Postmodern Investigation.* San Francisco: Androgyne Books, 1989.

Acker, Kathy. "Blood and Guts in High School." In *Blood and Guts in High School: Plus Two*, 5–165. London: Picador, 1984.

Amnasan, Michael. *I Can't Distinguish Opposites.* San Francisco: Hoddypoll, 1983.

Ashbery, John, and Mark Ford. *John Ashbery in Conversation with Mark Ford.* London: Between the Lines, 2003.

Baker, Paul. *Polari: The Lost Language of Gay Men.* New York: Routledge, 2002.

Baker, Timothy C. "The Whole Is Untrue: Experience and Community in *The Sluts*." In *Dennis Cooper*, edited by Paul Hegarty and Danny Kennedy, 52–67. Brighton, UK: Sussex Academic Press, 2008.

Bakunin, Mikhail. "The Paris Commune and the Idea of the State." In *Bakunin on Anarchy: Selected Works by the Activist-Founder of World Anarchism*, edited by Sam Dolgoff, 259–73. London: Allen & Unwin, 1971.

———. "The Reaction in Germany: From the Notebooks of a Frenchman." Marxists.org, (1842) 2019. http://www.marxists.org/reference/archive/bakunin/works/1842/reaction-germany.htm.

Baldessari, John. "John Baldessari: *Wrong*, Curator Notes." Los Angeles County Museum of Art (LACMA). Accessed February 8, 2018. https://collections .lacma.org/node/237769.

Barbéris, Isabelle. *"Jerk*, de Gisèle Vienne et Jonathan Capdevielle." *Communications*, no. 92 (2013): 159–72.

Barnes, Djuna. *Nightwood*. London: Faber & Faber, 2007.

Beachy, Stephen. "Who Is the Real JT LeRoy? A Search for the True Identity of a Great Literary Hustler." *New York*, October 10, 2005. http://nymag.com /nymetro/news/people/features/14718/.

Beauvoir, Simone de. "Must We Burn Sade?" In Sade, *The 120 Days of Sodom*, translated by Richard Seaver and Austryn Wainhouse, 3–64. New York: Grove Press, 1987.

Bedoya, Roberto. "'Outside Is the Side I Take' An Interview with Roberto Bedoya." By Robin Tremblay-McGaw. *X Poetics* (blog), October 17, 2008. http://xpoetics.blogspot.co.uk/2008/10/outside-is-side-i-take-interview -with.html.

Bellamy, Dodie. "Digression as Power: Dennis Cooper and the Aesthetics of Distance." In *Enter at Your Own Risk*, edited by Leora Lev, 97–104. Madison, NJ: Fairleigh Dickinson University Press, 2006.

———. *The Letters of Mina Harker*. 2nd ed. Madison: University of Wisconsin Press, 2004.

Bellamy, Dodie, and Kevin Killian. "Introduction: New Narrative Beginnings 1977–1997." In *Writers Who Love Too Much*, edited by Dodie Bellamy and Kevin Killian, i–xx. New York: Nightboat, 2017.

———. "Notes." In *Writers Who Love Too Much*, edited by Dodie Bellamy and Kevin Killian, 465–505. New York: Nightboat, 2017.

———, eds. *Writers Who Love Too Much: New Narrative, 1977–1997*. New York: Nightboat, 2017.

Benderson, Bruce. "Bruce Benderson Interview." By Alexander Laurence. The Write Stuff, 1994. http://www.altx.com/int2/benderson.html.

———. "Terminator." *New York Press*, January 27, 1998. http://www.nypress .com/terminator/.

———. "Toward the New Degenerate Narrative: A Literary Manifesto." Alternative-X, 1994. http://www.altx.com/manifestos/degenerate.html.

Benkler, Yochai. *The Wealth of Networks: How Social Production Transforms Markets and Freedom*. New Haven, CT: Yale University Press, 2006.

Bering-Porter, David. "The Automaton in All of Us: GIFs, Cinemagraphs and the Films of Martin Arnold." *Moving Image Review & Art Journal* 3, no. 2 (2014): 179–92.

Bernstein, Charles. "Narrating Narration: The Shapes of Ron Silliman's Work." In *Content's Dream: Essays, 1975–1984*, 305–20. Evanston, IL: Northwestern University Press, 1986.

Bersani, Leo. *A Future for Astyanax: Character and Desire in Literature*. New York: Columbia University Press, 1984.

Between C & D. Papers. Fales Library and Special Collections, New York University Libraries.

Bey, Hakim. "Part 3—TAZ: The Temporary Autonomous Zone, Ontological Anarchy, Poetic Terrorism." Hermetic Library, 1990. http://hermetic.com /bey/taz3.html#labelTAZ.

Blake, Nayland, and Dennis Cooper. *Jerk*. San Francisco: Artspace Books, 1993.

Blanchot, Maurice. "Friendship." In *Friendship*, translated by Elizabeth Rottenberg, 289–92. Stanford, CA: Stanford University Press, 1997.

———. "Sade." In *Justine, Philosophy in the Bedroom, and Other Writings* by D. A. F. Sade, translated by Richard Seaver and Austryn Wainhouse, 37–72. New York: Grove Press, 1965.

———. *The Space of Literature*. Translated by Ann Smock. Lincoln: University of Nebraska Press, 1989.

Block, Adam. "Scanning the 'Zine Scene." *Advocate*, January 30, 1990.

Blood, Rebecca. "How Blogging Software Reshapes the Online Community." *Communications of the ACM* 47, no. 12 (December 2004): 53–55.

Boone, Bruce. *Century of Clouds*. Callicoon, NY: Nightboat Books, 2006.

———. "Language Writing: The Pluses and Minuses of the New Formalism." *SOUP*, no. 2 (1981): 2–9.

———. "Stoned Out of My Gourd." *FUSE*, December 1982.

Boyd, Bruce. "Venice Recalled." In *The New American Poetry*, edited by Donald Allen, 159–60. New York: Evergreen Books, 1960.

Bradley, Paige K. "Dennis Cooper's Haunted HTML Novel." Bookforum.com, April 10, 2015. https://www.bookforum.com/pubdates/14456.

Brainard, Joe. *The Collected Writings of Joe Brainard*. Edited by Ron Padgett. New York: Library of America, 2012.

Bredbeck, Gregory W. "The New Queer Narrative: Intervention and Critique." *Textual Practice* 9, no. 3 (1995): 477–502.

Burt, Stephen (Stephanie). *The Forms of Youth: Twentieth-Century Poetry and Adolescence*. New York: Columbia University Press, 2007.

———. "Okay I'll Call You / Yes Call Me: Frank O'Hara's 'Personism.'" Poets .org, February 21, 2014. https://www.poets.org/poetsorg/text/okay-ill-call -you-yes-call-me-frank-oharas-personism.

Burton, Peter. "The Gentle Art of Confounding Naffs: Some Notes on Polari." *Gay News*, 1977.

CAConrad and Dale Smith. "Dorn, AIDS, and Community That Holds Us Together & Holds Us to It." PhillySound, October 31, 2009. http://phillysound .blogspot.co.uk/2009_10_01_archive.html.

Caffentzis, George, and Silvia Federici. "Commons against and beyond Capitalism." *Community Development Journal* 49, no. 1 (January 2014): 92–105.

Calson Analytics. "Blog Statistics and Demographics." Calson Analytics, October 2007. http://www.caslon.com.au/weblogprofile1.htm#ephemerality.

Cavalli, Lauren. "Google Deletes Dennis Cooper's Blog, Erasing Years of Artistic Output." Artforum.com, July 13, 2016. http://artforum.com/news /id=62177.

Chun, Rene. "Naked Breakfast, Lunch, and Dinner." *New York Times*, April 23, 1995.

Clarke, Roger. "Over Their Dead Bodies." *Observer*, September 25, 1994.

———. "The Tuesday Book: A Protégé with Plenty to Learn from His Master." *Independent*, May 17, 2005.

Colby, Georgina. *Kathy Acker: Writing the Impossible*. Edinburgh: Edinburgh University Press, 2016.

Cooper, Dennis. "#19." In *The Terror of Earrings*, 15. Arcadia, CA: Kinks Press, 1973.

———. "80s Then: Mike Kelley Talks to Dennis Cooper." In *Smothered in Hugs*, 343–50. New York: Harper Perennial, 2010.

———. "Amy Gerstler's Skinny Columns." *DC's* (blog), March 20, 2008. http:// denniscooper-theweaklings.blogspot.co.uk/2008/03/amy-gerstlers-skinny -columns.html?zx=442d3a8530cb5a7b.

———. "The Art of Fiction No. 213." Interview by Ira Silverberg. *Paris Review* 198 (Fall 2011): 172–98.

———. "Bill McCall." In *Idols*, 18. New York: Amethyst Press, 1989.

———. "Boy Talk." In *Tiger Beat*, n.p. Los Angeles: Little Caesar Press, 1978.

———. "The Charismatic Voice." Interview by Kate Wolf. *Los Angeles Review of Books*, June 28, 2012. https://lareviewofbooks.org/article/the-charismatic -voice/.

———. *Closer*. London: Serpent's Tail, 1994.

———. "Combustible Romanticism." Interview by Brandon Stosuy. *Prose Acts*, October 18, 2001, 18–21.

———, ed. *Coming Attractions: An Anthology of American Poets in Their Twenties*. Los Angeles: Little Caesar Press, 1980.

———. "Craig Tedesco." In *Idols*, 10. New York: Amethyst Press, 1989.

———. "Darkens." In *The Tenderness of the Wolves*, 45. Traumansberg, NY: Crossing Press, 1982.

———. "David Cassidy." In *Tiger Beat*, n.p. Los Angeles: Little Caesar Press, 1978.

———. "DC on Mark Lewis, the Inspiration for 'My Mark.'" Dennis-cooper .net. Accessed February 26, 2018. http://www.dennis-cooper.net/other _mymark.htm.

———. "DC on the Cycle." Dennis-cooper.net. Accessed June 21, 2012. http:// www.dennis-cooper.net/georgemiles.htm.

———. "DC's Writers Workshop #13: Hyrule Dungeon's THE GRAVAMINA." *DC's* (blog), October 20, 2012. https://denniscooperblog.com/dcs-writers-workshop-13-hyrule-dungeons-the-gravamina/.

———. "DeAundra Peek Teenage Superstar Day—DC's." *DC's* (blog), September 2, 2016. https://denniscooperblog.com/deaundra-peek-teenage-superstar-day/.

———. "Dennis Cooper (Interview)." By Robert Glück. In *Enter at Your Own Risk*, edited by Leora Lev, 241–59. Madison, NJ: Fairleigh Dickinson University Press, 2006.

———. "Dennis Cooper Interviewed by Larry-bob." By Larry-bob Roberts. *Holy Titclamps*, 1991. https://www.prismnet.com/~larrybob/cooperint.html.

———. "Dennis Cooper: On Avant-Garde Today." Interview by Donatien Grau. *Purple Diary*, Fall/Winter 2015. http://purple.fr/magazine/fw-2015-issue-24/dennis-cooper/.

———. "Dennis Cooper on Writing as Sculpture." Interview by Brandon Stosuy. Creative Independent, October 18, 2016. https://thecreativeindependent.com/people/dennis-cooper-on-writing-as-sculpture/.

———. "Dennis Cooper on Zine Days (They Were Good) and Transgressive Blogs (There Is Such a Thing)." Interview by Steve Lafreniere. *VICE*, November 30, 2007. http://www.vice.com/read/dennis-cooper-v14n12.

———. "Dennis Cooper's New 'Gif' Novel Is His Weirdest Work Yet." Interview by Niamh McIntyre. *Dazed*, November 30, 2016. http://www.dazeddigital.com/artsandculture/article/33862/1/dennis-cooper-s-new-gif-novel-might-be-his-weirdest-work-yet.

———. "Dinner." In *The Tenderness of the Wolves*, 36–39. Traumansberg, NY: Crossing Press, 1982.

———, ed. *Discontents: New Queer Writers*. New York: Amethyst Press, 1992.

———. "Early Riser." In *Idols*, 23. New York: Amethyst Press, 1989.

———. "The East Village and Its New Gay Ways." *Advocate*, March 19, 1985.

———. "First Sex." In *Idols*, 20–21. New York: Amethyst Press, 1989.

———. *Frisk*. New York: Grove Weidenfeld, 1991.

———. "Gisèle Vienne Day." *DC's* (blog), July 29, 2017. https://denniscooperblog.com/gisele-vienne-day-2/.

———. *God Jr.* New York: Black Cat, 2005.

———. "Greg Tomeoni." In *Idols*, 11. New York: Amethyst Press, 1989.

———. "Grip." In *The Tenderness of the Wolves*, 44. Traumansberg, NY: Crossing Press, 1982.

———. *Guide*. London: Serpent's Tail, 1998.

———. "Halloween Countdown Post #1: 2012 All New Animatronic Prop Showroom." *DC's* (blog), September 10, 2012. https://denniscooperblog.com/halloween-countdown-post-1-2012-all-new-animatronic-prop-showroom/.

———. "A Herd." In *The Tenderness of the Wolves*, 51–75. Traumansberg, NY: Crossing Press, 1982.

———. "Hero." *Dennis Cooper's* (blog), February 26, 2006. http://denniscooper .blogspot.com/2006/02/hero.html.

———. "High School Basketball." In *Idols*, 26. New York: Amethyst Press, 1989.

———. "Homocore Rules." In *Smothered in Hugs*, 1–7. New York: Harper Perennial, 2010.

———. "I Am Very, Very Happy to Be Able Announce That the Two Month-Long Google-Related Nightmare Is Over." Facebook, August 26, 2016. https:// www.facebook.com/permalink.php?story_fbid=1114019298684536&id=2140 73142012494&__xts__[0]=68.ARADQy4DoyhVxYUpZQ5qhLzm_ERyebDae KjUNgl-RCWiCmDkomX2-m1NF5e4dQ-XyUcbNeD1b9yCLmdUsy94No4Ji A1hCunR31Wcyd5aLRmOoDIfWMy2FBQSDYSd8JKqoJWdcGTO2NYml QLqrcMpvgJQrYAeN1cLkpSeU3xtqnQqDvemyMiQOLoR1D9BYvWxx -uqP7H5SJxCXQINuiVlWlTplzaTF-QgDV5Aotdupc9EMQ3voKC3WjYA6I cxil7itWskT6i92j37YFS_Hq5m8psuIPLNk3LXXlT8dq9llLXqrmmg3sYaBZ -GyjM-r8MoqQbpD8Q9MrAaPx1eGvb3QA&__tn__=-R.

———. "*I Apologize*: Extracts from the Text." Presented to the Audience at Le Quartz, Brest, France, March 8, 2007.

———. "I Really, Really Hate Nostalgia: Juliet Escoria Interviews Dennis Cooper." *Fanzine*, September 9, 2014. http://thefanzine.com/i-really-really-hate -nostalgia-juliet-escoria-interviews-dennis-cooper/.

———. "I Think I'm Ill-Suited to Blogging." *Dennis Cooper's* (blog), May 15, 2005. http://denniscooper.blogspot.com/2005/05/i-think-im-ill-suited-to -blogging.html.

———. "I Used to Throw These Literary Parties." *Dennis Cooper's* (blog), March 4, 2006. http://denniscooper.blogspot.com/2006/03/i-used-to-throw -these-literary-parties.html.

———. *Idols*. New York: Amethyst Press, 1989.

———. "If I Were Peter Frampton." In *Idols*, 30. New York: Amethyst Press, 1989.

———. "I'm Still Reeling From News Yesterday . . ." *Dennis Cooper's* (blog), June 17, 2005. http://denniscooper.blogspot.com/2005/06/im-still-reeling -from-news-yesterday.html.

———. "In a State of Confusion and Being Lucid as I Can." Interview by Joyelle McSweeney. *Fanzine*, July 4, 2015. http://thefanzine.com/an-excitable -collaborator-joyelle-mcsweeney-interviews-dennis-cooper/.

———. Interview by Diarmuid Hester, Paris, August 31, 2018.

———. Interview by Martin Bladh. In *Gone: Scrapbook 1980–1982*. London: Infinity Land Press, 2014.

———. Interview by Matthew Byloos. *Fishwrap*, 2000.

———. Interview by Tim Guest. *Bomb*, April 1, 1989.

———. "An Interview with Dennis Cooper." By Alexander Laurence. *Free Williamsburg*, January 2001. http://www.freewilliamsburg.com/still_fresh /january/dennis_cooper.html.

———. "An Interview with Dennis Cooper." By Dan Epstein. *3:AM Magazine*, 2001. http://www.3ammagazine.com/litarchives/2001_dec/interview _dennis_cooper.html.

———. "Interview with Dennis Cooper from *Honcho Magazine*." By Slava Mogutin. Slava Mogutin, July 2000. http://slavamogutin.com/dennis-cooper/.

———. "Interviews: Dennis Cooper Talks About His Film *Permanent Green Light*." By Jennifer Krasinsky. Artforum.com, August 30, 2018. https://www .artforum.com/interviews/dennis-cooper-talks-about-his-film-permanent -green-light-76484.

———. "Introducing Horror Hospital." In *Wrong: Stories*, 43–58. London: Serpent's Tail, 2004.

———. "Introducing Little House on the Bowery." Akashic Books, 2003. https:// web.archive.org/web/20080706115901/http://www.akashicbooks.com /dcstatement.htm.

———. "'It's the Shift That Creates': An Interview with Dennis Cooper, 12 July 2007." By Danny Kennedy. In *Dennis Cooper*, edited by Paul Hegarty and Danny Kennedy, 191–209. Brighton, UK: Sussex Academic Press, 2008.

———. "Jeff, After a Long Time." In *Idols*, 86. New York: Amethyst Press, 1989.

———. "Late Friends." In *The Tenderness of the Wolves*, 47. Traumansberg, NY: Crossing Press, 1982.

———. "LC#1 Introduction." *Little Caesar*, no. 1 (1976): 1.

———. *The Marbled Swarm: A Novel*. New York: Harper Perennial, 2011.

———. "Meet Hucow, CreatingPerfection, Jellyboy, Horriblehuman, and DC's Other Select International Male Slaves for the Month of July 2017." *DC's* (blog), July 31, 2017. https://denniscooperblog.com/meet-hucow-creatingperfection -jellyboy-horriblehuman-and-dcs-other-select-international-male-slaves-for -the-month-of-july-2017/.

———. "My Dark Places." Interview by Caroline Simpson. *Foggy Sapphires* (blog), June 5, 2011. https://foggysapphires.wordpress.com/2011/06/05/interview -with-dennis-cooper/.

———. "My Fear Arouses Me." Interview by Mike Meginnis. *HTML Giant*, January 5, 2012. http://htmlgiant.com/author-spotlight/an-interview-with -dennis-cooper/.

———. *My Loose Thread*. Edinburgh: Canongate, 2002.

———. "*My Loose Thread* Interview." By Michael Silverblatt. *Bookworm*. KCRW, October 10, 2002.

———. "My Type." In *Idols*, 29. New York: Amethyst Press, 1989.

———. "Not Evil." Interview by Steve Lafreniere. *Babble Magazine*, 1994.

———. "Novelist Dennis Cooper Thinks the Kids Are Alright." Interview by Ezra Marcus. *Interview Magazine*, May 11, 2018. https://www.interview magazine.com/culture/novelist-dennis-cooper-thinks-kids-alright.

———. Papers. Fales Library and Special Collections, New York University Libraries.

———. *Period*. London: Serpent's Tail, 2000.

———. "Phoner: The Sonic Youth Liner Notes (November 1994)." In *Smothered in Hugs*, 101–5. New York: Harper Perennial, 2010.

———. "The Plague and Boredom Are Getting Married." In *The Terror of Earrings*, 30. Arcadia, CA: Kinks Press, 1973.

———. "PS." *Dennis Cooper's* (blog), May 24, 2005. http://denniscooper.blogspot .com/2005/05/ps.html.

———. "Queercore." In *The Material Queer: A LesBiGay Cultural Studies Reader*, edited by Donald Morton, 292–96. Boulder, CO: Westview Press, 1996.

———. "Safe." In *Wrong: Stories*, 99–158. London: Serpent's Tail, 2004.

———. "Saturday." *Dennis Cooper's* (blog), August 13, 2005. http://denniscooper .blogspot.com/2005/08/saturday.html.

———. "Scott Van Der Karr." In *Idols*, 12. New York: Amethyst Press, 1989.

———. *The Sluts*. New York: Carroll & Graf, 2005.

———, ed. *Smothered in Hugs: Essays, Interviews, Feedback, and Obituaries*. New York: Harper Perennial, 2010.

———. "Solving the Puzzle of Sex and Violence with Dennis Cooper." Interview by Joshua Chaplinsky. *LitReactor*, November 3, 2011. http://litreactor .com/interviews/solving-the-puzzle-of-sex-and-violence-with-dennis-cooper.

———. "Some Adventures of John F. Kennedy Jr. (9. in School)." In *Idols*, 71. New York: Amethyst Press, 1989.

———. "Some of You Asked About Rules . . ." *Dennis Cooper's* (blog), March 5, 2006. http://denniscooper.blogspot.com/2006/03/some-of-you-asked-about -rules-and.html.

———. "Some Stuff." *Dennis Cooper's* (blog), June 2, 2005. http://denniscooper .blogspot.com/2005/06/some-stuff.html.

———. *The Tenderness of the Wolves*. Traumansberg, NY: The Crossing Press, 1982.

———. *The Terror of Earrings*. Arcadia, CA: Kinks Press, 1973.

———. "This Is Not an Isolated Incident: An Introduction." In *Userlands: New Fiction Writers from the Blogging Underground*, edited by Dennis Cooper, 11–13. New York: Akashic Books, 2007.

———. *Tiger Beat*. Los Angeles: Little Caesar Press, 1978.

———. *Try*. London: Serpent's Tail, 2004.

———. *Violence, faits divers, littérature*. Paris: P.O.L., 2004.

———. "Winners and Whatever Else." *Dennis Cooper's* (blog), July 12, 2005. http://denniscooper.blogspot.com/2005/07/winners-and-whatever-else.html.

———. "Wrong." In *Wrong: Stories*, 63–73. London: Serpent's Tail, 2004.

———. *Wrong: Stories*. London: Serpent's Tail, 2004.

Cooper, Dennis, and Zac Farley. Document distributed at UK premiere of *Permanent Green Light*, Cabinet Gallery, London, September 14, 2018.

———. "Language, and How It's Used, Is Extremely Important in *Permanent Green Light*." Interview by José Sarmiento-Hinojosa. *Desistfilm*, November 14, 2018. http://desistfilm.com/dennis-cooper-zac-farley-language-and-how-its -used-is-extremely-important-in-permanent-green-light/.

Cooper, Dennis, and Eileen Myles. "Afterword. The Scene: A Conversation between Dennis Cooper and Eileen Myles." In *Up Is Up But So Is Down: New York's Downtown Literary Scene, 1974–1992*, edited by Brandon Stosuy, 463–82. New York: NYU Press, 2006.

Cooper, Dennis, and Joel Westendorf. "A Raver Runs Through It." In *Smothered in Hugs*, edited by Dennis Cooper, 199–212. New York: Harper Perennial, 2010.

Cox, L. J., and R. J. Fay. "Gayspeak, the Linguistic Fringe: Bona Polari, Camp, Queerspeak and Beyond." In *The Margins of the City*, edited by S. Whittle, 103–27. Aldershot, UK: Ashgate, 1994.

The Cult of JT LeRoy. Directed by Marjorie Sturm. San Francisco: 2015.

Davis, Vaginal. Interview by Abbe Schriber. Studio Museum Harlem, May 2010. https://www.studiomuseum.org/article/vaginal-davis.

Debord, Guy. *Society of the Spectacle*. Detroit, MI: Black and Red, 1970.

Delany, Samuel R. *About Writing: Seven Essays, Four Letters, and Five Interviews*. Middletown, CT: Wesleyan University Press, 2005.

Deleuze, Gilles, and Félix Guattari. *A Thousand Plateaus*. Minneapolis: University of Minnesota Press, 1987.

Delp, Laurel. "A Small Circle of Bards: L.A.'s Poets Start a New Tradition of Their Own." *Los Angeles Herald Examiner*, January 31, 1982.

Dermody, Dennis. "The 10 Best and Worst Films of 2016." *PAPER*, December 19, 2016. http://www.papermag.com/10-best-and-worst-films-of-2016-2136144 903.html.

Diggory, Terence. "Community 'Intimate' or 'Inoperative': New York School Poets and Politics from Paul Goodman to Jean-Luc Nancy." In *The Scene of My Selves: New Work on New York School Poets*, edited by Terence Diggory and Stephen Paul Miller, 13–34. Orono, ME: National Poetry Foundation, 2001.

Dobson, Julia. "Troubling Matters: Mannequins, Murder, and Gisèle Vienne's 'Corps Troublants.'" In *Women Matter/Femmes Matière: French and*

Francophone Women and the Material World, edited by Maggie Allison and Imogen Long, 21–34. Oxford: Peter Lang, 2013.

Donne, John. "The Good-Morrow." In *The Norton Anthology of Poetry*, 5th ed., edited by Margaret Ferguson, Mary Jo Salter, and Jon Stallworthy, 293. New York: W. W. Norton, 2005.

Dorn, Edward. *Edward Dorn: Collected Poems*. Edited by Jennifer Dunbar Dorn. Manchester: Carcanet, 2012.

Dorn, Edward, and Tom Clark. "AIDS Awards for Poetic Idiocy." *Rolling Stock*, no. 5 (1983): 13.

Dreher, Mark. "Homosexuals Are Enemies of the State." *J.D.s*, no. 5 (1989): 42.

Edelman, Lee. *No Future: Queer Theory and the Death Drive*. Durham, NC: Duke University Press, 2004.

Eliot, T. S. Preface to *Nightwood* (1936), by Djuna Barnes, xvii–xxvii. London: Faber & Faber, 2007.

Elkind, David. "Egocentrism in Adolescence." *Child Development* 38, no. 4 (December 1967): 1025–34.

Ellingham, Lewis, and Kevin Killian. *Poet Be like God: Jack Spicer and the San Francisco Renaissance*. Hanover, NH: University Press of New England, 1998.

Eppink, Jason. "A Brief History of the GIF (So Far)." *Journal of Visual Culture* 13, no. 3 (2014): 298–306.

Epstein, Andrew. *Beautiful Enemies: Friendship and Postwar American Poetry*. Oxford: Oxford University Press, 2006.

Equi, Elaine. "The Switchboard: Interview with Elaine Equi." By Jesse Tangen-Mills. *Guernica*, August 1, 2011. http://www.guernicamag.com/interviews /tangen_mills_elaine_equi_8_1_11/.

Fallon, Claire. "If You Write A Novel In GIFs, Is It Still A Novel?" *Huffington Post*, September 15, 2015. https://www.huffingtonpost.co.uk/entry/if-you -write-a-novel-in-gifs-is-it-still-a-novel_us_55f72e77e4b0c2077efbade6.

Feuerzeig, Jeff. "Jeff Feuerzeig Talks Author: The JT LeRoy Story, Amazon and Amazing True Stories." Interview by Ivan Radford. VODzilla.co, July 30, 2018. http://vodzilla.co/interviews/interview-jeff-feuerzeig-talks-author-the -jt-leroy-story-amazon-and-amazing-true-stories/.

Fisher, Mark. *Capitalist Realism: Is There No Alternative?* Ropley, UK: Zero Books, 2009.

———. *The Weird and the Eerie*. London: Repeater, 2016.

Fitch, Andy. *Pop Poetics: Reframing Joe Brainard*. Champaign, IL: Dalkey Archive, 2012.

Flanagan, Bob. "Houses." In *Coming Attractions*, edited by Dennis Cooper, 66–68. Los Angeles: Little Caesar Press, 1980.

Foster, Hal. "Obscene, Abject, Traumatic." *October* 78 (October 1, 1996): 107–24.

Foucault, Michel. *Discipline and Punish: The Birth of the Prison*. Translated by Alan Sheridan. New York: Vintage Books, 1995.

France, David. *How to Survive a Plague: The Story of How Activists and Scientists Tamed AIDS*. London: Picador, 2017.

Freud, Sigmund. "The Uncanny." In *The Complete Psychological Works of Sigmund Freud, Volume XVII*, edited by James Strachey, 219–52. London: Hogarth Press, 1955.

Frisk. Directed by Todd Verow. San Francisco: 1996.

Galloway, Alexander, and Eugene Thacker. *The Exploit: A Theory of Networks*. Minneapolis: University of Minnesota Press, 2007.

Gardner, James. "Transgressive Fiction." *National Review*, June 17, 1996: 54–56.

Genecand, Marie-Pierre. "Critique: *I Apologize*, de Gisèle Vienne, à l'Arsenic, Festival International de Danse de Lausanne." *Le Temps*, September 26, 2008. https://www.letemps.ch/culture/critique-i-apologize-gisele-vienne-larsenic -festival-international-danse-lausanne-charnier.

Glück, Robert. "Caricature." In *Communal Nude*, 83–94. South Pasadena, CA: Semiotext(e), 2016.

———. *Communal Nude: Collected Essays*. South Pasadena, CA: Semiotext(e), 2016.

———. *Jack the Modernist*. New York: Serpent's Tail, 1995.

———. "Long Note on New Narrative." In *Communal Nude*, 13–25. South Pasadena, CA: Semiotext(e), 2016.

———. "Sanchez and Day (from Elements of a Coffee Service)." In *Writers Who Love Too Much*, edited by Dodie Bellamy and Kevin Killian, 1–3. New York: Nightboat, 2017.

Goldman, Emma. *Anarchism and Other Essays*. Toronto: Dover, 1969.

———. Preface to *Anarchism and Other Essays*, 41–45. Toronto: Dover, 1969.

———. "The Tragedy of Woman's Emancipation." In *Anarchism and Other Essays*, 213–26. Toronto: Dover, 1969.

Gooch, Brad. *City Poet: The Life and Times of Frank O'Hara*. New York: Knopf, 1993.

Goodman, Paul. "Advance-Guard Writing in America: 1900–1950." In *Utopian Essays and Practical Proposals*, edited by Paul Goodman, 191–216. New York: Random House, 1962.

———. "Post-Christian Man." In *Utopian Essays and Practical Proposals*, edited by Paul Goodman, 80–91. New York: Random House, 1962.

———. Preface to *Utopian Essays and Practical Proposals*, edited by Paul Goodman, xi–xvii. New York: Random House, 1962.

———, ed. *Utopian Essays and Practical Proposals*. New York: Random House, 1962.

———. "Utopian Thinking." In *Utopian Essays and Practical Proposals*, edited by Paul Goodman, 3–22. New York: Random House, 1962.

Goodman, Paul, and Percival Goodman. "Banning Cars from Manhattan." In

Utopian Essays and Practical Proposals, edited by Paul Goodman, 145–55. New York: Random House, 1962.

Grattan, Sean Austin. *Hope Isn't Stupid: Utopian Affects in Contemporary American Literature*. Iowa City: University of Iowa Press, 2017.

Griffith, Patricia. "Michael Lally Used to Explain . . ." *Washington Review*, September 1988.

Guattari, Félix. "Cinema of Desire." In *Chaosophy: Texts and Interviews, 1972–1977*, edited by Sylvère Lotringer, 235–46. Los Angeles, CA: Semiotext(e), 2009.

Hagman, Hampus. "The Digital Gesture: Rediscovering Cinematic Movement through Gifs." *Refractory*, December 29, 2012. http://refractory.unimelb.edu.au/2012/12/29/hagman/.

Hall, G. Stanley. *Adolescence, Its Psychology and Its Relations to Physiology, Anthropology, Sociology, Sex, Crime, Religion, and Education*. 2 vols. New York: D. Appleton, 1925.

Halperin, David M. *How to Be Gay*. Cambridge, MA: Harvard University Press, 2012.

Halpern, Rob. "Realism and Utopia: Sex, Writing and Activism in New Narrative." *Journal of Narrative Theory* 41, no. 1 (Spring 2011): 82–124.

Hardt, Michael. "The Common in Communism." *Rethinking Marxism* 22, no. 3 (July 2010): 346–56.

Hardt, Michael, and Antonio Negri. *Commonwealth*. Cambridge, MA: Belknap Press, 2009.

Harris, Kaplan Page. "New Narrative and the Making of Language Poetry." *American Literature* 81, no. 4 (2009): 805–32.

Hayles, N. Katherine. "Chance Operations: Cagean Paradox and Contemporary Science." In *John Cage: Composed in America*, edited by Marjorie Perloff and Charles Junkerman, 226–41. Chicago: University of Chicago Press, 1994.

Hegarty, Paul. "The Self-Contained and Its Emptying in *Frisk*." In *Dennis Cooper*, edited by Paul Hegarty and Danny Kennedy, 175–86. Brighton, UK: Sussex Academic Press, 2008.

Hegarty, Paul, and Danny Kennedy, eds. *Dennis Cooper: Writing at the Edge*. Brighton, UK: Sussex Academic Press, 2008.

Heil, T. "It's Impossible to Figure out How Many Stars to Give This Book." Amazon.com, January 13, 2016. https://www.amazon.com/review/R1HZV5RAG98SIG/ref=cm_cr_srp_d_rdp_perm?ie=UTF8&ASIN=0061715638.

Heise, Thomas. *Urban Underworlds: A Geography of Twentieth-Century American Literature and Culture*. New Brunswick, NJ: Rutgers University Press, 2011.

Henry, Casey Michael. "How Dennis Cooper Turns GIFs Into Fiction," *New Yorker*, September 4, 2015. https://www.newyorker.com/books/page-turner/how-dennis-cooper-creates-fiction-from-gifs.

Herd, David. *John Ashbery and American Poetry*. Manchester, UK: Manchester University Press, 2009.

Hester, Helen. *Beyond Explicit: Pornography and the Displacement of Sex*. Albany: State University of New York Press, 2014.

Hirsch, Jean-Paul. *Dennis Cooper: The Marbled Swarm Le Fol Marbre*, March 29, 2016. https://www.youtube.com/watch?v=Z14KHd4X7Tw.

HIV Epidemology and Field Services Program. "AIDS Diagnoses and Persons Living with HIV/AIDS by Year, Pre-1981 to 2016, New York City." New York City HIV/AIDS Annual Surveillance Statistics 2016. NYC Department of Health and Mental Hygiene, 2016. http://www1.nyc.gov/assets/doh/down loads/pdf/ah/surveillance-trend-tables.pdf.

Honeywell, Carissa. "Paul Goodman: Finding an Audience for Anarchism in Twentieth-Century America." *Journal for the Study of Radicalism* 5, no. 2 (Fall 2011): 1–33.

Houlbrook, Matt. *Queer London: Perils and Pleasures in the Sexual Metropolis, 1918–1957*. Chicago: University of Chicago Press, 2005.

Jackson, Earl Jr. "Bruce Boone." In *Contemporary Gay Male Novelists: A Bio-Bibliographical Sourcebook*, edited by Emmanuel S. Nealon, 25–28. Westport, CT: Greenwood Press, 1993.

———. "Death Drives Across Pornotopia: Dennis Cooper on the Extremities of Being." In *Enter at Your Own Risk*, edited by Leora Lev, 151–74. Madison, NJ: Fairleigh Dickinson University Press, 2006.

Jennings, Tom. "What the Fuck Is HOMOCORE?" *HOMOCORE*, December 1988.

Kane, Daniel. *All Poets Welcome: The Lower East Side Poetry Scene in the 1960s*. Berkeley: University of California Press, 2003.

———. "Angel Hair, The Second-Generation New York School, and the Poetics of Sociability." In *Don't Ever Get Famous*, 90–121. Champaign, IL: Dalkey Archive Press, 2006.

———, ed. *Don't Ever Get Famous: Essays on New York Writing After the New York School*. Champaign, IL: Dalkey Archive Press, 2006.

———. *"Do You Have A Band?" Poetry and Punk Rock in New York City*. New York: Columbia University Press, 2017.

———. "'Nor Did I Socialise with Their People': Patti Smith, Rock Heroics and the Poetics of Sociability." *Popular Music* 31, no. 1 (2012): 105–23.

Kermode, Mark. "*Love* Review—One for Hardcore Fans Only." *Guardian*, November 22, 2015. https://www.theguardian.com/film/2015/nov/22/love -review-hardcore-fans-only-gaspar-noe.

Kikel, Rudy. "Dennis Cooper: New Moves for the Poet of Distances." *Advocate*, November 24, 1983.

———. "Review of *Tiger Beat*." *Gay Community News*, September 11, 1978.

Killian, Kevin. *Bedrooms Have Windows*. New York: Amethyst Press, 1989.

————. "Open Letter to the Editors of Apex of the M." In *Writers Who Love Too Much*, edited by Dodie Bellamy and Kevin Killian, 424–27. New York: Nightboat, 2017.

————. "A Xerox Coup D'État: Sophie Seita Interviews Kevin Killian About Editing *Mirage* and *Mirage #4/Period[ical]*." By Sophie Seita. Front Porch Commons, August 11, 2015. http://www.joewoodsworks.com/fpc/?p=223.

Kinkel, Kipland. "Kip's Writings & Statements." PBS *Frontline*, January 2000. https://www.pbs.org/wgbh/pages/frontline/shows/kinkel/kip/writings.html.

Kinkel, Kipland, and Al Warthen. "Transcript of Kip Kinkel's Confession (5.21.1998)." PBS *Frontline*, January 2000. https://www.pbs.org/wgbh/pages/frontline/shows/kinkel/etc/confesst.html.

Kissack, Terence S. *Free Comrades: Anarchism and Homosexuality in the United States, 1895–1917*. Edinburgh: AK, 2008.

Koestenbaum, Wayne. *Hotel Theory*. New York: Soft Skull, 2007.

————. "John Ashbery's Lazy Susan." In *My 1980s and Other Essays*, 84–86. New York: Farrar, Straus and Giroux, 2013.

LaBruce, Bruce. "Hard Driving Fiction: The Adventures of a Teenage J. D. and His Young, Eager-to-Please Punk." *J.D.s*, no. 2, 1985.

LaBruce, Bruce, and G. B. Jones. "Don't Be Gay, Or, How I Learned to Stop Worrying and Fuck Punk Up the Ass." *HOMOCORE*, February 1991.

Lee, Craig. "The Little Caesar of L.A.'s Poetry Scene." *L.A. Weekly*, 1980.

Lehman, David. *The Last Avant-Garde: The Making of the New York School of Poets*. New York: Anchor Books, 1999.

LeSueur, Joe. *Digressions on Some Poems by Frank O'Hara*. New York: Farrar, Straus and Giroux, 2004.

Lev, Leora. "The Center Cannot Hold: My Loose Thread." In *Enter at Your Own Risk*, edited by Leora Lev, 231–37. Madison, NJ: Fairleigh Dickinson University Press, 2006.

————, ed. *Enter at Your Own Risk: The Dangerous Art of Dennis Cooper*. Madison, WI: Fairleigh Dickinson University Press, 2006.

————. "Next: Vampiric Epistolarity, Haunted Cyberspace and Dennis Cooper's Positively Mutant Multimedia Offspring." In *Dennis Cooper*, edited by Paul Hegarty and Danny Kennedy, 88–105. Brighton, UK: Sussex Academic Press, 2008.

Love, Heather. "Truth and Consequences: On Paranoid Reading and Reparative Reading." *Criticism* 52, no. 2 (Spring 2010): 235–41.

Lovink, Geert. *Zero Comments: Blogging and Critical Internet Culture*. New York: Routledge, 2008.

Macfarlane, Robert. "The Eeriness of the English Countryside." *Guardian*, April 10, 2015. http://www.theguardian.com/books/2015/apr/10/eeriness-english-countryside-robert-macfarlane.

Mac Low, Jackson. Interview by Nicholas Zurbrugg. In *Light Years: An Anthology on Sociocultural Happenings (Multimedia in the East Village, 1960–1966)*, edited by Carol Bergé, 380–401. New York: Spuyten Duyvil, 2010.

Manovich, Lev. "The Practice of Everyday (Media) Life: From Mass Consumption to Mass Cultural Production?" *Critical Inquiry* 35, no. 2 (Winter 2009): 319–31.

Marcus, Sara. *Girls to the Front: The True Story of the Riot Grrrl Revolution.* New York: Harper Perennial, 2010.

Marhoefer, Laurie. "From Gay Nazis to 'We're Here, We're Queer': A Century of Arguing about Gay Pride." *Conversation*, June 22, 2017. http://the conversation.com/from-gay-nazis-to-were-here-were-queer-a-century-of -arguing-about-gay-pride-78888.

Masi, Bruno. "Giséle Vienne, diptyque fantasmatique." *Libération*, July 23, 2005. http://next.liberation.fr/culture/2005/07/23/gisele-vienne-diptyque -fantasmatique_527372.

McGann, Jerome J. "Contemporary Poetry, Alternate Routes." *Critical Inquiry* 13, no. 3 (April 1, 1987): 624–47.

McHale, Brian. "Poetry as Prosthesis." *Poetics Today* 21, no. 1 (Spring 2000): 1–32.

Miller, D. A. *Place for Us: Essay on the Broadway Musical.* Cambridge, MA: Harvard University Press, 1998.

Moffet, Penelope. "Poetic License: Beyond Baroque Center in Venice Has Helped Nurture and Launch the Careers of Aspiring Writers. More than Two Decades Later, the Avant-Garde Still Reigns." *Los Angeles Times*, May 1, 1994. http://articles.latimes.com/1994-05-01/news/we-52760_1_beyond-baroque -center.

Mohr, Bill. *Hold-Outs: The Los Angeles Poetry Renaissance, 1948–1992.* Iowa City: University of Iowa Press, 2011.

Monte, Bryan. "The Political as Personal: My Memoir of Steve Abbott, 1980–1990." *Amsterdam Quarterly*, Spring 2016. http://www.amsterdamquarterly .org/aq_issues/aq15-war-peace/bryan-r-monte-the-political-as-personal-my -memoir-of-steve-abbott/.

Morrison, Toni. "On the First Black President." *New Yorker*, September 28, 1998. https://www.newyorker.com/magazine/1998/10/05/comment-6543.

Muñoz, José Esteban. "'Gimme Gimme This . . . Gimme Gimme That': Annihilation and Innovation in the Punk Rock Commons." *Social Text* 31, no. 3 (Fall 2013): 95–109.

Myles, Eileen. "An American Poem." In *Not Me*, 14–17. New York: Semiotext(e), 1991.

Nair, Sashi. *Secrecy and Sapphic Modernism: Reading "Romans à Clef" between the Wars.* New York: Palgrave Macmillan, 2012.

Nault, Curran. *Queercore: Queer Punk Media Subculture*. New York: Routledge, 2018.

Nelson, Maggie. *Women, the New York School, and Other True Abstractions*. Iowa City: University of Iowa Press, 2007.

Noé, Gaspar. *Enter the Void* press kit. Wild Bunch Productions, 2010. https://www.wildbunch.biz/movie/enter-the-void/.

Noland, Carrie. "Rimbaud and Patti Smith: Style as Social Deviance." *Critical Inquiry* 21, no. 3 (Spring 1995): 581–610.

O'Hara, Frank. *The Collected Poems of Frank O'Hara*. Edited by Donald Allen. Berkeley: University of California Press, 1995.

———. "Personism: A Manifesto." In *The Collected Poems of Frank O'Hara*, edited by Donald Allen, 498–99. Berkeley: University of California Press, 1995.

———. "Poem Read at Joan Mitchell's." In *The Selected Poems of Frank O'Hara*, edited by Donald Allen, 113–15. Manchester: Carcanet, 1991.

———. "Today." In *The Collected Poems of Frank O'Hara*, edited by Donald Allen, 15. Berkeley: University of California Press, 1995.

Olbermann, Keith. "Heartbreaking Hoax." *Countdown with Keith Olbermann*. MSNBC, April 8, 2006. https://www.youtube.com/watch?v=fdanXu2GDFw.

O'Reilly, Tim. "What Is Web 2.0." O'Reilly, September 30, 2005. http://www.oreilly.com/go/web2.

Padgett, Ron. *Ted: A Personal Memoir of Ted Berrigan*. Great Barrington, MA: Figures, 1993.

Peters, Robert. "Youth-an-Agia: Nurtured Fantasies: Dennis Cooper's Idols." *San Francisco Review of Books*, April 1980.

Prager, Robert. "An Author Who Explores the All-Consuming Gay Culture." *San Diego Gayzette*, January 31, 1985.

Press, Joy. "The Cult of J.T. LeRoy." *Village Voice*, June 12, 2001. https://www.villagevoice.com/2001/06/12/the-cult-of-j-t-leroy/.

Prix Sade. "Lauréat 2007—Prix Sade." Accessed December 13, 2012. http://prix-sade.over-blog.com/categorie-10216755.html.

Proudhon, Pierre-Joseph. "System of Economical Contradictions: Or, the Philosophy of Poverty. Chapter VIII. Of the Responsibility of Man and of God, under the Law of Contradiction, or a Solution of the Problem of Providence." Marxists.org, (1847) 2019. https://www.marxists.org/reference/subject/economics/proudhon/philosophy/ch08.htm.

Quandt, James. "Flesh and Blood: Sex and Violence in Recent French Cinema." In *New Extremism in Cinema: From France to Europe*, edited by Tanya Horeck, 18–25. Edinburgh: Edinburgh University Press, 2011.

Rahv, Betty T. *From Sartre to the New Novel*. Port Washington, NY: Kennikat Press, 1974.

Ramsay, Raylene L. *Robbe-Grillet and Modernity: Science, Sexuality, and Subversion*. Gainesville: University Press of Florida, 1992.

Rathe, Adam. "Queer to the Core." *OUT*, April 12, 2012. http://www.out.com
/entertainment/music/2012/04/12/history-queer-core-gay-punk-GB
-JONES.

Rault, Erwan. *Théorie et expérience romanesque chez Robbe-Grillet: "Le Voyeur."*
Paris: La Pensée Universelle, 1975.

Reynolds, Simon. *Energy Flash: A Journey Through Rave Music and Dance Culture.* London: Faber & Faber, 2013.

Rich, B. Ruby. "New Queer Cinema." In *New Queer Cinema: A Critical Reader,*
edited by Michele Aaron, 15–22. New Brunswick, NJ: Rutgers University
Press, 2004.

Rimbaud, Arthur. "Childhood." In *Illuminations and Other Prose Poems,* translated by Louise Varese, 11. New York: New Directions, 1957.

Robbe-Grillet, Alain. *The Voyeur.* Translated by Richard Howard. Cornwall:
Oneworld Classics, 2009.

Ronell, Avital. "The Philosophical Code: Dennis Cooper's Pacific Rim." In *The
ÜberReader: Selected Works of Avital Ronell,* edited by Diane Davis, 188–99.
Chicago: University of Illinois Press, 2008.

Ross, Kristin. *The Emergence of Social Space: Rimbaud and the Paris Commune.*
Minneapolis: University of Minnesota Press, 1988.

Rubin, Gayle S. "Thinking Sex: Notes for a Radical Theory of the Politics of
Sexuality." In *Culture, Society and Sexuality: A Reader,* edited by Richard
Parker and Peter Aggleton, 143–78. London: UCL Press, 1999.

Sade, D. A. F. *The 120 Days of Sodom and Other Writings.* Translated by Richard
Seaver and Austryn Wainhouse. New York: Grove Press, 1987.

Scemama, Celine. "Robert Bresson and the Voices of an Inner World: 'You,' or
the Impossible Identification." In *Subjectivity: Filmic Representation and the
Spectator's Experience,* edited by Dominique Chateau, 99–117. Amsterdam:
Amsterdam University Press, 2011.

Schildcrout, Jordan. *Murder Most Queer: The Homicidal Homosexual in the
American Theater.* Ann Arbor: University of Michigan Press, 2014.

Schjeldahl, Peter. "Dennis Cooper's Molten Miracle." *Village Voice Literary
Supplement,* October 19, 1984.

Schulman, Sarah. *Gentrification of the Mind: Witness to a Lost Imagination.*
Berkeley: University of California Press, 2012.

Sedgwick, Eve Kosofsky. "Paranoid Reading and Reparative Reading: Or, You're
So Paranoid You Probably Think This Essay Is About You." In *Touching Feeling: Affect, Pedagogy, Performativity,* 123–51. Durham, NC: Duke University
Press, 2003.

Shaw, Lytle. *Frank O'Hara: The Poetics of Coterie.* Iowa City: University of Iowa
Press, 2006.

She Said Boom: The Story of Fifth Column. Directed by Kevin Hegge. Canada:
2012.

Shields, David. *Reality Hunger: A Manifesto*. London: Penguin, 2011.

Sifry, David. "Blog Usage Statistics and Trends: State of the Blogosphere." Robin Good's Master New Media, April 26, 2006. http://www.masternewmedia.org/news/2006/04/27/blog_usage_statistics_and_trends.htm.

Silliman, Ron. *TJANTING*. Cambridge, UK: Salt, 2002.

Silverblatt, Michael. "Shock Appeal: Who Are These Writers, and Why Do They Want to Hurt Us? The New Fiction of Transgression." *Los Angeles Times*, August 1, 1993. http://articles.latimes.com/1993-08-01/books/bk-21466_1_young-writers.

Skelley, Jack. "Juvenile Loitering." In *Coming Attractions*, edited by Dennis Cooper, 127. Los Angeles: Little Caesar Press, 1980.

Solomon-Godeau, Abigail. "The Rightness of *Wrong*." In *Failure*, edited by Lisa Le Feuve, 30–32. London/Cambridge, MA: Whitechapel Gallery/MIT Press, 2010.

Sontag, Susan. "On Paul Goodman." In *Under the Sign of Saturn*, 3–12. New York: Vintage Books, 1981.

Soulellis, Paul. "The Download: Dennis Cooper's GIF Novels." Rhizome, November 14, 2016. https://rhizome.org/editorial/2016/nov/14/the-download-dennis-coopers-gif-novels/.

St. John, Warren. "The Unmasking of JT LeRoy: In Public He's a She." *New York Times*, January 9, 2006. https://www.nytimes.com/2006/01/09/books/the-unmasking-of-jt-leroy-in-public-hes-a-she.html.

Stefans, Brian Kim. "The Lost Poets of Los Angeles." *Paul Revere's Horse*, no. 5 (March 2011): 131–62.

Steiner, Melissa. "Queercore U Kno the Score: She Said Boom—The Story of Fifth Column." *Quietus*, April 11, 2013. http://thequietus.com/articles/11858-5th-column-review-melissa-steiner.

Stogdill, Frances. "Mrs. Thompson, Prominent Club Woman, Talented Artist, Dies." *McKinney Courier-Gazette*, October 25, 1968.

Stone, Laurie, ed. *Close to the Bone: Memoirs of Hurt, Rage, and Desire*. New York: Grove Press, 1997.

———. "Introduction: Recalled to Life." In *Close to the Bone*, xi–xxviii. New York: Grove Press, 1997.

Strobel, Marion. "Middle-Aged Adolescence." In *William Carlos Williams: The Critical Heritage*, edited by Charles Doyle, 75–76. New York: Routledge, 1980.

Sturm, Marjorie. "Dennis Cooper, George Miles, and JT Leroy: Outtake from *The Cult of JT LeRoy*." July 12, 2016. https://www.youtube.com/watch?v=nye1Zk_Mcps.

Supree, Burt. "Men with Men." *Village Voice*, December 22, 1986.

Taylor, Marvin. "'A Dorian Gray Type of Thing': Male-Male Desire and the Crisis of Representation in Dennis Cooper's *Closer*." In *Enter at Your Own*

Risk, edited by Leora Lev, 175–99. Madison, NJ: Fairleigh Dickinson University Press, 2006.

———. "Geometries of Desire: The Structures of Dennis Cooper's George Myles Cycle." Presented at the Launch of *Closer*: The Dennis Cooper Papers, Amsterdam, Netherlands, March 22, 2012.

Terminator. "Baby Doll." In *Close to the Bone*, edited by Laurie Stone, 14–47. New York: Grove Press, 1997.

Terranova, Tiziana. *Network Culture: Politics for the Information Age*. London: Pluto, 2004.

Texier, Catherine. "Love Among the Damned." *New York Times*, March 20, 1994.

Thorne, Harry. "'The New York School Is a Joke': The Disruptive Poetics of *C: A Journal of Poetry*." In *Don't Ever Get Famous*, edited by Daniel Kane, 74–89. Champaign, IL: Dalkey Archive Press, 2006.

Tillman, Lynne. Papers. Fales Library and Special Collections, New York University Libraries.

Tremblay-McGaw, Robin. "A Review of *LIAR* by Mike Amnasan." *X Poetics* (blog), December 20, 2008. https://xpoetics.blogspot.co.uk/2008/12/review-of-liar-by-mike-amnasan.html.

Trinidad, David. Interview by D. A. Powell. *Electronic Poetry Review* 5, February 2003. http://www.epoetry.org/issues/issue5/text/prose/powell2.htm.

———. "The Party." In *Coming Attractions*, edited by Dennis Cooper, 141–43. Los Angeles: Little Caesar Press, 1980.

Uhlin, Graig. "Playing in the Gif(t) Economy." *Games and Culture* 9, no. 6 (2014): 517–27.

Viegener, Matias. "Philosophy in the Bedroom: Pornography and Philosophy in Dennis Cooper's Writing." In *Dennis Cooper*, edited by Paul Hegarty and Danny Kennedy, 130–44. Brighton, UK: Sussex Academic Press, 2008.

Vienne, Gisèle. "Entretien avec Gisèle Vienne." Interview by Laure Fernandez. *Registres*, Winter 2008.

———. "Érotisme, mort et méchanique. Sur une expérience de travail autour des rapports du corps au corps artificiel." *Registres: Revue d'Études Théâtrales*, Winter 2008.

———. "*Showroomdummies*, 2001: Presentation." Gisèle Vienne, undated. http://www.g-v.fr/en/shows/showroomdummies-2/.

———. "Uncanny Landscapes." Interview by Anna Gallagher-Ross. *Theater* 47, no. 2 (May 2017): 34–45.

Walsh, John. John Walsh Column. *Independent*, March 14, 1996.

Waters, John. "Best Films of 2016." Artforum.com, December 2016. https://www.artforum.com/print/201610/john-waters-64773.

Weaver, Andy. "Divining the Derivers: Anarchy and the Practice of Derivative Poetics in Robert Duncan and John Cage." *Jacket* 40 (2010).

Weinberger, Eliot. "A Case of AIDS Hysteria." In *Written Reaction: Poetics, Politics, Polemics (1979–1995)*, 39–41. New York: Marsilio, 1996.

Weinger, Mackenzie. "Bill Clinton: Occupy Wall Street Must Get Specific." *Politico*, October 13, 2011. http://www.politico.com/news/stories/1011/65846.html.

Weissman, Benjamin. Interview by Raul Deznermio. Akashic Books, 2014. http://www.akashicbooks.com/extra/interview-with-benjamin-weissman-by-raul-deznermio/.

Welt, Bernard. Interview by Troy Elliott. *Washington Review*, September 1988.

——. "Silent Radio." *Gay Anarchist Circle*, June 1983: 1–2, 6.

White, Edmund. "Out of the Closet, Onto the Bookshelf." *New York Times Magazine*, June 16, 1991.

Young, Elizabeth. "Death in Disneyland: The Work of Dennis Cooper." In *Shopping in Space*, edited by Elizabeth Young and Graham Caveney, 235–63. London: Serpent's Tail, 1992.

Young, Elizabeth, and Graham Caveney. Introduction to *Shopping in Space*, v–viii. London: Serpent's Tail, 1992.

——, eds. *Shopping in Space: Essays on American "Blank Generation" Fiction*. London: Serpent's Tail, 1992.

Index

Abbott, Steve, 46, 77–78, 91–93, 102, 109; "Notes on Boundaries/New Narrative," 99–101; *SOUP*, 98, 103

Acker, Kathy, 129, 253; correspondence with Cooper, 86–88, 90, 134; and Grove Press, 135; and New Narrative, 96, 99; and "transgressive writing," 147–148

adolescence, 23–29; choreography of, 199–200; egocentrism of, 31–32; high school, 23–24, 171–176; as influence, 6, 184; in *My Loose Thread*, 175; poetics of, 23–32; and Rimbaud, 26–29, 31, 60; temporality of, 24–31. *See also* teenagers

AIDS, 106–107, 123; activism, 125, 141, 237–238, 245; and Cooper's work, 82, 131; deaths, 132, 145–146, 167, 181; exploitation of, 167, 178–182

AIDS Awards for Poetry (Clark and Dorn), 77–79, 82, 91, 111

Albert, Laura. *See* LeRoy, JT

Allen, Karen, 111

Allison, Dorothy, 171

Amnasan, Mike, 92, 99, 101–102, 104–106, 109

anarchism, 30–31, 63–64, 245; and community, 62, 204, 206; friendship as a form of, 269; literary engagements with, 66–71, 152–164; networks, 206–208, 227; and punk rock, 60, 115, 120, 124, 125; sex radical, 112–115. *See also* Cage, John; commons, the; Gay Anarchist Circle, the; Goldman, Emma; Goodman, Paul; Mac Low, Jackson; Proudhon, Joseph

Apfelschnitt, Carl, 130, 146

Araki, Gregg, 123

Ashbery, John, 216, 253

asses, 27–28, 77, 82; anal sex, 83; fisting, 72; rimming, 145

Ayrton, Pete, 147

Bakunin, Mikhail, 30, 124

Baldessari, John, 1–4, 7

Baraka, Amiri. *See* Jones, LeRoi

Barnes, Djuna, 240; *Nightwood*, 240–241

Barthelme, Donald, 130

Bataille, Georges, 96, 99, 186

Baudelaire, Charles, 16, 18, 96

THE NEW AMERICAN CANON